# That's Weird!

## Awesome Science Mysteries

### Kendall Haven
### Illustrated by Jason Lynch

fulcrum resources
Golden, Colorado

*This book is dedicated*
*to those who have dared to consider the unpopular,*
*dared to think beyond the human understanding of their time*
*and dared to risk their careers and reputations to pursue a driving curiosity.*
*It is dedicated to those who have stretched our knowledge of the*
*universe and of ourselves.*

Text copyright © 2001 Kendall Haven
Illustrations copyright © 2001 by Jason Lynch

Book design by Patty Maher

Library of Congress Cataloging-in-Publication Data
Haven, Kendall F.
  That's weird! : awesome science mysteries / Kendall
Haven.
     p. cm.
Includes bibliographical references and index.
  ISBN 1-55591-999-5
  1. Science—Miscellanea. I. Title.
Q173 .H376 2001
001.94—dc21
                                          2001001700

Printed in the United States of America
    0  9  8  7  6  5  4  3  2  1

Fulcrum Publishing
16100 Table Mountain Parkway, Suite 300
Golden, Colorado 80403
(800) 992-2908 • (303) 277-1623
www.fulcrum-resources.com

# Contents

# Introduction

Science is a formal process of rigorous, systematic, logical discovery. A mystery is something that cannot be explained. Science mysteries, then, are phenomena that formal, rigorous investigation cannot explain. But a science mystery is much more than that. Science mysteries stir the imagination and chill the blood. They make the heart race and the adrenaline pump. They conjure images of wonders and terrors beyond our control, beyond our world, beyond our imagining.

Every natural event began as a mystery: lightning, gravity, radiation, rain, life itself. Then science collected observations through field studies and laboratory experiments. From observations came hypotheses that were tested to become theories. After years of further testing and verification, theories become factual knowledge. Science is the process of turning mystery into knowledge. Yet many mysteries stubbornly elude explanation, and some have so fascinated us that we stubbornly reject any attempt to rationalize away the mystery.

Mysteries touch the realm of superstition and wonder. Mysteries speak of uncharted possibilities, of supernatural intervention. Science is rooted in the realm of logic and rational fact. We need scientific reasoning. But we also seem to need the enchantment of mystery and are dismayed by the possibility that mystery might be snuffed out by plodding science.

Science mysteries, then, lie at the edge of a delicate and fascinating dance. Science has sworn to eradicate mystery. Mystery has pledged to defy and survive science's probing. These forces explode in a head-on collision in the heart of every major science mystery. Sixteen of these mind-twisting, heart-stopping thrill rides are presented in this book.

Science mysteries are not foreign and unknown to me. I am not dispassionately objective about most of them. Most of them have been deeply etched into my psyche for years. They rumble around in my brain unanswered, making me dream and wonder and wish. I've hiked the wild and rugged forests of the Pacific Northwest. On each outing, I remember wondering—hoping that—this time, I'd meet Sasquatch, or see him across a small ravine, or at least find his footprints in the soft earth. I wanted to be able to shout to the world, "I've found him! He's real!"

I've stepped on hot coals—accidentally—twice (both times barbecue briquettes that had fallen out of the family grill). I never put my full weight on either coal. Still, both times my foot was horribly burned and didn't heal for weeks. I am in awe of the thought of intentionally walking across a long bed of glowing briquettes, with the heat wafting up in billowing waves that make your eyes burn, and your feet crunching on glowing coals more than 1,000 degrees hot. My heart, mind and soul are totally convinced that I would be barbecued like a burnt chicken wing long before I reached the far end of the pit. Still, people firewalk every day and walk away without even one tiny blister.

I have four friends who have seen and been touched by ghosts—real ghosts. I didn't believe in ghosts until I heard their stories and watched their faces as they told them. They were serious. Each is totally convinced that the experience really happened. I trust these people. None is prone to exaggeration or inventing wild stories. How could they all be wrong?

I have an uncle who toured Easter Island and said his first sight of the stone giants was the most profoundly moving moment of his life. I have a friend who visited Stonehenge and said the same thing of that experience. They both said that part of the power came from the mystery of their destination.

I have peered through a backyard telescope at Mars and searched for the signs of life I *knew* existed on our next-door neighbor in space. I have been fascinated by Loch Ness and have always longed for—almost needed—the monster to be real, as if I would lose something precious and be somehow lessened if it were not. I also have always rooted for the existence of Atlantis the way we root for a badly outmatched underdog. I have always wished that UFOs were real too—not just as UFOs, but as real alien spaceships zipping in to visit Earth and say "Howdy do!" I am sure I would be deeply crushed if any of these things proved to be fake and nonexistent. Somehow, my world would then be smaller, less appealing. My life would be duller and less colorful without them.

Still, I can't help but ponder: What are we searching for in the way we cling to these seemingly unexplainable mysteries? What are we hoping to find and to gain? Or to hold onto? Wonder? Inspiration? Newness? A sense that excitement still exists in the universe and that there still are things out there for us to discover? Simply that science doesn't know everything yet? (I was thrilled by the discovery of a new shark species, the megamouth shark, in 1972. I was in oceanography graduate school at Oregon State University and remember reveling in the notion that we still didn't know everything there was to know about the ocean.) Or is it that we long to disprove our rational, skeptical, "scientific" disbelief in natural magic and wonder and open our world to more limitless possibilities? Is it, after all, simply to be able to say (and believe) that anything is possible?

The mysteries that nag at the fringes of our all-powerful science allow us to wrestle with the limits of how we define our world and our understanding of the rules that govern it. These mysteries seem to help us fight against rigid order and commonplace reality. If Loch Ness can actually have a monster, if the myth of Atlantis can turn into real history, then why *can't* I go time-traveling to whenever I want? Why can't elves and unicorns be real? Why can't there be a pot of gold at the end of a rainbow? Why can't magic hover at the fringes of our world to zip in at its own random discretion to grace our lives?

I believe that we humans *need* mysteries. We need something for our beliefs and our values to wrestle against, to test themselves against. I believe that mysteries are essential to developing and holding our sense of wonder and our sense of the grandeur of life and of the universe around us. Mysteries keep us alive and fascinated with our surroundings and our very existence. If there were no mysteries left, nothing we needed to unravel, life would seem gray and pointless.

How we deal with, honor and approach mysteries helps define who we are as a culture and how we approach our world and our universe. I believe that watching how science and scientists approach the mysteries that confront them helps us define what our science is, and helps us gain a sense of the function and role of science in our lives.

This book presents sixteen fascinating mysteries for you to ponder, challenge and debate. They span across the major disciplines of science. Many of them have endured for centuries, some are new within the last half of the twentieth century. Some have captivated and thrilled the public but have elicited only disdain and indifference from the scientific community. Some have fascinated and excited scientists but have elicited only bored apathy from the public. A few have captivated both.

Because there is a dual purpose to the presentations in this book—present the wonder and magic of each mystery as well as the grinding, logical processes of science—I have split the entry for each mystery into two main sections. Each mystery is presented first in story form (The Mystery), the most powerful way to revel in and fully appreciate the mystery. Stories allow us to experience the emotional depths of a mystery.

Each mystery also includes a factual section (The Science) presenting what science currently knows about this mystery and how scientists have studied it. This section includes the theories that various scientists have developed to explain the mystery. Where there remains controversy (and there often does), I have tried to include both sides of the argument and the evidence and data to support each side. The resulting combination should allow the reader to fully evaluate each mystery from all perspectives and vantage points and draw their own conclusions.

I owe deep debts of thanks to a number of people for their contributions to this book. First, thank you to Suzanne Barchers, who created the idea for the book and talked me into writing it. Second, my biggest thanks go to Roni Berg, the love of my life, a talented graphic designer, conceptualizer and editor, for her invaluable efforts in researching these mysteries and in editing and shaping each story. Thanks also to May Haven for her efforts to review and edit the stories. I also owe a great debt of thanks to the following teachers—Peggy Swearingen, Debbie Leonard, Susan Ferlotta, Carla Briente, Linda Yancy and Merl Williams—and to their students (ranging from the fifth through the seventh grade), who have graciously read, discussed and critiqued these stories. Their comments and ideas have been immensely helpful. Thanks are also due to the librarians at the Salizar Library at Sonoma State University who greatly assisted in the research on many of these stories.

Finally, I owe thanks to you, the reader, for grappling with and pondering these incredible treasures we call science mysteries. Become curious as you read, be skeptical, become passionately opinionated. Research, pontificate, explore and enjoy those mysteries that strike a resonant chord in you. But don't stop there. Identify and research other science mysteries to fascinate and excite us all.

There are only sixteen mysteries in this book. The world abounds with incredible mysteries, enough to enthrall us all for a lifetime. As Carl Sagan once said, "Somewhere, something incredible is waiting to be known." And as Albert Einstein once said, "The most beautiful thing we can experience is the mysterious."

Enjoy!

# Using This Book

The entry for each mystery in this book is divided into seven sections, with selected references included at the end. It is important that each student understand exactly what is in each of these sections and which are factually authenticated and which are not.

At a Glance. This section creates background context and perspective for the science mystery and following story. It includes a brief review of the events and historical figures that led up to, and set the stage for, the events depicted in the story and subsequent science discussion. All information included in this section represents common belief and may be considered factually authenticated and reliable.

The Mystery. Stories are included to propel students into the middle of the wondrous worlds of these natural mysteries and unexplained wonders. Each story is designed to help students experience and appreciate the mystery and its awe, wonder, thrills-and-chills, glory and terror. Each story also represents one major current or historical viewpoint concerning the science mystery being presented.

Some of these stories are historically accurate accounts of actual events and are completely reliable as sources of accurate information. Some are based solely on the testimony and experiences of one or two participants and have not been verified or authenticated. Some are my interpretation and extension of historical events. The source material for each story is specified in the About This Story section.

About This Story. I am often asked, "Is that true?" But I am rarely sure how to answer. Some of each story is accepted as fact by the general science community. Some of the stories are based on the experiences of one or more individuals or on their own version of the truth. Some of the stories have been created based on available scientific information. There is no one, simple answer. This brief section provides details about the type of information on which the story is based so that students can better interpret the story and fold it into their understanding of the science and the mystery.

The Science. This section is reserved for the hardest science knowledge, evidence, hypothesis, theory and understanding available. Often I present some historical context, showing how science knowledge and understanding have evolved over time. Where there is still significant controversy within the scientific community, I present and compare the various viewpoints, presenting objections to, and limitations of, each theory. In part, I use this section to help students evaluate and assess the story and gain a more informed perspective on story events. Finally, I also try to define the current limits of science understanding regarding the mystery, and present the remaining questions and challenges for future scientists.

Fact or Fiction? This section presents a capsulized summary of the evidence for and against the mystery, and draws the best-available conclusions to related key questions based on current scientific understanding.

Follow-On Questions to Explore. The goal of this section is to help students personalize the mystery and internalize the science concepts. Follow-on questions seek students' opinions and experiences and ask them to compare their opinions and experiences to the body of available scientific information. They prompt science discussion and present themes developed in the story that merit further attention and research by students. The questions in this section also ask students to evaluate and compare the evidence and decide what they believe and do not believe. Finally, the follow-on questions lead students to scrutinize the scientific process as it applies to these mysteries to gain a better understanding of the approach scientists use to study any topic.

Follow-On Activities. Follow-on activities are designed to demonstrate and bring to life elements and themes central to the story and the key science concepts presented in the subsequent science discussion. Few of these activities require equipment or supplies. Each teacher should feel free to modify and restructure the activities to best meet their own needs and those of their students.

References. Selected references are included for further reading of the various views and scientific opinions.

# That's Weird!

# Sunken City

## Atlantis—Lost Splendor or Greek Myth?

### At a Glance

Plato started it. In two of his books he described a glorious land that had existed ninety-five hundred years before his time (twelve thousand years before the present), a land of marble buildings crowned with gold and silver, of fruits and vegetation never before seen in his Mediterranean world. Plato described in detail mighty irrigation canals and elaborate structures, hot and cold running water and domesticated horses, all of which would not reappear in human society for thousands of years. Most importantly, he described an advanced race of humans whose civilization, culture, science, technology and accomplishments all arrived in the Atlantean culture at least ten thousand years earlier than modern science thinks possible.

And then the entire island continent sank beneath the waves. In a single day, Plato tells us, Atlantis sank into the depths of the Atlantic and disappeared forever. What a day that must have been!

Through the 1700s, the existence of ancient Atlantis was accepted as fact. But as scientific skills and knowledge developed, doubts emerged. By the early 1900s, Atlantis was considered to be a myth, a work of fiction by crafty old Plato. Everyone agreed that the final nail in Atlantis's coffin was hammered home by the emergence of plate-tectonic theory in the late 1960s and early 1970s. North America and Europe had drifted apart over the previous several hundred million years. Before that they had fit together perfectly. There was no room for an island continent in the middle of the Atlantic. Atlantis was fiction. Period.

But more recent studies have found chinks in the armor of the Atlantis-as-fiction theory. Like a nine-lived cat, Atlantis refuses to die. New evidence hints at the possibility that a land mass might have existed in the mid-Atlantic as recently as twelve thousand years ago, and that advanced civilizations could have existed long before ancient Egypt (the first civilization from which we have written records).

Could Atlantis be real? Could this prehistoric paradise really have been destroyed in a single fiery day of destruction? Suddenly the questions are back on the table for us to ponder, study and dream about.

# The Mystery: Sunken City

Early morning sunlight sparkled off the thin plates of gold that covered the dome of the great Temple of Poseidon, more than 100 feet high and 600 feet long. Palaces and lesser temples of marble and silver radiated outward from the Temple of Poseidon, across the great inner circle of this capital city. Graceful bridges over perfectly carved circular canals joined together buildings as well as wide parks filled with breathtaking statuary. Towering seawalls tamed the stormy Atlantic Ocean, named for Atlas, eldest son of the god Poseidon and first king of these lands.

Towering above the seawalls rose the king's palace, built of black and red marble and lined with sheets of a red-bronze metal, called orichalcum, that shone more brightly than gold. Lush, rippling green fields spread west from the capital city for miles before curving up into the foothills of towering, snowcapped mountains. The city and the land were more beautiful than a fairy tale.

But on this spring day King Atlan was not pleased. A tall and muscled man, he planted himself on the wall of his palace, wearing flowing silken robes sewn with gold threads, and gazed steadily seaward. Without turning his head, King Atlan demanded at the sound of approaching feet, "What news from my brother's lands in the west?"

The general, wearing a gold breastplate and plumed helmet, dropped to one knee and bowed. "Everything beyond the western mountains is flooded with seawater, my lord. The entire province has sunk below the waves."

The king slowly shook his head, but did not turn away from the sea. "I feared as much. My scientists have been measuring shifts in those lands for over a month. Were all the people safely evacuated?"

The general nodded. "Yes, my king. Your engineers were able to build the amazing ships and canals that carried everyone and all the kingdom's wealth beyond danger."

"The same fate has already befallen two of the northern provinces, my lord," moaned a gray-haired adviser carrying a bulging armful of scrolls. "Over one-quarter of Atlantis has sunk!"

The king concluded, "I fear our beloved Atlantis is doomed. We must prepare the people to move to a new land."

The two glowering bodyguards who always hovered around their golden king, waiting to serve his every whim and order, began to wail and moan. "Our dear Atlantis cannot sink!" "What will happen to our great city? To my home and wealth?"

"Silence with your whining!" bellowed the king. He pointed toward the rising Sun, shimmering like an orange disk just above the blue horizon. "A messenger ship is overdue with a report of my army's success. There are rich lands surrounding the sea beyond the Pillars of Hercules to the east. If the army completes its conquest, we will move there before dear Atlantis sinks forever to the depths of Lord Poseidon's ocean realm."

The bodyguards gushed soothing responses. "There are only uncivilized savages in the lands to the east, my lord. Your glorious army *must* be victorious. Savages can never stop trained troops."

The tottering adviser agreed. "Fear not, my king. Good news will surely arrive."

The general from the west protested, "Atlantis cannot sink, my king. It is the land given to us by Lord Poseidon and Atlas, themselves. They will protect it forever!"

"They have not protected my brother's western province!" snapped King Atlan. Finally the king turned away from the sea and glared at a small, bent man covered in a ragged black robe. "What say you, soothsayer? Will the army's news be good or bad? Will Atlantis sink or reside above the waves forever? Speak, old man. I command you."

The soothsayer closed his eyes and hummed while his fingers seemed to paw and mold the air before him into a vision. "Where arrogance and cruelty reign, forces greater than Poseidon will gather to take revenge."

"What mean you?" demanded King Atlan. "It is not arrogance to *know* we are the greatest civilization on Earth. It is fact. All others are crude savages. And it is not cruel to kill those we encounter. They are better off dead than living in caves and huts as animals."

The general and bodyguards chuckled in agreement.

"Only Zeus is more powerful than Poseidon," muttered an adviser.

But the soothsayer continued without acknowledging the interruptions. "I see that the army's messenger will arrive this very day. But his news will do you no good, nor will you ever call him to your side to deliver it to you."

"Of course I'll call him to me!" The king waved his hand and sneered, "I asked for simple answers and you speak in riddles, old man."

A slight tremor rumbled through Atlantis, causing the buildings to sway and small waves to ripple down the long canals. The old adviser squealed and dropped to his knees, clawing at the smooth stone wall for a handhold. Scrolls clattered across the walkway. The others laughed at him. Small earthquakes were common in Atlantis. Most people ignored them and went about their daily duties.

A second, stronger tremor rattled through the capital city, followed by a thunderous explosion. A boiling plume of ash and smoke rose from one of the lower mountains. Thin red lines of lava oozed on its flanks. Screams and shouts of people in the vast city of splendor could be heard above the freight-train rumble of the volcano.

"My king, you must away!" squealed one of the bodyguards.

"Nonsense," scoffed King Atlan. "That volcano is leagues distant from us and poses no threat. Besides, we have had volcanoes before in Atlantis." He snapped his fingers at his adviser, still regathering his precious scrolls. "When was the last volcano?"

The frazzled, gray-haired man nervously rummaged through scrolls. "Ah, here it is, my lord. Seventy-eight years ago, in the southern mountains."

"There," shrugged the king. "A common occurrence. Have my science advisers draw up any necessary plans to protect populated areas. And despite what my learned soothsayer claims …" The king paused and sneered at the bent, ragged man. The general and bodyguards dutifully chuckled. "… It is only the news from the army I care most about, for that is our future."

The entire top half of the volcanic mountain exploded in a ball of red-orange flame that rivaled the Sun. The explosion's shock wave slammed into the glittering city, flattening people and trees. Water sloshed dangerously high in the canals that ringed the city walls. Towering fountains of glowing lava burst from a dozen gashes in the mountain's sides like a dazzling fireworks display. Building-sized boulders smashed through the city and raised great geysers as they smacked into the bay.

"We must away!" whimpered one bodyguard, now trembling on hands and knees.

"Look!" cried King Atlan, pointing out to sea. "A sail! News arrives!"

"But the danger …," whined his adviser.

"There is no danger as long as the army's news is favorable!" snapped the king. "Have my engineers do what they must to protect the city and prepare the people to evacuate." Still pointing to the tiny white dot on the eastern horizon, he added, "I will remain here until that ship arrives. A king must always look to the future."

The earth groaned and shook like a sapling being shaken by an angry bear. Statues tumbled. Graceful columns buckled and crashed to the ground in showers of splintered marble and dust. Walls cracked. Buildings screeched in protest and wobbled like rubber toys.

"My king!" screamed the bodyguards. "You must flee to safety!"

"Stay!" ordered King Atlan, ignoring the chaos behind him, staring only at the white dot that had grown into a spreading sail with the blue flag of Atlantis fluttering high above. "Have the army deployed to maintain order and move our citizens to the hills for safety." The general from the west bowed and staggered off, as if on the deck of a ship being tossed about by a fierce storm, to deliver the king's orders.

Tremor after tremor, rolling like one unending earthquake, turned the land to jelly. Buildings collapsed. Bridges disintegrated. A great cloud of marble dust and debris hung like a death shroud over the city. Great fissures and gashes tore through the land, creating instant canyons where flat city and fields had been moments before.

A second mountain exploded in a giant fireball. Jets of high-pressure lava sprayed a thousand feet into the air. Fiery ash, screeching red-hot lava and molten rocks rained down thick as snow. A thousand fires roared through the city, spreading to join into a mighty funeral pyre for the great capital. The screams of the crushed, burned and dying were drowned by the thunder of volcanoes, the roar of the shifting earth, the whine of a gale-force volcanic wind and the howl of dying buildings being torn apart.

Even as the walls crumbled around him, King Atlan stood transfixed at the seawall, straining to see a sign of his army's victory. "Look! The messenger stands in the bow eager to report!"

"We will all die!" wailed the bodyguards.

Propelled by a strong eastern wind, the boat sped toward the royal dock. Now King Atlan could see his general's brother, the royal messenger, standing in the bow—battered, blood-spattered, humbled, filled with bitter sadness, head lowered. The look said more than any detailed report could. It confirmed the king's nightmarish fears. His army had lost. The Athenians had somehow defeated his unstoppable legions.

Finally the king perceived that deadly danger lay all around him.

Before the boat could draw close enough to be roped to dock, the water in the bay washed out to sea as if the ocean's plug had been pulled. The boat hit bottom and listed far to one side. Sailors were thrown across the deck like rag dolls. The bay's bottom rocks, kelp and clam beds were exposed to dry air. Canals drained to bottom mud as water rushed out to the empty bay.

King Atlan stood rooted in fascination. The ocean seemed to have disappeared. Slowly, his eyes were drawn far out to sea, where the dark line of a monstrous wave had begun to rise, stretching across the horizon.

The land of Atlantis rose, fell and twisted like a rodeo bucking bronc, and rumbled like deafening thunder. Fire, ash and billowing smoke hid the great city in a black haze. White-hot wildfires raced across the fields. Giant plumes of ash and rock rose from the volcanoes 60,000 feet into the mid-Atlantic sky. Rivers of lava raced toward the city and the sea.

The monster wave grew like a menacing shadow towering high above the city walls. Like a thundering avalanche roaring in at 60 miles per hour and rising almost a thousand feet into the air, the wave sent uncountable tons of water slamming across the city, erasing every building, bridge, wall, tree and sign of human habitation from the face of the land.

The land itself groaned under the onslaught of these millions of tons of water. The mighty wave boiled and churned all the way to the distant foothills. With a final trembling groan the entire plateau of Atlantis sank deep into the ocean, settling thousands of feet down into the crust of the earth.

It was over in a flash, as seawater surged in to replace the land. Waves, scattered debris and muddy waters sloshed where fertile fields and palaces had stood. Circling gulls screeched in confusion at the loss of their perches. All that remained of the mighty nation were a few scattered islands, the high Atlantis mountaintops that had not sunk, peopled by simple shepherds who had not ventured down from their mountain huts in years and knew nothing of the greatness of the now-lost cities, armies and canals of the valleys far below.

Mighty Atlantis was gone.

## About This Story

This story is conjecture. It is a series of imagined events portraying what the last day of Atlantis might have been like, if there was an Atlantis, if it was destroyed in a single day—both ideas based on Plato's writings and on indigenous legends from both sides of the Atlantic Ocean. However, all descriptions of Atlantis included in this story are taken from translations of Plato's descriptions of the island nation. The descriptions of the cataclysm that destroyed Atlantis are taken from scientific records and on-site observations of volcanic, seismic and tsunami events recorded on islands around the world. The characters, too, are based on Plato's descriptions.

## The Science

Before the 1950s, investigating the existence of Atlantis involved historical writings, legends, mariner diaries and logs, ship soundings and the disciplines of geology, geography, biology, linguistics and archaeology. After 1950 came scuba and sonar, which permitted humans to peer directly under the oceans. After 1970, satellites, computers and the new plate-tectonic theory were added to the tools scientists could use. In the late 1970s, deep-sea submersibles were invented to actually cruise the ocean floor. In the 1980s, multispectral satellite mapping was developed to produce detailed images of Earth's surface, including the ocean floor. Some of the evidence uncovered by these various scientific tools points toward the existence of Atlantis, and some points against it.

There are four key points in the evidence against the existence of Atlantis. First, there is no direct supporting evidence to prove that Atlantis existed—no written records, no artifacts, no land and no sites to study and catalog—and science cannot accept anything without physical evidence and proof. Second, plate-tectonic theory (currently accepted as fact) does not allow for the existence of a great landmass between North America and Europe. Third, multiband satellite mapping indicates that the mid-Atlantic shelf where Atlantis supposedly lay is 5,000 to 8,000 feet deep. There is no evidence of any massive shift in the shape of the earth's crust over the past fifteen thousand years, and a large landmass couldn't have sunk more than 5,000 feet without leaving telltale traces and clues in the surrounding land and seabed. Finally, modern anthropologists have developed a detailed theory for the development of human civilization. The level of sophistication that Atlantis supposedly possessed fifteen to eighteen thousand years ago comes almost ten thousand years too early to mesh with the timetable of modern theory (for example, humans supposedly didn't domesticate animals until 5000 B.C.; cities supposedly didn't develop until 4000 B.C.; etc.).

Still, there is strong circumstantial evidence, and some tantalizing bits of hard data, to support Plato's Atlantis. In the late 1980s, an ancient African metal mine forty-three thousand years old was discovered. But that is long before a metal mine could have existed according to modern theory. Cro-Magnon cave drawings at San Michele d'Arudy and Lamarche (both in France) showing horses with bridles have been carbon-dated at twenty-two to twenty-five thousand years old. But modern theory says horses were not tamed until 3000 B.C. Giant stone ruins at Gozo on the island of Malta have been dated to 8000 B.C., and show advanced human engineering long before modern theory says it should have occurred. If modern theory can be wrong about these three places, it can be wrong about a fourth—Atlantis. The ancient Babylonian city of Nineveh was thought to be a myth until it was recently discovered. Maybe the myth of Atlantis is real.

The traditional lore of virtually every indigenous culture surrounding the Atlantic holds a central story of a great island land that sank and whose advanced civilization was destroyed. Every European story says this land lay to the west (the Atlantic). Every American story says it lay to the east (the Atlantic). Most of these cultures had no contact with one another, and most of these stories predate Plato's writings. The story as recorded by Egyptian and Aztec scholars, for example, was written in stone more than three thousand years before Plato's time. And more than thirty indigenous cultures surrounding the Atlantic have a name for this land that sounds like the word Atlantis—Atlala (Berber), Avalon (Welsh), Atlaintika (Basque), Atlantida (Portuguese), Atli (Viking), Arallin (Babylonian), Atda (Arab), Azatan (Aztec), Atlan (Venezuela) and so forth. Only one name, Valhalla (Teutonic), is not remarkably similar to the word Atlantis.

Identical stories of a sinking Atlantic island grew independently in each culture. It is very unlikely that each of these cultures, separated by thousands of years and thousands of miles, could have invented the same fictional story. They had no direct contact with one another, and yet each claimed to have had contact with Atlantis. An ancient Egyptian papyrus now displayed in the Hermitage Museum in St. Petersburg, Russia, says that in approximately 3000 B.C. the pharaoh sent an expedition to the west to search for the land from which, thirty-five hundred years before, ancestors had sailed to Egypt. What else could that land be but Atlantis?

At least four other famous "mythical" cities have turned into fact in recent years when modern technology has made it possible to discover their sites. Homer's city of Troy has been discovered, and both the desert trading center of Nineveh and the desert city of Ubar have been detected by wideband satellite imaging. The space shuttle *Atlantis* took pictures that detected the site of the ancient Thai city of Ankor Wat. All these cities were dismissed as myths until modern technology found them and made them fact. Atlantis could be next on the list to be discovered.

Evidence has also been compiled on the ocean floor. In 1984, Dr. Maria Klenova of the Soviet Academy of Sciences reported that ocean bottom rocks taken in samples from a 6,000-foot depth north of the Azores Islands (on the mid-Atlantic ridge) had to have been formed at atmospheric pressure less than fifteen thousand years ago. Dr. Pierre Termier, a French oceanographer, studied ocean bottom rocks from about 500 miles off the Azores and discovered that they were made from a type of lava called tachylyte, which is only formed in the presence of air and which will dissolve in seawater in fifteen to twenty thousand years. Both of these small studies show that what is now deep ocean floor in the mid-Atlantic—exactly where Atlantis supposedly lay—was dry land until around twelve to fifteen thousand years ago—just when Atlantis supposedly sank.

Mid-Atlantic core samples drilled by the United States Geologic Survey (USGS) in 1980 led to the same conclusion. They show a layer of volcanic ash laid down between twelve and fifty thousand years ago—a sure indication of local, above-water volcanic activity. Finally, the shape of the mid-Atlantic plateau generally matches ancient descriptions of the shape and size of Atlantis.

More intriguing, a tip of ancient Atlantis might have been seen. On March 1, 1882, the British ship *S. S. Jesmond,* sailing from Sicily to New Orleans, found muddy water and millions of dead fish floating on the surface of the mid-Atlantic. On the horizon the crew saw smoke. By March 2, the *Jesmond* had sailed close enough to see that the smoke was billowing from an island—an island sitting where the charts showed no land for more than 1,000 miles in any direction.

The experienced British captain, Joseph Robson, led a landing party onto the barren, lava-rock island and, in two days of exploration, found arrowheads, bronze swords and the crumbling remains of massive walls. The few artifacts he took he showed to reporters in New Orleans, who reported them in the local paper. The captain and all hands aboard swore that they had truthfully found a new island. Four other ships reported seeing mysterious smoke rising along the horizon in the mid-Atlantic during the same week. Their stories were reported in the *New York Times* and other East Coast papers.

The *Jesmond*'s British shipping company claimed ownership of Robson's artifacts. They were returned to London without further study and supposedly housed in the company warehouse until it was destroyed by German rockets during World War II. Now we will never know if they really were from Atlantis. Still, *something* happened out in the mid-Atlantic that March, even though Robson's island was never seen again. It apparently sank back below the waves.

There is a great body of circumstantial evidence that says Plato's Atlantis could have existed. However, no physical, tangible evidence exists to offer as proof. But there is one final question to ask: Where does science think Atlantis lay? Various theories have placed it in the Sahara Desert, in Antarctica, in the North Sea, off Greenland, in the Caribbean Sea and in the Mediterranean Sea, as well as throughout the Atlantic.

Submerged roads and walls have been found by divers scattered across the western Caribbean—evidence of an advanced ancient civilization if not actually of Atlantis itself. Psychic Edgar Casey claimed that Atlantis would be found near the Caribbean Island of Bimini. But studies have discounted this area as a possible site for Atlantis.

In the 1970s, Dr. James Mavor of the Woods Hole Oceanographic Institute in Massachusetts discovered that small Santorini Island (originally called Thera), located near Crete in the Mediterranean, had been blown apart by a massive volcanic explosion around 3500 B.C. This explosion was far bigger than that of Krakatau in 1883 (the most massive modern volcanic explosion), and blew out much of the island. A large chunk of the island sank during the explosion.

Several of Santorini's land sites, as well as areas that sank during the explosion, have been excavated and studied. Evidence of a major port city of an advanced civilization was found both on land and under several hundred feet of water—a civilization that existed before the 3500 B.C. volcanic explosion. This evidence is currently being studied. With artifacts, photos and hard evidence to prove that something was on Santorini Island six thousand years ago, many scientists have accepted Santorini as the real Atlantis.

## Fact or Fiction?

There is no proof that Atlantis was fiction. Unfortunately, neither is there any direct evidence or hard proof that it was real. Without physical evidence, most scientists discount the existence of Atlantis, or are at least highly skeptical. It runs counter to the nature of science to accept anything without tangible, physical evidence. Besides, the existence of Atlantis's advanced culture fifteen thousand years ago runs counter to too many current and dominant theories.

The case of Santorini Island, however, has changed much of this thinking. Santorini is real. It has been studied. Ancient artifacts are present there. So many scientists have assumed that Plato wrote about Santorini and just changed the name, the location and the dates, and exaggerated a few details. Because Santorini Island has been generally accepted as Plato's Atlantis, intriguing bits of pro-Atlantis data from the mid-Atlantic have been ignored and have never been studied to see if they lead to hard evidence.

Still, it is most probable that Santorini is not Atlantis. The dates, size and location are all wrong. A small Mediterranean island nation does not fit with folklore and linguistic studies from all around the Atlantic. But the case of Santorini does establish that an advanced civilization existed at least seven thousand years ago, stretching modern theory. Maybe funding will be acquired to pursue the small clues hinting that Atlantis lay in the Atlantic, where Plato said it was. Without detailed (and expensive) searches of the mid-Atlantic ridge, the existence of Atlantis will remain inspiring but doubtful.

## Follow-On Questions to Explore

1. Compare the types of evidence used to support and discount the existence of Atlantis. For example, which do you think has more scientific weight: recent plate-tectonic theory holding that North America and Europe used to be joined, or linguistic and folklore studies showing that virtually every ancient civilization surrounding the Atlantic has a myth and name matching the story of Atlantis? Which do you believe more? Why? Which do you think is a more believable site for Atlantis: Santorini Island (which can be seen and studied, even though no ancient stories place Atlantis there), or the mid-Atlantic (which so many stories indicate as the site of Atlantis, even though there is no physical evidence)? Why?

2. Why do you think Atlantis (a lost paradise) has been so popular over the centuries? What makes it interesting to you? Do you think Atlantis would be as interesting if there were any proof one way or the other of whether it ever really existed? Why?

# Follow-On Activities

1.  Identify and research other lost worlds (Shangri-La, Babylon, lost cities of the desert such as Nineveh, etc.). Make a list of all the lost paradises you can find. Who believed/believes in them? What happened to them? Mark on a map their supposed locations. Why weren't they ever found again? Were lost cities thought to be myths or stories before they were found? How did they stop being myths and stories and become historical fact? What does this mean for Atlantis?

2.  Create a lost-world myth of your own. What will you call your lost world? Why? Where was it? Why? What special properties/attributes will you give to the land and its inhabitants? Who founded it—humans or gods? How and why was it lost? What does the new finder get? Keep a log of both the difficult and fun parts of creating your lost-world myth. How can you make your story fascinating to other people?

# References

Berlitz, Charles. *Atlantis, the Eighth Continent.* New York: G. P. Putnam's Sons, 1984.

———. *The Mystery of Atlantis.* New York: G. P. Putnam's Sons, 1972.

Bowman, John. *The Quest for Atlantis.* New York: Doubleday, 1971.

Cazeau, Charles. *Exploring the Unknown.* New York: Doubleday, 1980.

Cohen, Daniel. *Mysterious Disappearances.* New York: Dodd, Mead, 1976.

Ellis, Richard. *Imagining Atlantis.* New York: Alfred Knopf, 1998.

Leonard, R. *Quest for Atlantis.* New York: Franklin Watts, 1979.

Mavor, James. *Voyage to Atlantis.* New York: Scribner's Sons, 1973.

Spence, Lewis. *The History of Atlantis.* New York: Gramercy Books, 1996.

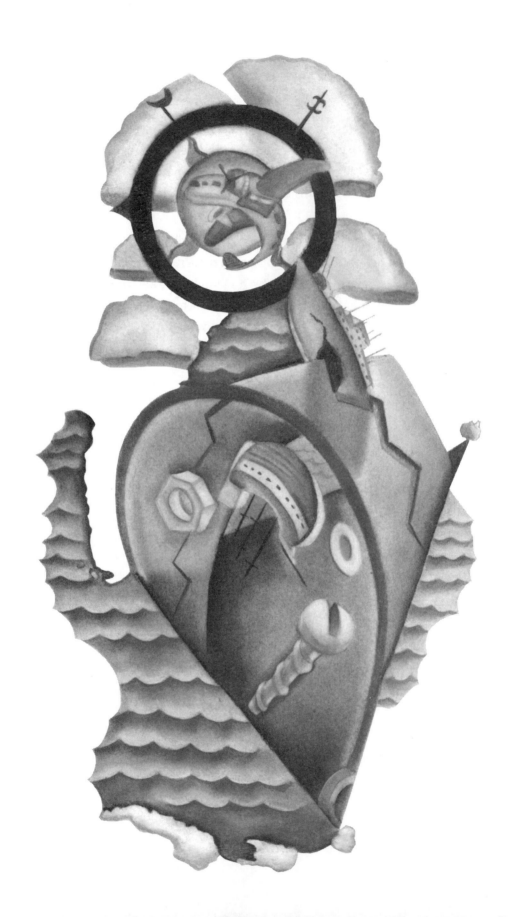

# Disappearing Act
## Bermuda Triangle—
## Annoying Anomalies or Terrifying Tales?

## At a Glance

The words "Bermuda Triangle" conjure up as much terror for most sailors as "Pirates off the port bow!" The many ship and plane disappearances and unexplained events in the area have become one of the most famous of all mysteries. However, this long-standing oceanic region of deadly mystery didn't get its name until an article in the August 1968 issue of *Argosy* first used the words "Bermuda Triangle." Although there is no official definition for the Triangle, there is general agreement that it covers the half million square miles inside a triangle with corners at the island of Bermuda (NE), Puerto Rico (S) and Miami, Florida (SW).

Columbus reported problems with compass readings and navigation when he sailed through this area. Hundreds of ships and planes have disappeared in the Triangle. Seemingly perfectly good ships have been mysteriously abandoned in the Triangle. Ships and planes disappear without sending a distress call or warning call of any kind. Compasses stop pointing faithfully north and begin to spin, electronic equipment mysteriously fails and pilots become inexplicably disoriented—all within the Bermuda Triangle. The question lingers, begging for a answer: Is there really something strange about this particular patch of ocean?

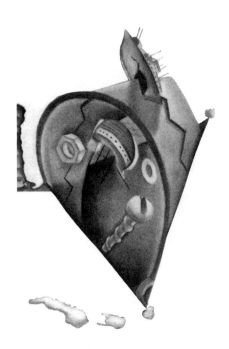

# The Mystery: Disappearing Act

Twenty-eight-year-old charter airline captain Robert Linquist stuffed both hands grumpily into his pockets and slouched against the front landing strut of his Douglas DC-3 charter plane. Even though it was the evening of December 27, 1948, his leather flight jacket was unzipped in the balmy tropical air at the San Juan, Puerto Rico, airport. His hat was cocked far back on his head. In disgust, he reared back and kicked the plane's tire.

Twenty-two-year-old copilot Ernest Hill whistled to himself as he half danced, half walked across the dark tarmac of the airport wearing an aloha shirt and swimming trunks. He, at least, had made a point of enjoying his twelve hours of off-duty time in Puerto Rico, even if Linquist had insisted on staying at the airport to nurse their plane back into airworthiness.

"Our little angle ready to fly?" Hill asked.

Linquist shook his head and hunched his shoulders. "Engines are fine. But the batteries are drained. They were almost out of battery fluid. Some jerk at the company never filled them. They're full now, but they won't be recharged in time for the flight. We can't check electronics, and we won't be able to transmit."

Hill shrugged and smiled his boyish confidence. "No big deal. The plane's generator will recharge the batteries during flight."

Linquist's thirty-two hundred hours of commercial flying experience pushed nagging doubts into his mind. It would be safer to wait until morning, when the batteries would be fully charged, to make sure they'd work and then check out the electronics before taking the plane into the air and across ocean waters. Hill was a rookie. Sure, he was a licensed pilot. But with less than two hundred hours in the air, he didn't have the experience to develop gut instincts about a plane or a flight. So Linquist lingered, torn by doubts and cautions.

Now Hill frowned. "You're not thinking of scrubbing the flight?"

"It would be safer—"

"No!" Hill blurted. "We gotta do this flight *tonight.* If we cancel, these people will demand refunds from the company. The company will get angry at *us,* and there goes our year-end bonus—which I'm gonna need if I'm going to pay for that new house my wife and I are buying."

Linquist slouched back against the landing strut. "I got my own troubles, pal. I got a wife and a five-year-old kid waiting in Miami. My wife threw a fit when I told her I had a six-day charter over Christmas, even though we need the extra holiday pay rates. I promised to show up by breakfast tomorrow bringing Christmas with me, or else. If I cancel the flight now, she'll kill me."

Hill playfully punched his captain's shoulder. "Then it's settled. We fly tonight."

"But the batteries …"

"The plane got us here all right. She'll get us home, too."

Again Linquist kicked the tire and reluctantly nodded. "File the flight plan. Notify the tourists. Let's load up and get outta here."

"Yahoo!" Hill cheered as he dashed for the control tower. Over his shoulder he called, "It's only a six-hour flight! What can go wrong?"

At 9:30 P.M. that evening, Linquist's DC-3 lumbered out to the end of the runway. Scattered puffy clouds drifted playfully across a sky of dazzlingly clear stars. With the plane's batteries still drained, Linquist heard the tower's instructions, but couldn't use the plane's radio to transmit back to the control tower. The tower refused to clear him for takeoff until he acknowledged their radio instructions. A thirty-minute stalemate followed as Linquist sat idling his plane's engines on the runway while his twenty-seven holiday passengers laughed, partied and sang Christmas carols in the back.

At 10:03 P.M. Linquist roared down the runway and into the night, cleared on the condition that he would circle San Juan long enough for his batteries to charge so he could transmit his revised flight plan. At 10:20 P.M. copilot Hill radioed the Federal Communications Center in San Juan that, for unknown reasons, they were unable to contact the tower and were proceeding to Miami.

At 11:23 P.M. the Overseas Air Traffic Control Center in Miami received a radio call from the DC-3 stating that they were flying at 8,500 feet, that all was well and that they would land in Miami at 4:05 A.M. The center radioed back that the wind was changing. The forecast for a northwest wind of 15 to 20 miles per hour had been changed to a northeast wind of 20 to 30 miles per hour, and Linquist was advised to adjust accordingly. The DC-3 never acknowledged. The center tried two more times to radio the wind-change information to Linquist's plane, but never received a reply.

Over the next three hours, the plane's twin engines droned monotonously, the tourists slowly drifted off to sleep and the stewardess, Mary Burks, plopped into a seat to get off her feet and begin her paperwork for the flight. Linquist and Hill alternated shifts at the controls with stretch walks up and down the aisle past the fitfully dozing passengers.

"Anything on the radio?" Linquist asked, squeezing back into his leather seat.

"Nothing," Hill answered, gazing out the side window at the endless black ocean below. "All quiet."

"I'm surprised we haven't heard anything," Linquist answered. "A revised weather forecast, other traffic, … *something*."

Hill simply shrugged and stared at the reflection of the half-moon dancing along the water.

At 3:30 A.M. Linquist's wife, Carol, and his son, Robert Jr., arrived at the Miami airport to greet the returning plane. Because Mrs. Linquist was a pilot's wife and there was little activity, they were allowed to wait and watch in the tower. But not wanting to alarm Mrs. Linquist, the tower duty officers didn't mention that they had never received confirmation when they radioed the wind change to her husband's plane.

As 4:00 A.M. neared and no word had been received, the tower officers grew steadily more expectant and more tense. In hushed conversations, tower staff began to whisper to one another about other planes that had disappeared on that same flight route. All eyes glanced from the clock to the radio speaker.

At 4:05 A.M. the planned arrival time for Linquist's plane, the tower chief tried to radio the DC-3. He received no reply. Tension slowly turned to fear in everyone except Robert Jr., who marveled at the rows of colored and blinking lights. He said it looked like a Christmas tree in the tower—a tree his daddy could put the presents under when he landed.

At 4:13 A.M. the tower speaker blared to life. With hardly a hiss of static to distort his voice, Linquist announced that he was 50 miles south of Miami, that all was fine, that he could see the glow of the city on the horizon and that he would land in twenty minutes. He requested landing instructions.

"That's my daddy's voice!" Robert Jr. squealed, laughing and clapping with joy. "Christmas is here!"

A cheer and a sigh of relief erupted across the tower. Tears of relief crept into Carol's eyes. Her growing dread evaporated. She realized she had been biting her lip while she had stared helplessly at the speaker. Now she happily dabbed her tongue at the pinprick of blood on her lip. The tower chief quickly plotted the landing approach for Linquist's plane. He radioed the details.

Linquist didn't acknowledge.

The chief radioed again, and again heard nothing.

Frantically, the tower crew changed transmitters and radioed again. Everyone stared at the speaker, praying to hear Linquist's voice.

No word was ever heard again from Robert Linquist's DC-3. The plane had simply vanished within sight of its destination.

The next morning a massive search was begun. The water in the area south of Miami is shallow—less than 50 feet deep in most parts. Any plane that went down in these waters would be clearly visible from above. Hundreds of ships and planes scoured thousands of square miles from Key West to Cuba to the Bahamas. Yet no sign of Linquist's plane was ever found—not the plane, not an oil slick, not one bit of debris, not even a single life vest. The investigation report from the

Civil Aeronautics Board simply said that the plane had disappeared for unknown reasons.

Another victim had vanished into the Bermuda Triangle.

Perhaps even more eerie, Robert Linquist Jr., as a young Air Force radar technician, was on duty in the Bermuda control tower on June 7, 1965, when an Air Force C-119 Flying Boxcar radioed its approach to the Bermuda airfield—and then disappeared without a word while on final approach to Bermuda. The C-119 disappeared in exactly the same way his father's plane had disappeared seventeen years before near Miami. And as with his father's plane, no trace of the Air Force C-119 was ever found.

## About This Story

The characters and events in this story are historical record, taken from the FAA Board of Inquiry and the reports by the several towers and communications centers involved. The charter DC-3 Robert Linquist flew that day did disappear and has never been found. The dialog between pilot and copilot presented in this story is based on the brief character sketches included in the official record and on the sequence of events presented in that record.

## The Science

Most scientists refuse to discuss the Bermuda Triangle, fearing that, if they are associated with a topic considered to be frivolous pseudoscience by their peers, their credibility and standing in the scientific community will be permanently destroyed. Those who have studied the Bermuda Triangle extensively say that there is no mystery. How, then, do they explain the vast number of disappearances and other strange reports?

Supporters of the Bermuda Triangle mystery say that hundreds of ships and planes have disappeared there—without any trace of debris ever being found, and usually without any distress call ever having been made. The disappearances often occur in good weather without any apparent explanation. As perfect examples, supporters often cite Linquist's DC-3 and the tanker *S.S. Marine Sulfur Queen*, which steamed out of Beaumont, Texas, in early 1963 with an experienced crew of thirty-nine. Early in the afternoon on February 3, en route to its destination of Norfolk, Virginia, the ship made a standard radio position call, reporting its location as being near Key West, Florida, and reporting that it was on schedule and steaming normally. The *Marine Sulfur Queen* was never heard from again. Three days later, one of the ship's life jackets was found bobbing in calm seas 50 miles southwest. The ship had vanished.

University scientists and the U.S. Navy and Coast Guard, all of whom have conducted extensive studies of the Bermuda Triangle, say that the three most famous disappearances—Navy Training Flight 19 (1946), the *Cyclops* (1918), and the *Marine Sulfur Queen* (1963)—as well as the host of smaller boat and plane losses, are easily explainable. The area covered by the Triangle is the pleasure-boat capital of the world, and one of the busiest shipping routes in world. Although ships do disappear there, they do so at no faster a rate than in any other patch of ocean, considering the particularly dense use of the Triangle. The Coast Guard responds to an average of twenty-three distress calls each day in the Bermuda Triangle (more than eight thousand calls per year). A few of those calls are bound to end in mysterious disaster.

More importantly, the ocean in this area features some of the world's most inviting-looking waters—warm and azure, beckoning every novice with a boat out for a pleasure ride. However, this area is also as treacherous as any other in the world's oceans. Storms brew up fast and mean with no warning. Waves pile up 10 to 20 feet high (and often higher) in minutes. The current is fast and relentless and quickly disperses any sign of debris. Sudden microstorms arise, last a few minutes and dissipate, even on an otherwise clear day. But those momentary storms can be electrically intense and exceptionally violent—often creating vicious water spouts and chaotic waves capable of flipping the boats of even seasoned sailors.

Winds shift erratically and suddenly. In fact, it is most likely that a simple wind shift from northwest to northeast doomed Robert Linquist's DC-3 in 1948. If he never received the wind-change report, and never adjusted for it, the wind would have pushed his plane well south of Miami—so far south that he would have missed the entire Florida peninsula and flown into the expanse of the Gulf of Mexico, where he would have run out of fuel and crashed, unable to report his position because of recurring onboard electrical problems.

Finally, this is an area frequented by rogue waves, single powerful waves that roar through the ocean at heights of 20 to 30 feet (and sometimes reaching heights of more than 100 feet). If a ship is hit by such a wave and can't survive being momentarily but completely submerged, it is doomed. Rogue waves can't be predicted or tracked. They hit with no warning, but are known to frequent the area of the Gulf Stream off southern Florida because of the current and wind configurations there. The truth is, it is a wonder that more ships aren't lost in these inviting but treacherous waters.

Believers in the mystery of the Bermuda Triangle point to pilot reports of temporary disorientation, of strange lights in the water and sky, of an inability to relocate the Sun. Some pilots have reported feeling like they were flying through Jell-O. Compasses, radios and magnetometers all go haywire during these events. Waves and currents can't explain occurrences such as these.

Florida State University and U.S. Navy geologists have documented the presence of large gas domes under the ocean floor in this vicinity. It is probable, they say, that great bubbles of gas leak from these undersea gas domes. The gas would mix with water as it rises, bubbling to the surface as a thick foam. To any observer, the water would mysteriously seem to froth and boil.

This mixture of water and gas would lack buoyancy and cause any ship caught in it to sink. As the mixture rose into the atmosphere as a thick, foamy cloud, it would cause sudden gaseous whiteouts for planes, which could account for pilots' loss of orientation and loss of visual contact with the Sun. It would also temporarily interfere with engine operation. Skeptics theorize that it is contact with these gaseous leaks and not some mysterious alien force that pilots are reporting.

Bermuda Triangle supporters say that, especially near the island of Bimini, plane and boat compasses begin to spin wildly, and radios and other electronics conk out at the same moment. Some unearthly magnetic anomaly or force is creating this electrical havoc in the Triangle. Sometimes these electromechanical devices come back online, sometimes they don't. Famed Navy Training Flight 19 was lost when the instructor reported that both his compasses mysteriously malfunctioned. Compasses of several of his students' planes did too. That is far too strange to be a coincidence.

The U.S. Navy's Project Magnet has mapped Earth's magnetic field all over the globe for twenty years and, says Henry Stockard, the project's director, "has passed over the area [of the Bermuda Triangle] hundreds of times and never noticed any unusual magnetic disturbances." Florida State University geophysicists have investigated hundreds of reports of magnetic disturbances. But no test, no measure, no piece of investigative equipment has ever detected any anomaly—not ever. Scientists' best guess to reconcile pilot reports with their own test results is that the pilots in question probably flew too near to one of the Florida strait's famous electric microstorms. The strong electric field of such a storm would blow out onboard electronics and disrupt compasses.

It is also true that pilots in this area often believe that their compasses aren't working correctly, even though they are, because the area off south Florida is one of two places in the world where magnetic north and true north are exactly in line with each other. (The other is the Devil's Sea off Japan, which is the other spot in all the seas known for mysterious ship disappearances.) Maps are aligned to true north, and lead to the North Pole as defined by lines of longitude. Compasses point to the north magnetic pole, a point that moves slowly over time and is now located about halfway between the North Pole and the northern coast of Greenland. In most of the United States, magnetic compasses do not point toward true north (as determined on a map), but north-northeast. Their readings must be "corrected" to show where true north lies.

In the western part of the Bermuda Triangle, compasses naturally point to true north because magnetic north and true north lie along the same line. So compasses here do not need the usual correction of 7 to 15 degrees. Sailors used to correcting compasses for true north could easily misreckon their course and become lost and disoriented.

Scientists conclude that there is no great mystery in the Bermuda Triangle, only unforgivingly treacherous and demanding seas and skies that quickly turn any human error into deadly tragedy. Thorough investigation and known oceanographic phenomena easily explain more than 98 percent of Bermuda Triangle mysteries. But not all. Some defy all reasonable explanation.

In 1952, Captain Martin Gaiden flew an Air Force B50-D Superfortress from the Azores Islands to Bermuda. For one hour of that flight, the plane stood still in the sky even with all engines revving at full throttle. Bermuda radar had the plane on their screen the whole time as a stationary blip. The plane could climb up or drop down or drift sideways, but not advance a single inch. After an hour, as if worming itself out of a thick glue, the plane crept forward and then broke free to continue its flight on course. The plane landed with 760 pounds less fuel than it should have had (one hour's consumption).

The crew of twelve, as well as half a dozen ground radar personnel, all witnessed this event, but no one could offer an explanation. The official Air Force report concluded that the event had no explanation.

# Fact or Fiction?

The idea that things mysteriously disappear in the Bermuda Triangle is fiction. Things disappear there at the same rate as they do in any other part of the oceans. Research data compiled by the Navy, the Coast Guard, university studies and private investigators have proven this beyond a shadow of a doubt.

But the question of disappearances is not the only question to ask about the Bermuda Triangle. Do an unusually large number of unexplained and mysterious events happen in the Triangle. Here, the answer seems to be yes. Far too many strange sightings, equipment malfunctions, breakdowns and unexplainable reports of boiling seas, pudding-thick air and other phenomena have been documented in the Bermuda Triangle to be dismissed. Incredible occurrences have been and continue to be reported in the Bermuda Triangle at a much higher rate than in any other part of the oceans. Official explanations seem inadequate. Something more is going on in those ocean waters.

Until scientists undertake a serious, large-scale study to understand and explain the reported anomalies in the area, there is plenty of mystery left in the Bermuda Triangle.

# Follow-On Questions to Explore

1. Is there a place in or near your town where strange things are supposed to have happened: a haunted mansion or house, maybe? Has anyone researched the place? How much of what is supposed to have happened there is fact? How much is just rumor? Why do you think most people are eager to jump to wild conclusions about supposedly mysterious places? Do you like having a haunted house or spookily mysterious place in your town? Why? If you don't, do you wish you did? Why?

2. Why do we humans want to believe in things like the mysterious Bermuda Triangle? Why are most people so eager to believe, and so reluctant to listen to scientific explanation if it takes away the mystery? What does a belief in the mysterious do for us?

# Follow-On Activities

1. Research commercial ship disappearances in the last hundred years. Mark them on a map. How many did you find? Where did they disappear? Did you find any real pattern to their disappearances, or do they seem pretty evenly spread out all over? Where are the major oceanic shipping lanes? Have most disappearances happened along major shipping lanes? How many disappearances were eventually explained? How many weren't? Are your unexplained disappearances evenly scattered across the map, or congregated in a few concentrated areas? Why?

2. Find pilots and sailors in your local community and interview them. See if they can offer explanations for the mysterious happenings in the Bermuda Triangle. Why do they think ships and planes mysteriously disappear? Do they think it would be as likely to happen now as it was twenty or fifty years ago? Why? Have they ever gotten lost or disoriented? When? How? What happened?

# References

Berlitz, Charles. *The Bermuda Triangle.* New York: Avon Books, 1979.

Cazeau, Charles. "Great Mysteries of the Earth." *Journal of Geological Education* 24, no. 4 (1986): 102–107.

Dolan, Edward. *The Bermuda Triangle and Other Mysteries of Nature.* New York: Bantam Books, 1980.

Edwards, Frank. *Stranger than Science.* Secaucus, N.J.: Citadel Press, 1987.

Fraknoi, Andrew. "A Skeptic's Bookshelf: Responses to Pseudoscience." *Mercury* 13, no. 4 (1984): 121–126.

Gaffron, Norma. *The Bermuda Triangle: Opposing Viewpoints.* San Diego, Calif.: Greenhaven Press, 1995.

Kusche, Larry. *The Bermuda Triangle Mystery: Solved.* Amherst, N.Y.: Prometheus Books, 1995.

Naval Historical Center. *The Bermuda Triangle Fact Sheet.* Washington, D.C.: Department of the Navy, Naval Historical Center, 1996.

Rosenberg, Howard. "Exorcizing the Devil's Triangle." *Sealift* 24, no. 6 (June 1984): 11–15.

Smith, Warren. *Triangle of the Lost.* New York: Zebra Books, 1985.

Titler, Dale. *Wings of Mystery: True Stories of Aviation History.* New York: Dodd Mead, 1991.

Winer, Richard. *The Devil's Triangle.* New York: Bantam Books, 1974.

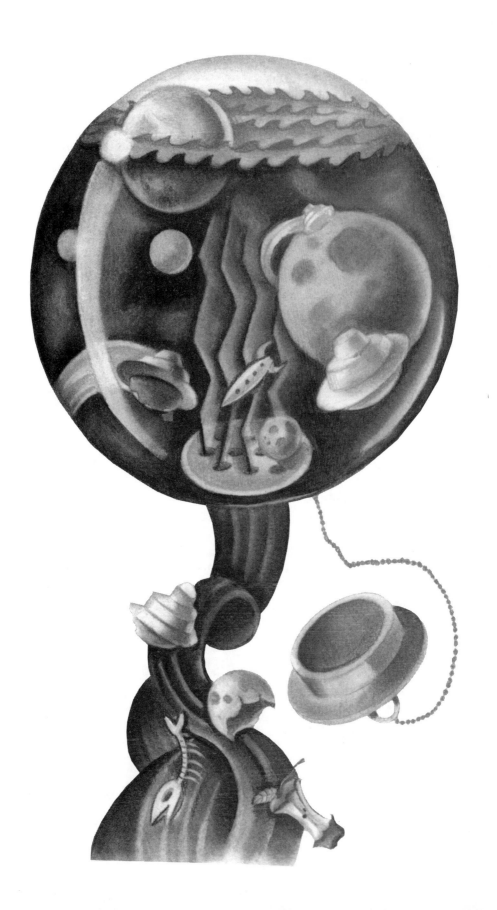

# "No Light" Matter
## Black Holes—
## Garbage Dumps or Space Doors?

## At a Glance

Up through the nineteenth century, scientists thought that the universe was an orderly, tame place inhabited by stars, planets, a few wandering comets and chunks of rocks called asteroids. Since then, an explosion of new celestial bodies has been discovered, each weirder than the last—galaxies, nebulae, quasars, pulsars, white dwarves, supernovas, neutron stars and so forth. But the most mysterious and bizarre of all are the unseeable black holes.

What is a black hole? White dwarves, neutron stars, pulsars and black holes are all the highly condensed remains of a burned-out star. When ordinary-sized stars, like our Sun, run out of fuel, their gravity forces the star's matter to collapse in on itself, forming an incredibly dense chunk of burned-out matter—a white dwarf. Many larger stars end their lives in a magnificent explosion so violent and powerful that it jams all the star's free electrons inside protons, so that all that's left is an even denser pack of neutrons—a neutron star. If that neutron star spins, it is a pulsar. Some larger dying stars, though, collapse in on themselves with such incredible force that they form the densest mass of matter of all. The gravitational field of such a chunk of matter is so powerful that not even light can escape. This is a black hole.

A black hole is a region of space. At its center lies the dense mass of a collapsed star with its monstrous gravitational field. Anything coming near that collapsed star will be pulled into the star, no matter how fast it is traveling. Even a photon of light, traveling at light-speed, cannot escape, unless it starts out some minimum distance away from the black hole. Outside that distance, fast-moving objects can escape. Inside that distance, nothing escapes. A sphere around the black hole's central core at that minimum distance is called the event horizon. That horizon marks the edge of the black hole. Like a galactic vacuum cleaner, a black hole sucks in all matter, light and energy that carelessly wander too near.

How dense is the material at the core of a black hole? A cubic inch of earth weighs a few ounces. A cubic inch of a white dwarf weighs hundreds of *tons*. A cubic inch of a neutron star weighs *millions* of tons, a whole mountain on Earth compressed into one tiny cubic inch. A black hole is hundreds of times more dense than a neutron star.

A black hole cannot be seen because light cannot escape from the clutches of its gravitational field. But the effect of a black hole's gravity can be seen in the movements of nearby stars. If the motion of a star suggests that some great gravitational force is pulling on it, but no other stars are visibly present to account for that pulling, a black hole is suspected.

The general idea of a black hole was first theorized in 1783 by English physicist John Mitchell. Mathematically, black holes were first predicted by Einstein's relativity equations in 1933. They were named black holes in 1967 by American physicist John Wheeler. The first black hole ever discovered was found in 1970 in the Cygnus constellation, 6,000 light-years from Earth, and was named Cygnus X-1.

Since their first discovery, cosmologists and physicists have gazed with awe and eager anticipation at black holes. What is inside a black hole? What happens if someone enters a black hole? Are black holes really tunnels, short-cuts, through the fabric of space and time? Are they the long-sought cosmic mass-transit system? Do black holes eventually die? If so, what happens to them? Are they links to other universes? Was it an exploding black hole that created our universe? Certainly, these unseeable holes in space are current mysteries of the first order.

# The Mystery:
# "No Light" Matter

Jocelyn Bell didn't feel like a graduate student. She felt like a slave, chained to the endless drudgery of backbreaking, mindless toil. Calluses had grown over her blisters. New blisters formed over her calluses. She had been digging and lugging heavy poles and giant rolls of wire for so long that it was hard for her to stand up straight. Mud and dirt were permanently ground into all her clothes, as well as the skin of her fingers and face.

In this soggy July of 1967 in Cambridge, England, it didn't seem to matter much that her herculean task of constructing the world's biggest, most sensitive radio antenna was almost complete. She still faced another week of stringing wires through the antenna field. And one more week seemed like an eternity.

Jocelyn's radio antenna was really a forest of 8-foot-high poles spaced 4 feet apart and topped with 4,096 metal antenna rods, all of which stretched over a five-acre field in the rolling English countryside on the outskirts of Cambridge. It looked like a forest of giant toothpicks. Wires were strung like a loose net across the tops of the poles and connected through an elaborate system of junctions. From the junction boxes, thick cables snaked back to a squat, one-story lab building where the radio equipment was housed.

Twenty-four-year-old Jocelyn had been hired by Professor Antony Hewish to assist him in his planned study of quasars and solar wind. Her interpretation of the recordings their equipment produced would qualify for her doctoral thesis. Only after she signed on did Jocelyn learn that the first part of her study would be to sweat and strain through the English mud for four months to build and wire the antenna field they would use to detect faint radio-wave signals coming from deep space.

"Wiring finished?" asked Professor Hewish, who had just strolled over from campus and was leaning against the lab building. He dabbed his forehead with a handkerchief as if he, wearing his tie and tweed coat, had been the one slaving in the antenna field.

"Another week," Jocelyn answered. When Hewish grunted and seemed displeased, she snapped, "You *could* help!"

"I'll start calibration and diagnostics of the radio equipment." And he turned for the temperature-controlled comfort of the lab.

By mid-July the system was ready. Jocelyn stepped up from construction laborer to lab technician. Her job would be to analyze the three tracks of wavering lines printed continuously onto recording paper and spit out by the electronic equipment. The equipment measured any signal detected by the antenna field, and each track monitored a different frequency band.

The system produced 60 meters of printout paper each and every day. Jocelyn had to note the exact sky position of each recorded signal and see if it had changed in any way when the antenna array next swept through that same spot in the sky five days later. It was painstaking, tedious work to measure and track each of the thousands of signals the antenna detected. It took a strip of paper one and a half football fields long to cover the sky once. And the paper kept right on rolling out of the printer.

On August 6, Jocelyn noted what she called "a tiny bit of scruff" on one of the lines of the printout recorded at about midnight. It was a rapid squiggle in the line, only about a centimeter long. Because the antenna was pointing directly away from the Sun when it recorded this odd scruff, it couldn't be solar wind or a quasar. Jocelyn shrugged and dismissed it. It wasn't part of what she and Hewish were searching for, and she had no time to dally with nonessential signals. She was already slipping behind, and it appeared likely that she would never catch up as the monstrous electronic machine gorged out long strips of paper for her to analyze, every day, without ever a day off.

At 2:00 A.M. during one early September morning, bleary-eyed Jocelyn again noticed that same bit of scruff on one of the charts. She calculated that it came from the same part of the sky, in the constellation Vulpecula. But she was too tired to pay it any mind.

By the end of September, with more than a quarter mile of printouts backed up, waiting to be read, Jocelyn realized she had spotted that same, unique, wavy-line pattern six times. Each time it had been recorded when the antenna's narrow beam swept across Vulpecula.

She mentioned it to Hewish. He shrugged, saying that it was probably a star that periodically erupted with solar flares. Just to make sure, he decided to hook up a high-speed recorder during the antenna's next pass through Vulpecula. But for six weeks the signal disappeared.

While reading the November 21 printout, which she finally got to on November 27, Jocelyn paused to call Hewish. "It's back."

"When will we next scan through Vulpecula?"

Jocelyn checked the detailed tables she had created back in September. "Tomorrow night."

Just after 11:00 P.M. on November 28, the antenna beam began its brief scan across Vulpecula. The high-speed recorder showed regular, short pulses that blipped across the recorder once every 1.25 seconds. Each pulse lasted only about one-seventh of a second.

Hewish huffed, "That settles it. It must be human-made."

"Why?" asked Jocelyn.

"No astronomical phenomenon occurs at so fast a tempo. The fastest stars spin at rates of once every eight hours."

"But what *is* it?" Jocelyn insisted.

Hewish shrugged, "Probably radar signals bounced off the Moon, or reflections from some orbiting satellite."

"But …"

"Forget it," ordered Hewish. "It's human-made. I'm going home."

At the December 1 staff meeting, Jocelyn reported that, during the times they had recorded her scruff, the Moon was never in a position where it could reflect human-made signals back to their antenna. She had also checked all orbiting satellites and found that none was in the correct orbital position to affect their antenna.

Hewish barked, "Then it's interference from the corrugated roof on the building just south of the antenna field. Forget it, Miss Bell."

Two days later Jocelyn reported that, although she had tried to bounce signals off the corrugated roof to interfere with their antenna, she couldn't create any interference. The antenna hadn't been receiving interference from the roof.

"Stop wasting time on this nonsense!" Hewish ordered. "Who cares what it is!"

"I do."

"It could be anything. A faulty automobile ignition circuit … A faulty connection in a nearby refrigerator … Anything!"

Jocelyn refused to back down. "But I want to find out what it *is,* not just what it could be."

By mid-December, Jocelyn had twice more recorded the rapid, rhythmic pulses from Vulpecula. At her insistence, Hewish agreed to analyze the pulses. To his astonishment, they were incredibly precise. Each pulse lasted exactly 0.16 second. They occurred at a rate of one pulse every 1.33730113 seconds, precisely. They never varied, not even as much as one part in ten million! No human-made signal could do that.

The frequency and size of the pulses showed that they were coming from a small body—a sphere much smaller than Earth, not from a giant star. Far more frightening, there was no known celestial phenomenon that could create such signals—other than some intelligent life-form.

Unable to talk above a whisper, Hewish said, "They're not from Earth. They aren't even from this solar system." He shuddered as he added, "These signals come from deep space."

Hewish and Bell were suddenly faced with recordings of a regular, radio-frequency signal, apparently artificially created, coming from a planet-sized body circling far beyond the Milky Way. They both stared at the squiggle lines on the printout—most probably the first-ever-recorded signal from an alien civilization. They named the source of the signal LGM-1 (for Little Green Men).

Jocelyn asked, "What do we do? Who do we tell?"

Hewish snapped, "Tell no one! Not a living soul!" He knew well that several other astronomers had become laughingstocks when their claims of alien contact had turned out to be reflected human-made signals. Certainly, he had been far more careful than they had been to eliminate that possibility. But still, he had no desire to risk his good reputation on some outlandish, headline-grabbing claim.

"But this work is my thesis," Jocelyn protested. "I have to regularly share our findings with my review committee."

"You will not mention this to anyone, and these printout pages may not leave this building. Period!"

"What will we do with them?" she asked.

"We will find a way to be much more sure of our results. That is what we will do."

One week later, just before the Christmas break, Jocelyn walked into Hewish's office to find a high-level meeting in progress. Top university, military and government officials were present. The military officials wanted to confiscate all of their results and classify them top secret.

"But this is my thesis!"

"Not anymore, Miss. Now it's national security."

Frustrated and depressed, Jocelyn wandered back to the lab for more chart analysis. Within an hour she found another bit of scruff on her charts recorded from a different part of the sky. She checked earlier recordings of the same region and found that this new signal, also, had occurred regularly before. Trembling with excitement, she checked her schedule charts. That same patch of sky would cross through the antenna's beam at 1:00 A.M. this very night.

The night was bitter cold. The high-speed recorder did not work well in cold weather. Several of its connectors tended to freeze. By 12:20 A.M. the recorder had conked out. Jocelyn rubbed the connectors. She breathed warm air on them. She held a cup of hot tea under them so the steam would thaw them out. She yelled and cursed at them.

Between 12:45 and 1:15 A.M. she was able to coax the recorder into working for only five minutes. Luckily, they were the right five minutes. She captured the pulses from this new source. Except that the period of these pulses—longer than 1.25 seconds—was different from that of LGM-1.

Within a week of intensive review of the miles of printouts, Jocelyn found three other sources of regular pulses. The new sources were labeled LGM-2 through LGM-5. It seemed that the antenna had found not just an inhabited planet, but an advanced civilization that had spread out across the cosmos.

The high-level debate as to what to do with the findings raged on. Then Hewish and two of his colleagues realized the pulses couldn't be coming from inhabitable planets. Planets orbit around stars. A distant planet would be moving in its orbit sometimes toward Earth, sometimes away. That motion would affect the frequency of the pulses. But no such effect had been seen.

This meant that these mysterious signals had to be coming from stars—a new kind of tiny pulsing star that no one had ever seen or dreamed of before! Hewish was even more excited by this result than he had been when he thought he had discovered Little Green Men. Other Cambridge scientists deduced that Hewish's stars had to be a new kind of neutron star—the incredibly dense, collapsed remnant of a former large star. But these neutron stars had to be spinning at an incredibly fast rate to create the pulses. Hewish named them pulsars.

By the early 1970s, when Hewish finally published these findings, others who were working with Einstein's equations had calculated that black holes and wormholes were possible—theoretically. The theory claimed that black holes might be gateways to parallel universes. But no physical evidence to support the theoretical calculations had ever been found.

Then Bell and Hewish discovered pulsars—tiny, compact collapsed stars almost as compact as a black hole, with an incredibly strong gravitational field almost as strong as that of a black hole. If some stars could shrink to a diameter as small as 10 or 20 miles and become pulsars, then surely other stars could shrink even further and become black holes. Cosmologists searching for proof of the theoretical black hole, and others seeking the elusive wormhole (a tunnel through space and time that spans many light-years in a few seconds), both realized that Jocelyn Bell's little bits of scruff, and the pulsars they revealed, were the first concrete evidence that might lead toward confirmation of these two most mysterious and fascinating celestial bodies.

As a sidenote to this story, Jocelyn graduated in 1970 and went on to other work. Years later, when Hewish was awarded a Nobel Prize for the discovery of pulsars, he never once mentioned Jocelyn or gave her credit for her role in the discovery. Many in the scientific community were rightly outraged by this omission and considered it an unforgivable affront to a highly deserving and dedicated researcher.

## About This Story

All the names, events and details of this story are real and accurate. The last paragraphs of the story compress the decade-long jump between the discovery of pulsars and the application of pulsars as a practical steppingstone to black holes and wormholes. Still, the jump was eventually made from one event to the other.

## The Science

Black holes are invisible. No one has ever seen a black hole or studied one. Everything science has discovered about black holes has been determined from observations of what happens just outside a black hole, and from calculations based on Einstein's theory of relativity and the principles of quantum mechanics.

The concept of escape velocity was first identified in the late 1700s. Throw a ball into the air and gravity pulls it back down. It can't escape from Earth's gravity. The harder (faster) you throw the ball, the higher it gets before gravity drags it back to the ground. If you could throw the ball fast enough, it could escape into space. That minimum initial speed (velocity) an object needs to escape the pull of gravity is called the escape velocity.

The escape velocity on Earth is 11.5 kilometers per second. On massive Jupiter it is 654 kilometers per second. On the Sun it is greater than 8,000 kilometers per second. On a neutron star, it may be as much as 80,000 kilometers per second. To escape from a black hole, an object would have to travel much faster, faster even than light itself, which travels at about 300,000 kilometers per second. But Einstein has told us that nothing can travel faster than light. According to Einstein's theory, then, nothing can escape from a black hole. Not even a photon of light blasting off from the surface of the collapsed star inside a black hole travels fast enough to overcome the star's gravity.

Science does know how black holes are initially formed. Start with a large star (at least six times the size of our Sun) that has burned up all its nuclear fuel. When the heat of the star's internal combustion no longer pushes its matter outward, gravity will collapse the star in upon itself. The strength of a star's gravity is partly dependent on its density. The greater its density, the stronger the pull of its gravity. The more it collapses, the harder its own gravity pulls it in. If that collapsing star does not explode and spray its mass across space, it can crush in on itself to form a black hole. Once a black hole is formed, scientists can learn nothing more about it, because neither light nor any other radiation can escape to give scientists information about the black hole.

So, what happens inside a black hole? As a particle approaches a black hole, the hole's gravity accelerates the particle. It speeds faster and faster as it approaches the event horizon, until, just as it crosses the event horizon, it reaches the speed of light and disappears inside. But what's in there? No one knows exactly. By watching the gravitational effects of black holes on nearby stars, scientists have been able to calculate that black holes come in all sizes, having masses from six times that of our Sun, up to many millions of times that of our Sun. Roger Penrose discovered mathematical proof that somewhere inside every black hole there is a spot where matter has been compressed to an infinite density and raised to an infinite temperature. Such a spot is called a singularity.

Is all the matter sucked into a black hole compressed into this one, infinitesimally small point of infinitely dense matter? No one knows for sure. Is it possible to enter a black hole and *not* be sucked into the singularity at its center? Some say yes. Some say no. No one knows for sure. Everyone has equations and theories that support their view. But what would happen if a person were to be sucked into a singularity? For that question science does know the answer. The gravitational forces are so strong near a singularity that, literally, every atom in a person's body would be ripped apart. If you approach a singularity, you will die.

All of the information generated before 1990 about black holes was based on Einstein's equations and theories. But Einstein never incorporated quantum (subatomic) effects into his theory. In the early 1990s, Stephen Hawking made a startling discovery. The quantum uncertainty principle allowed subatomic particles to travel faster than light. If that is true, then some particles should be able to escape from a black hole after all. At first the entire scientific community ridiculed Hawking's idea. But within two years others had confirmed his calculations and space telescopes had detected faint streams of primary particles flowing out of black holes. Black holes aren't completely black after all!

Beyond this basic information, the ideas put forth about black holes are still theory and logical guesses. Einstein claimed that nature loved symmetry. If nature allowed black holes to suck particles in and not send any back out, then nature would have also created some other object that spewed particles out and never took any in. He called such hypothetical objects white holes.

Einstein suspected that black holes and white holes were somehow joined, so that matter that flowed into a black hole would flow back out of a white hole. Others thought this concept sounded like the perfect description of a wormhole—a shortcut tunnel for long-distance space travel. Enter a black hole and zoom back out of a distant white hole, instantly traversing countless light-years of space. That is exactly what wormholes are supposed to do. For the next thirty years black holes were suspected of being wormhole tunnels through space-time.

Then Roger Penrose showed that there existed an all-powerful singularity at the center of every black hole. Science adapted its belief, contending that all matter entering a black hole would be sucked into the singularity and destroyed. If it were to be spit back out later through a white hole, it would be as protons, quarks and electrons, not as whole, living bodies. The idea that black hole–white hole tunnels could be used as wormholes for actual space travel was abandoned.

Then, in the late 1980s, astronomers realized that small quasars shine more brightly than whole galaxies and must be radiating huge amounts of matter and energy. Cosmologists suspected that quasars could be Einstein's white holes, and the black hole–white hole tunnel theory was revived. In the mid-1990s, work by Kip Thorn and Stephen Hawking showed that, if black hole–white hole tunnels did exist, they would be inherently unstable. Any disturbance—such as the entry of a spaceship into the black hole side of the tunnel—would destabilize and collapse the whole system. Others claimed that Thorn and Hawking's conclusions were flawed because they were based on unrealistic assumptions. The debate still rages, but most scientist believe that the singularity in a black hole is an inescapable deathtrap.

Kip Thorn, at Cal Tech, and George Chapline, at Lawrence Livermore Lab (California), independently estimated that as many as ten million black holes exist in our galaxy alone. As many as half a dozen small ones could be lurking unseen in our own solar system, waiting to gobble up future space travelers. Some scientists scoffed and said this was impossible. But at about the same time, Stephen Hawking proposed that a large batch of primordial mini–black holes were created during the Big Bang explosion and were scattered across the universe.

Hawking theorized that the tiny cores of some of these mini–black holes were as small as a single atom, but would still weigh thousands of tons. He also theorized that these tiny black holes emitted constant streams of high-energy subatomic particles. The more matter they emitted, the smaller and hotter they became. The hotter they became, the more matter they emitted. The end of this shrinking spiral would always come when the black hole grew so small that it became unstable and self-destructed in a massive explosion. As farfetched as this theory might seem, several of these mini–black hole explosions have been detected and recorded.

Other prominent scientists shuffled Penrose's hypothesis (each black hole contains a central singularity) together with Big Bang theory (the universe began with the explosion of a singularity) to conclude that every black hole is a new universe waiting to be born. They theorized that black holes, gaining mass continuously over the eons, eventually suck in so much matter that they grow too large and explode. This explosion, they believe, most probably doesn't release the matter back into our universe, but into another, or even into a new, parallel universe.

Finally, recent work by George Chapline and others shows that black holes (especially Hawking's mini–black holes) could be the ultimate power source. Their powerful gravitational fields, thermal fields and spinning masses could be tapped to create virtually endless sources of energy. This might be done by building giant structural rings around a black hole just outside its event horizon. According to Chapline and others, black holes are not to be feared and avoided, nor are they to be viewed as possible wormholes. Rather, black holes should be sought out as the needed energy source to power human exploration into deep space.

## Fact or Fiction?

Do black holes physically exist? Yes. Collapsed stars have formed black holes and there is strong evidence to support the existence of Hawking's primordial mini–black holes. Do black holes exist in our solar system? Quite possibly, but none have been found. Are black holes useful tunnels through space to other parts of the universe? The best-guess answer is no. Although a few still believe this is possible, most scientists are now convinced that any person entering a black hole will be ripped apart atom by atom by the immense gravitational forces.

If you were sucked into a black hole, could you ever escape? No and yes. No, you would not live to escape. But the basic matter and energy that made up your body would sometime, somehow, somewhere emerge from the black hole. Some think it would emerge into another universe. Some think it would emerge back into our universe through a quasar. Some think that eventually black holes explode and self-destruct.

Does anyone know what happens inside a black hole, or even what is in there? No, not for sure, because it is impossible to see into a black hole, and impossible for a person or machine to escape once inside—it is still all just theory. Are black holes the ultimate galactic energy source? Quite possibly, but to harness their energy they would need to be small and located nearby.

## Follow-On Questions to Explore

1. Scientists can't see black holes. How can they detect and study something they can't see? Discuss all the ways you might be able to detect something you can't see, and create a list of your schemes. Can scientists see through a black hole to what lies behind it? Does a black hole affect the path and speed of particles and radiation that pass by it? Does a black hole affect the movement of nearby stars?

2. According to current cosmological theory, all stars live a very orderly and normal life. They all burn, some hotter, some cooler. As a star consumes its fuel, it enlarges into a red giant. Once it has burned all its fuel, it dies and either explodes (a supernova) or collapses into a white dwarf, neutron

star, pulsar or black hole. Countless billions of stars have already burned out. Countless more are still burning. Many billions of stars are new and are just beginning their lives. Does the life cycle of stars affect you at all? Why or why not? Does it change the way you view yourself? Your planet? The universe? Why or why not?

# Follow-On Activities

1. Density is a critically important measure for determining the strength of a collapsed star's gravitational field. Density is a measure of the amount of matter packed into a certain space. Make some density measurements to gain an appreciation for how dense these collapsed stars are.

   Measure the volume of 5 pounds each of loosely packed feathers, tightly packed feathers, packing foam, flour, wood, water, iron and steel. Make a graph of your results.

   Now calculate the density of each substance you tested in pounds per cubic inch (total weight—5 pounds—divided by the total volume of the substance in cubic inches). Graph your results.

   Which substance is the most dense? Which is the least dense? How big a pile of each substance would you need to create a weight of 10 million tons (the weight of 1 cubic inch of a typical neutron star) and a weight of 1 billion tons (the probable weight of 1 cubic inch of the collapsed star inside a black hole)?

2. Albert Einstein believed that nature insists on symmetry and flowing cycles of life and death, increase and decrease. That belief led him to predict that white holes must exist. Do you agree with his general belief? Do you observe that "things seem to eventually balance out"? Do things around you seem to flow in orderly cycles? Search for, and research, examples of these cycles. Can you find abundant examples in nature? In human life? In history? In sports? In your own life?

   Make a list of the cycles you have found and how long it takes them to balance out. Did you find any exceptions to Einstein's belief? List these and explain how they don't cycle, how they don't eventually balance out.

# References

Al-Khalili, Jim. *Black Holes, Worm Holes and Time Machines.* Philadelphia: Institute of Physics, 1999.

Branley, Franklyn. *Journey into a Black Hole.* New York: T. Crowell, 1989.

Cornell, James. *Bubbles, Voids, and Bumps in Time: The New Cosmology.* New York: Cambridge University Press, 1990.

Davies, Paul. *The Edge of Infinity.* New York: Simon and Schuster, 1991.

Ferguson, Kitty. *Black Holes in Spacetime.* New York: Franklin Watts, 1991.

Gribbin, John. *Spacewarps.* New York: Delacorte, 1987.

Haven, Kendall, and Donna Clark. *100 Most Popular Scientists for Young Adults.* Englewood, Colo.: Libraries Unlimited, 1999.

Hawking, Stephen. *Black Holes and Baby Universes.* New York: Bantam Books, 1993.

———. *A Brief History of Time.* New York: Bantam Books, 1998.

Kaufmann, William. *Black Holes and Warped Spacetime.* San Francisco: W. H. Freeman, 1989.

Lampton, Christopher. *Black Holes and Other Secrets of the Universe.* New York: Franklin Watts, 1988.

Layzer, David. *Constructing the Universe.* New York: Scientific American Library, 1994.

Macvey, John. *Time Travel.* Chelsea, Mich.: Scarborough House, 1993.

Sullivan, Walter. *Black Holes.* Garden City, N.Y.: Anchor Press, 1989.

Thorn, Kip. *Black Holes and Time Warps.* New York: W. W. Norton, 1994.

Wheeler, John. *Geons, Black Holes and Quantum Foam.* New York: W. W. Norton, 1998.

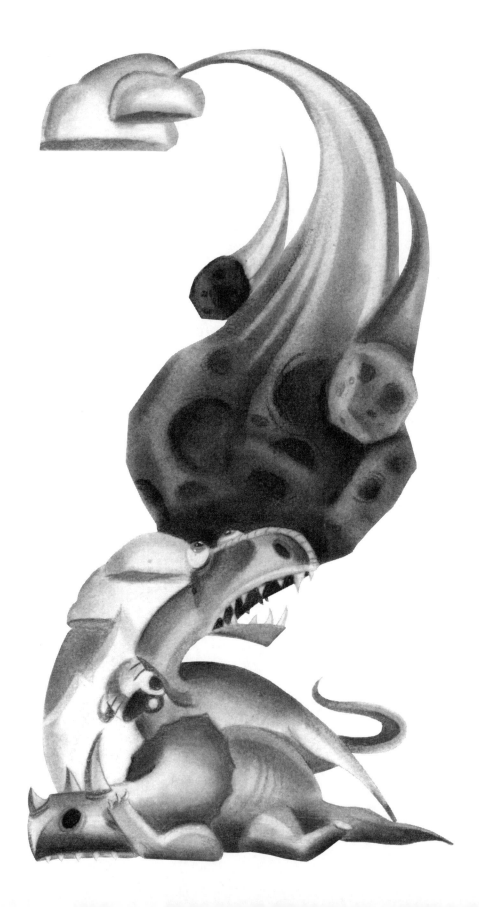

# Fallen Might
## Dinosaur Extinction—
## Asteroid or Toxic Terrain?

## At a Glance

**H**umans first learned that monstrous dinosaurs had once roamed the earth when, in the nineteenth century, French scientist Baron Georges Cuvier discovered a thighbone so large it could not be dismissed as coming from "a large cow or an overgrown lizard." British scientist Richard Owen invented the name *dinosaur* in 1841 to mean "terrible lizard." He pictured fierce, snarling giants that stomped across the earth, always ready for deadly combat.

There followed a flurry of scientific interest in dinosaurs up to the early 1900s. By then, it had been well established that giant dinosaurs had once lived on Earth but had become extinct. All agreed that dinosaurs had been dimwitted, sluggish, cold-blooded sloths—evolutionary mistakes—that had deserved to die. They simply petered out because of their own limitations. Given such a pronouncement, interest in dinosaurs waned.

But as scientific tools, technology and techniques improved in the 1950s and 1960s, contemplating the demise of the dinosaurs regained its popularity. Now it was possible to scientifically investigate possible hypotheses describing the cause of their demise. Did some plaguelike disease doom the dinosaurs? Did they all die because of a long period of intense volcanic activity? Did a climate change seal their fate? Was it a change in carbon dioxide levels in the atmosphere?

In the midst of this eager new questioning, Nobel Prize–winning physicist Louis Alvarez proposed that a massive meteorite strike had killed the dinosaurs, and he offered substantial evidence of such a massive collision and its worldwide effects. Most of the lay world enthusiastically embraced the Alvarez theory, cheering that a great mystery had been solved. But most geologists, paleontologists and other earth scientists were skeptical. The theory of a meteorite impact left too many unanswered questions.

What can be said with certainty is that the dinosaurs first appeared around 225 million years ago, that by 215 million years ago they were the dominant life-form on Earth and that they ruled Earth for 150 million years. But something happened 65 million years ago at the boundary between the Cretaceous and Tertiary periods (called the K-T boundary). After their long, glorious, diversified and very successful reign, the dinosaurs—along with almost half of the other living species on Earth—suddenly disappeared.

What happened at this K-T boundary to so disrupt life on Earth? Why did so many of Earth's living creatures suddenly become extinct? If it could happen to the dinosaurs, could it also happen to us? Above all, what really killed the dinosaurs?

# The Mystery: Fallen Might

It was a warm, steamy morning as the mother triceratops and her two babies leisurely grazed through a lush field of grass and waving lime-green ferns. Scattered palm trees, which dotted the south side of the field facing toward the marsh and the shallow sea beyond, fluttered in the puffs of morning breeze. Thicker, denser groves of trees and tangled vines spread out east and west. To the north the ground gently rose through a wide, grassy plain toward rolling hills and distant mountains. The ferns were thick here on the flatlands near the water. In sixty-five million years this scene would be a dry and dusty spot in western Wyoming.

A family of longnecks honked in a nearby lagoon, their voices echoing across the plain, their heads and necks gracefully swaying like leafless palm trees. Families and sprawling herds of grass-eating dinosaurs dotted the wide plain, shrinking to tiny specks along the distant rolling hills. Over the fields lay a drifting haze, the result of a rumbling volcano off to the west spewing ash, dirt and rock high into the sky, and fire and lava down its steep slopes. But volcanoes were commonplace—something to stay away from, but nothing to be too concerned about. All seemed quiet and peaceful.

Mother triceratops blinked her tiny eyes, which were almost hidden below the great, curving bone plate that protected her head. Her vision was weak, but good enough to see any danger within 50 or 60 yards. She slowly turned her head and sniffed the smoky air. Her three long spikes jutted out in front of her wherever she turned. It was hard to smell danger through the strong odor of a volcano.

Softly she bleated to her babies to stay close and to stay alert. One bleated in response and continued to chew contentedly. The other nestled close to her mother, rubbing softly against her mighty front leg.

Then the mother paused. It was not something she heard or smelled, but rather a tiny, distant vibration that she felt. Again she called to her young, more forcefully this time, and directed them toward a thick grove of trees near the edge of the field. Her daughter dutifully trotted at her side as she began her steady retreat toward cover. Her son squeaked out a high-pitched honk in protest and remained where he was, eating contentedly.

Again she bellowed, more forcefully, more insistently. Again her son refused to obey, barely lifting his head as he bellowed back at his mother. He was hungry. He wasn't finished. He'd come in a minute.

The vibrations grew stronger now. Small puddles of standing water rippled with every tremor. Now a deep thud accompanied each vibration. Mother recognized this sound. Giant longnecks made a similar sound when they raced across the plain. But this vibration and pounding thud carried more force, more power, more menace.

Small mammals—moles and mice—chattered nervously and scurried through the thick tufts of grass toward the safety of their burrows. A flock of birds chirped nervously and then rushed into the safety of the sky, wings noisily beating the quiet air.

The mother honked at her daughter to continue toward the cover of bushes and trees, then stomped back toward her son. Her voice was harsh and sharp. An edge of panic crowded into it, the ground now trembling with every pounding of the giant feet. Mother listened to the chitters and calls of unseen animals in the tree line to the east. That was where the danger lay.

Then the *Tyrannosaurus rex* roared, a deep throaty roar filled with hate and fury. The juvenile triceratops stopped his chewing and stared at the tree line. Mother honked her urgent demand to run. It would not be good to be caught with children in the open. Not good at all.

The mother knew she could most likely protect herself from a lone tyrannosaur. She was heavy and compact enough to keep from being bowled over. And as long as she could spin fast enough to remain face-to-face with her attacker, her armor plate and spikes would keep the predator from reaching her tender and defenseless sides.

But now she had her babies to worry about. Her daughter was bleating, crying in fright from just outside the safety of the thick trees for her mother to come and protect her. Her son now angrily turned toward the trees. He stomped one foot and bellowed his puny cry—as if a 500-pound baby, whose horns weren't sharp enough or hard enough to frighten even the tiniest attacker, could destroy the mightiest of all carnivores. One day her son would be able to threaten a tyrannosaur, using powerful spikes sent whistling through the air while shaking his mighty head from side to side. But not today. Today he must run or die.

Mother called again, pleading with her son to run to safety. Reluctantly he began his retreat—only after he issued a second tiny snort of a roar.

A mighty roar in response exploded from behind the eastern trees. The trees whipped from side to side as if caught in a gale. Limbs snapped. And the snarling tyrannosaur burst into the meadow, 7 tons of muscle and fury standing more than 30 feet tall. The *T. rex* bellowed his challenge to everyone or everything to withstand his might.

The baby triceratops spun to face the mighty *T. rex* and honked back, a tiny tricycle bell challenging a deafening steam locomotive's piercing blast.

The tyrannosaur roared his rage and leapt toward the baby. Trees shook under the pressure of his cry. Animals a mile away quivered. But the baby triceratops planted his feet, honked back his defiance and locked his miniature legs, ready for a fight.

Mother rushed forward to defend her son. Her bleating roar took on the fierceness only a desperate mother can produce. Like a streamlined missile, the *T. rex* bent low to the ground as he raced, deadly mouth gaping wide to devour the brazen baby.

A flicker of movement back in the western tree line behind her caught the mother triceratop's eye. A ruffian gang of six velociraptors slipped out of the trees, near where the mother triceratop's daughter whimpered, unprotected. Moving silently, evilly, they fanned out, sliding forward through the grass.

Mother tensed. She hesitated. This was quickly unraveling into disaster. Indecision and panic gripped her. Should she fight the *T. rex*? Rush to her daughter's side? Retreat to safety herself? There was no way to fight both a tyrannosaur and a pack of vicious velociraptors at the same time. Always some deadly killer would be at her back.

Who to save? Which way to turn? She honked her frustration and rage. This wasn't fair at all. She didn't deserve this cruel fate.

And then every dinosaur in the field froze as a thunderous whine tore at every ear and filled the air, as if the sky itself were being ripped to shreds, screeching in protest. A brilliant ball of fire, far bigger than the Moon, brighter than the Sun, hurtled across the sky, streaking from the west toward the southeast.

In a few seconds it was gone. The screech faded. The ball's glowing vapor trail slowly evaporated.

Then the fierce rumbling vibration of a distant explosion rattled the field. Trees swayed. Birds cried in protest and fear. A dense flock thumped their way into the air for safety.

And again all was deathly quiet. The velociraptors romped off, as if they had forgotten all about their attack and were preoccupied with some deep foreboding.

The tyrannosaur shook his mighty head and roared at the sky, infuriated that it had shouted louder than he could. Then he cocked his head, as if waiting for the sky to reply. When no sound issued from above in response to his challenge, the *T. rex* snorted—again he was the undisputed king—and roared his triumph, a deafening bellow that flattened the grass and rattled the trees.

Snarling and angry, he turned back toward the baby triceratops. But the ground began to rumble and buck. Trees rocked, snapped and toppled. A giant black plume rose into the southern sky, many miles across, 70,000 feet high, black and boiling. Again the dinosaurs paused to stare in wonder at this monstrous sight.

Balls of glowing fire and white-hot rock rained down from the sky. Mountains swayed as if made of Jell-O. It was hard to stand on ground that pitched like the deck of a ship being tossed by a hurricane. A fierce wind howled, flattening trees.

Then a new sound caught their ears—a rumbling, grinding sound as if some unstoppable force were chewing up the earth itself. The longnecks bellowed in panic and splashed toward shore. The shadow of a monster wave rose above the trees, above the longnecks, above the triceratop's field of vision. It seemed to cover the sky.

A single wave, traveling faster than any bird could fly, rising higher than the tallest hills and trees, sped toward the helpless land. It smashed into the coast with a force greater than that of ten thousand volcanoes.

In a blink the trees were gone, the lagoon was gone, the field was gone. The dinosaurs were gone. Every tree, bush, grass blade and loose boulder was gone. Every living thing all the way to the distant mountains, more than 100 miles inland, was stripped away by the hungry wave before it lost its power and sloshed back toward the sea. Only bare desolation stood where, moments before, rich ecosystems and countless lives had flourished.

The ash cloud boiled into the sky, carrying millions of tons of debris that spread into a thick dust layer and covered the earth. The smoke from a hundred new volcanoes, triggered by the violent shaking of the meteorite impact, rose thick and black to join the deadly layer of dust. Beneath this dense blanket, Earth was thrown into perpetual darkness and cold. Soft summer rains turned to blizzards of snow. Tropical lands froze in a week. Plants withered and died. Dinosaurs not killed by the tidal wave soon froze or starved under the dense shroud of the impact cloud, which did not dissipate for years.

And so ended the reign of the dinosaurs.

Or ... maybe not.

## About This Story

This story is fiction. However, the species described in this story are those that actually existed in North America near the end of the reign of the dinosaurs. Their behavior and mannerisms, as described, match current theory. The descriptions of the meteorite and the aftermath of its collision with Earth are based on Louis Alvarez's theory and are taken from scientific approximations of the global chaos such a major collision would create.

## The Science

Is that really what finally destroyed the dinosaurs, a giant meteorite impact? How can scientists even guess at what happened sixty-five million years ago? It is difficult enough to understand what is happening to Earth today while we are here to observe and study it. Pinpointing the cause of events sixty-five million years ago seems nearly impossible. Still, considerable scientific effort has been expended re-creating and studying the last days of the reign of the dinosaurs.

From 1800 through the mid-1900s, all dinosaur studies were limited to anatomical comparisons between dinosaur fossil bones and the bones of modern animals. Scientists deduced dinosaur anatomy and activity by comparing the size and thickness of various dinosaur bones with bone measurements of various animals alive today. Initial finds suggested that dinosaurs most closely matched lizards. So, lizards they were.

As tens of thousands of bones were found and studied over the 160 years from 1800 to 1960, scientists slowly constructed a more complete and accurate picture of dinosaur anatomy and life. Many of these findings didn't match the original model of dinosaurs as lumbering, dimwitted, cold-blooded lizards. By 1970 the fossil record forced scientists to change their view of dinosaurs to that of cunning, mobile, warm-blooded endurance runners. They were now recognized as highly successful evolutionary champions, as good parents, as intelligent survivalists. However, if dinosaurs were so intelligent and successful, then what killed them? If they weren't "evolutionary mistakes" that deserved to die, then something else must have done them in. But what?

With the advanced technology of the 1970s and 1980s, scientists used fossil bones and deep-sea core samples to study carbon dioxide levels and oxygen levels in the air of sixty-five million years ago. They used new radar techniques to measure prehistoric volcano activity. They used gas spectrometers to measure trace elements in the dinosaurs' environment. They used electron microscopes and DNA samples to search for nutritional deficiencies in dinosaur habitats.

In the midst of this burst of study, Louis Alvarez proposed his meteorite collision theory. Popular science and the public loved the notion. It finally explained why these superior species had become extinct. It wasn't their fault. A meteorite disrupted life on Earth. Mystery solved.

Except serious earth scientists knew that the theory left too many questions unanswered. Why did most bird and mammal species (all smaller and weaker than the dinosaurs) survive? Why did many—but not all—types of oceanic plankton become extinct at the K-T boundary? Why did shellfish die off, but turtles, crocodiles and snakes survive? Why did shallow-water fish die off, but sharks and deep-ocean fish survive?

The Alvarez theory couldn't explain these and dozens of other important questions. Scientists realized that the correct question wasn't, What happened to the dinosaurs? It was, What happened to *Earth* at the K-T boundary that destroyed half of all living species, including the dinosaurs?

Startling, but solidly supported, answers flooded in from this intensive study. Measurements at hundreds of sites confirmed that dinosaurs had pretty much died out at least five million years before the mass extinction at the K-T boundary. For the last several million years of their reign, dinosaurs existed only in North America. Further, very few species remained. *Tyrannosaurus rex* and *Triceratops* were the last two survivors. But the great diversity of dinosaur species were already long gone. With or without a mass-extinction event, the dinosaurs wouldn't have lasted very much longer. Their time was naturally up.

It has been suggested that the growing population of mammals destroyed the dinosaurs by eating their eggs. It's possible. But there is no direct supporting evidence. Without any evidence, it's just a guess.

In search of sounder theories, scientists discovered that a half a million years of intense, worldwide volcanic activity preceded the mass extinction at the K-T boundary, and that sea levels dropped several hundred meters just before the K-T boundary, then rose back after the mass extinction. With this evidence, scientists were finally able to build an accurate picture of the world in which the last of the dinosaurs lived.

The shallow North American seas dried up over several hundred thousand years. The land grew arid. The lush, tropical plant life that supported the dinosaurs diminished into semiarid grasslands that could not. Because of the intense volcanism, acid rain increased sharply, further diminishing plant life. Acidity levels in the ocean rose dangerously high, killing many plankton. Shellfish died due to a lack of shallow seas, low oxygen levels and high acidity levels.

The constant volcanic emissions also increased levels of several trace elements in the environment to millions of times greater than would normally exist. Most important in this group was the element selenium. Selenium is easily absorbed and concentrated in grasses and leafy bushes. Dinosaurs that ate great quantities of this infected vegetation would develop alkali disease. Horses of the Old West used to suffer from this disease when they ate locoweed. Infected dinosaurs would suffer intense behavioral changes and, ultimately, death.

## Fact or Fiction?

The vast majority of scientists now agree that it is very unlikely that a meteorite impact was the primary cause of the demise of the dinosaurs and the mass extinction at the K-T boundary. A few physicists and astronomers still cling to this belief. But the body of paleontologists, geologists and other earth scientists have disproved the theory to their own satisfaction.

The extinction did not happen fast enough for a single event to be the cause. It happened over four hundred thousand years (which looks "sudden" when viewing hundreds of millions of years of the fossil record). It was caused by sea-level changes and intense volcanic activity. This combination of bad-luck events drove the final nail into the dinosaurs' coffin. But the dinosaurs were well on their way to the grave of extinction long before either event triggered the K-T boundary mass extinction.

This current understanding seems complete. No major questions are left unanswered. Those few scientific groups who disagree have offered no new evidence to support their position. The case seems to be finally closed.

Still, there is no absolute proof of this chain of events, only a carefully supported set of logical conclusions based on everything scientists have learned about the way the world works now, and on the bits of evidence they have been able to retrieve from the long-ago world of the dinosaurs. Unless some startling new evidence is uncovered to reopen the extinction debate, the only real question left is whether dinosaurs were birdlike and had feathers. Did they really become extinct, or more correctly did they evolve into birds?

## Follow-On Questions to Explore

1. Why do you think the prevailing view of dinosaurs has changed so radically over time (from "terrible lizards," in the early 1800s; to slow, fat dullards, in the early 1900s; to crafty, smart, fast survivors that were good

parents and social creatures, in the late 1900s; to feathered creatures that evolved into birds, currently)? Was it new scientific information that changed the popular view, or was it changing social and political beliefs about the relationship between humans and the environment? Do you think it was a combination of both factors? Are there other factors that could have changed our view of the dinosaurs?

2. The notion of extinction was first conceived in the early 1800s. What did people believe before that? Why did they think that every creature placed on Earth still existed? Hadn't many species become extinct over the thousands of years that humans had been keeping written records of what they saw on Earth? Why hadn't anyone noticed that some species had become extinct?

# Follow-On Activities

1. Build life-sized versions of the final few dinosaurs to live on Earth, and also of the biggest and smallest dinosaurs ever to live on Earth. Make a chart comparing how long the dinosaurs lived and how long humans have lived and dominated Earth. If the length of time humans have "ruled" Earth were represented by a 1-inch line, how many feet long would a line representing the rule of dinosaurs be?

2. How much food do you think a 90-ton, warm-blooded dinosaur would have to eat each day? Measure the total weight of your own food intake for three days (track both food and water). Average your food weight for one day, and then scale up the food weight to a dinosaur's requirement by using the ratio of your body weight to a dinosaur's body weight.

   Find out how much food and water a cow eats in a day and scale that amount up to a dinosaur's requirement. Now compare your two estimates. Which estimate do you think is closer to a dinosaur's intake? Why?

3. Do an experiment to experience the difficulties scientists encounter trying to reconstruct the past from core samples (small columns of dirt and rock drilled out of the earth or ocean bottom). You will need a cardboard shoebox, about 1 pound each of four or five colors of modeling clay, several colors of glitter, a dozen straws and a craft knife.

   One student must secretly build a geologic structure for the other students to investigate. Do this by layering the different colors of clay into the shoebox, one on top of the other. The layers don't have to be uniform, and you don't have to use all of each color of clay. You could even change the order of the layers in different parts of the shoebox. Between several of the layers, sprinkle some of the glitter. These glitter layers don't have to be uniform either.

Other students must now use their straws to take twelve core samples to determine what the layers of clay and glitter in the shoebox look like. One student at a time "drills" into the shoebox structure by slowly inserting a straw all the way through the clay to the bottom of the box. Measure the position of the straw relative to the sides of the box and mark on a piece of paper where the sample was taken. Carefully remove the straw and (with adult supervision) cut it open with a knife so that the clay and glitter layers can be identified and measured.

After taking twelve core samples, see if the layering inside the shoebox can be accurately determined. If not, how many core samples do you think would be needed to gain an accurate image of the box's contents? Did you find this process easy or difficult?

# References

Alvarez, Louis, and Walter Alvarez. "Asteroid Extinction Hypothesis." *Science* 211 (1981): 654–656.

Alvarez, Walter. *T. rex and the Crater of Doom.* Princeton, N.J.: Princeton University Press, 1997.

Archibald, J. D. "Late Cretaceous Extinctions." *American Scientist* 70 (1982): 377–385.

Asimov, Isaac. *Did Comets Kill the Dinosaurs?* Milwaukee, Wis.: Gareth Stevens Publishing, 1988.

Bakker, Robert. *The Dinosaur Heresies.* New York: William Morrow, 1986.

Gore, Richard. "Dinosaurs." *National Geographic,* January 1993, 2–53.

Lauber, Patricia. *Living with Dinosaurs.* New York: Bradbury Press, 1991.

Officer, Charles, and Jake Page. *The Great Dinosaur Extinction Controversy.* Reading, Mass.: Addison-Wesley Publishing, 1996.

Seymour, Simon. *New Questions and Answers About the Dinosaurs.* New York: Morrow Junior Books, 1991.

Sloan, R. E., and J. K. Rigby. "A Reassessment of Reptilian Diversity Across the K-T Boundary." *Science* 232 (1986): 629–633.

Whitfield, Philio. *Why Did the Dinosaurs Disappear?* New York: Viking Books, 1991.

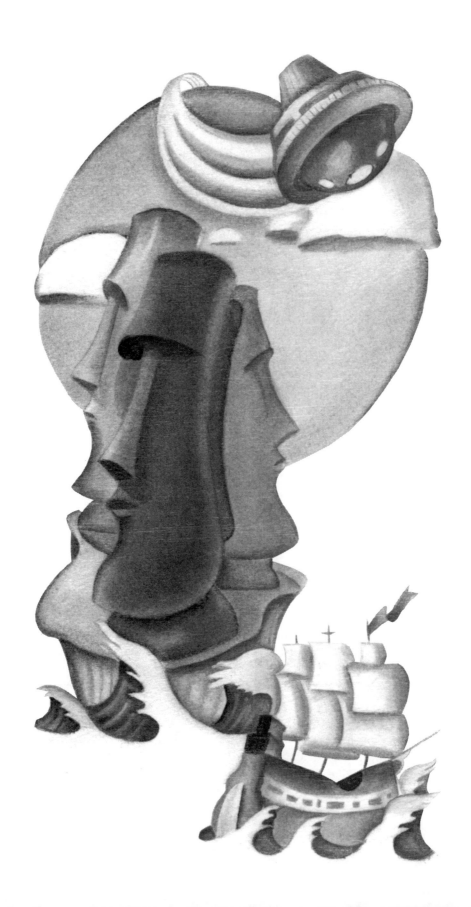

# Stone Giants
## Easter Island—Alien Monoliths or Island Madness?

## At a Glance

Tiny Easter Island is the most isolated spot on Earth. Just over 15 miles long and 6 miles across at its widest point, Easter Island is a 46-square-mile scrap of land 2,300 miles west of Chile and 2,500 miles east of Tahiti. The nearest land, tiny Pitcairn Island, lies 1,400 miles away. As far south of the equator as Houston, Texas, is north, Easter Island has a mild, pleasant climate. Still it only supports a small native population of about three thousand—mostly farmers and fishermen.

What makes Easter Island memorable is the presence of almost nine hundred giant stone statues—some as tall as 60 feet and weighing as much as 270 tons—scattered around the edge of the island. When the island was discovered by western explorers, no one—not even the island natives—knew how they were made, how they were moved into position, who built them or even why they were built. There are no trees or timbers on the island to use to construct machines or rollers for moving the mammoth statues. There are no vines or plants from which to make sturdy ropes. There seemed to have been no way to create them, move them or lift them into place. It almost seemed as if some giant hand had reached down to create the statues on a whim, or as if powerful sorcerers or aliens had built them and then disappeared.

Why didn't the natives know anything about them? Who built and moved them? How? Why? The Easter Island statues quickly became one of the most perplexing mysteries of the modern world.

# The Mystery: Stone Giants

First Mate Nicolass Dekker leaned over the rail to study the sparkling Pacific water. "The waves are piling up, Captain. There must be land nearby." Sunday, April 5, 1772—Easter Sunday—dawned clear and mild over the Pacific Ocean. The Dutch sailing ship *Rozamond Betje* seemed little more than an infinitesimal speck on the thousands of empty miles of endless blue ocean. Captain Jacob Roggeveen was on a trading mission, seeking faster routes to the exotic (and profitable) trading ports in the South Pacific Islands. The *Rozamond Betje* had survived the dangerous passage through the Straight of Magellan and now sped across the vast Pacific, well south of the equator, aiming first for Tahiti.

Rocking contentedly, heel to toe on the ship's quarterdeck, plump Captain Roggeveen stroked his steel wool–tough, muttonchop sideburns and called out, "Full sails! Steady as she goes!" He turned to short, thick Nicolass Dekker. "Light duty, today, Mr. Dekker, so the men have time for Easter worship."

But Dekker didn't hear it. He was leaning far over the side, holding his wide-brimmed hat on his head with one hand, studying the gentle, rolling waves. He straightened up this time before he spoke and turned excitedly toward the captain. "I said, the waves are piling up! There's land nearby!"

Captain Roggeveen chuckled and shook his head. "You're surely mistaken, Mr. Dekker. We're in the middle of the empty Pacific. There's no charted land for 2,000 miles in any direction." Then he tisked his first mate and lowered his voice. "I thought you were a better sailor than to make such a silly error, Mr. Dekker."

The mate turned beet red and muttered, "But the waves *are* piling up. Maybe it's a shallow shoal."

One of the sailors squinted into the early morning Sun and cried, "Look! A bird!"

The entire crew eagerly gazed where the sailor's outstretched arm pointed. They hadn't seen a bird in eight days. Birds meant land.

Captain Roggeveen wheeled around to peer into the sky over the ship's stern. He shook his head and smiled. "That's an albatross. They can easily fly a thousand miles out over the deep ocean."

"Down lower, Captain!" called the sailor. "Just over the waves!"

"By thunder! That's a gull!" bellowed Roggeveen. "A shore bird." He turned and called up to the lookout 45 feet up in the crow's nest. "We have indications of land, Mr. Van Eych! What see ye?"

The reply seemed to float down between the stretched sails. "Only ocean and waves, Captain."

"Keep a sharp eye, Mr. Van Eych!"

"Aye, Captain."

Easter worship was forgotten as the crew strained at the rails to catch a first glimpse of a new land. An excruciatingly long hour passed before the lookout cried, "Land ho! Off the starboard quarter!"

"Mr. Dekker, bring me my glass!" called the captain as the crew scrambled into the rigging for a look at the fuzzy black line on the horizon that was land.

"How large do you make it, Mr. Van Eych?" called Captain Roggeveen, sighting through his telescope.

"One small island, sir. Nothing more."

The captain closed his telescope and shivered. "The most isolated spot on Earth. I wonder if we're the first humans to stumble across the place." He shrugged to recover his usually jolly disposition. "Bring her around to the leeward side, Mr. Dekker. Trim the sails. Watch for coral reefs." After a minute's thought, he added, "I'll name it Easter Island, since we discovered it this Easter morning."

Over the next hour, the tiny black smudge on the horizon grew into sand-colored bluffs and a 1,500-foot-high mountain up on the island's north end. Mr. Dekker guided the *Rozamond Betje* slowly along the southern shore, leery of the jagged coral reels that surrounded so many Pacific islands.

"What are *those*—on the bluff above the shore?" asked Mr. Dekker from the helm.

Roggeveen peered through his telescope before answering. "Stone giants. Must be thirty of them lined along the bluff. It's the most amazing thing I've ever seen." He lowered the glass and pulled on his muttonchops. "What sort of place is this?"

"An enchanted island, like as not," answered Mr. Dekker. "Just like in the story of Jason and the Argonauts."

"That was a Greek myth, a story, Mr. Dekker, as far as we know."

"But those monster statues are real, Captain. And I don't think they're meant as a friendly greeting."

Rounding the point of land at the southern end of the island, the crew could see seventy or eighty more of the giant, dark statues, standing ominous watch over the island along the sandy bluffs.

"Prepare a landing party!" called the captain. Then he added, "Mr. Dekker, break out the muskets, pistols and cutlass. I want all those comin' ashore well armed."

"Captain! The natives are swimming out to meet us!" called the lookout, pointing at the crystal-clear waters of the bay.

"Swimming, you say? That's odd," muttered the captain. "I'd have thought they'd be in outrigger boats." Then he called louder, "What do you make of it, Mr. Dekker?"

Dekker studied the fifty brown-skinned natives clumsily splashing toward them, and the six paddling out in two canoes. "Their canoes aren't fit to cross a river. See there? They're only 40 yards out on a calm sea and already more are bailing than paddling."

Roggeveen's face wrinkled in thought and concern. "Odd ... Very odd ... How can islanders on such a tiny speck survive without good seamanship skills? How can a island community possess only two flimsy canoes?"

The first of the half-sunk, rickety canoes neared the *Rozamond Betje*. As they furiously bailed, the natives jabbered and pointed wildly at the Dutch ship and crew. Especially, they seemed fascinated by the wooden planks that made up the ship. The crew smiled and waved back from their perches in the rigging.

Roggeveen stood back from the rail. "Drop anchor! Where's that Tahitian interpreter we hired to handle trading in the South Pacific? Maybe he can help us communicate."

Kani Taauni, a stooped, white-haired native of Tahiti, had been leaning over the rail to listen to the native speech. He climbed onto the quarterdeck next to the captain. "It sounds like ancient Hawaiian, Captain."

"Hawaiian, you say?"

"I can understand most of it."

"These people came from Hawaii?"

"More likely they came from the same place the Hawaiians came from, Captain."

"Which is …?"

Taauni shrugged, then added, "They are very excited to see us, Captain."

"Are they hostile?"

"No. More afraid and in awe, I would say."

"Odd … Very odd."

"I believe that they were unaware that there were any other people on Earth, Captain."

Roggeveen frowned and shook his head. "Totally isolated on their tiny island. What a dismal life to have to live. And living under those giant statues would give anyone nightmares!"

A longboat was lowered and ten men made the final quarter-mile leg of the journey to Easter Island with Captain Roggeveen. The bay's water was so clear and clean that it looked as if the boat floated on air.

Upon landing, the Dutch found a barren land of brown, withered grass, without a single tree, and only scatters of small bushes—most of them scorched and burnt. Above the beach they stumbled over an endless array of odd-shaped, abandoned garden plots, most completely covered with small stones.

Once off the beach and away from the soothing rumble of waves, and now under the watchful eyes of the statues, Roggeveen shivered at the deep quiet. Not a single bird chirped. Hardly an insect flitted or buzzed past him. The only sound was the soft, constant clucking of chickens.

"Rats and chickens is all that seems to live on this island, Captain," whispered Mr. Dekker, so as not to be heard by the statues. "Them, and the statues, and those people," he continued thumbing toward the growing crowd of dirt-covered, matted-hair natives who followed the shore party at a short distance. They talked in hushed tones, and their wary gaze shifted constantly between Captain Roggeveen's landing party and the rolling hills and narrow gorges, as if expecting some attack. Many carried crude weapons—clubs, stubby bows, stone knives.

Roggeveen nodded. "Not a rabbit. Not a lizard. Not a dog. Odd … Very odd."

"Something's not natural at all here, Captain," whined Mr. Dekker. "We should leave."

"First, I intend to have a closer look at those incredible statues."

They walked the low, rolling coastal hills and found hundreds of stone statues, each a giant head and upper body—all facing inward, away from the sea. Each monstrous stone face glared angrily down at the intruders as if plotting revenge. Many statues were crowned with red rock topstones, like elaborate hats. Some stood 60 feet tall. Some were only 12 or 13 feet tall. Many stood side by side on raised stone platforms, often 500 feet long and 10 feet high.

Roggeveen pulled on his muttonchops and called for Taauni. Leaning close to the Tahitian and pointing back to the following crowd, he said, "Ask them who built these statues. It obviously wasn't them. By the looks of it, they can scarcely build a fire."

Kani Taauni nodded and walked back to the throng of natives. He spoke. They answered, often ten at a time. He spoke again. They answered, gesturing wildly in different directions. He spoke again. They answered, louder than before.

The sailors with Roggeveen clutched their muskets and drew into a tighter, nervous knot.

"I think he made them mad, Captain," whispered Mr. Dekker. "We should return to the longboat."

Roggeveen ignored his first mate and watched Taauni nod and march back up the hill. "They call the statues 'ahu' and 'maoi.' But they don't know who built them, Captain. This group is from one of four clans on the island. Apparently, none of the others know either."

"Don't know, eh?" Roggeveen pulled on his muttonchops. "Ask them how the statues were moved here."

Taauni marched back down the hill in the late morning warmth and held another heated, animated discussion with the natives. "They don't know how the maoi were moved, Captain."

"Don't know, eh? Are you sure you're translating right?"

"Correctly enough, Captain. Their speech is definitely Polynesian."

"But they know nothing about the statues?"

"They talked of an old man in another clan at the north end of the island who still knows stories about the statues. He says that the maoi walked to their appointed places—"

"Statues walked?" interrupted the captain.

Taauni shrugged. "Apparently one of the ancient ones said magic words and the maoi walked by themselves. Others said something about gods having flown here and made the statues move by magic powers."

Roggeveen scratched his muttonchops like a shopper haggling for a better price. "Magic powers, eh? Fifty-ton stone statues walk by themselves, eh?"

"It's a wicked magic land for sure, Captain," whined Mr. Dekker.

"It's just a story, Mr. Dekker. They're probably playing a joke on us."

"No, Captain. They are serious," insisted Taauni.

Mr. Dekker and most of the crew were beginning to tremble, glancing fearfully from statue to statue. "It *is* a magic land, Captain. We best leave, or some giant hand will rise up and crush us dead."

"Nonsense, Mr. Dekker. Statues don't walk by themselves." But most of the conviction had disappeared from his voice.

"But here the statues are, Captain. And look, not a single tree to form a timber for rolling the statues or to build a scaffold to lift them. No ropes. The natives know nothing. How else could they have been moved?"

Roggeveen muttered to himself before turning to his translator again. "Ask them if they came here by sea."

In five minutes Taauni was back. "They don't know. They never go out to sea because they have no boats. But it seems they have stories about ancestors who were great seafarers and sailed like magic over the ocean from a distant land—like us, Captain. They think maybe we are their ancient ancestors come back to save them."

"Odd … How very odd indeed." The wind picked up and began to whistle and moan past the statues. The crew pressed tightly together. All gazed longingly at the safety of the *Rozamond Betje,* floating quietly at anchor in the bay.

Captain Roggeveen stroked his muttonchops. "What do you make of it, Mr. Dekker? A crude, cave-dwelling, almost starving people, barely able to scratch out a living, with no wood, no timber, no machines, no wheels or rollers and no ropes—who sit on one of the greatest archaeological and engineering finds of all time. How do you explain it? How did they do it?"

Mr. Dekker mumbled that it was an evil land and that they should leave quickly before they were killed.

Captain Roggeveen said to Taauni, "Ask them *why* the statues were built."

The answer came back. "They don't know, Captain."

"Well what in blazes *do* they know?" thundered the captain.

"They know which statues belong to other clans and how to knock them down!"

"Clan wars, eh?" nodded the captain.

The natives began to scream. Those with weapons crowded into a tight line at the front as a hundred similarly dressed men raced out of a concealed gully, waving stone knives and crude spears and throwing rocks. Most rushed toward the crowd. Some veered off to attack Roggeveen's landing party.

"Firing line!" called the captain. "Prime your weapons! … Cock your muskets! … Aim! … Fire!"

Fire and smoke bellowed from the row of crude muskets. A thunderclap blasted across the plain. Four of the attackers sprang back and crumpled to the ground. All the natives—attackers and the following crowd alike—turned and fled in terror.

Two days later, Captain Roggeveen set sails to continue his appointed voyage. He marked Easter Island on the charts and carried away only questions, wonder and mystery. Who built the mighty statues on this desolate and isolated island, and how, and why? How could the natives not know? The lapping of Pacific waves against the hull revealed no answers.

## About This Story

The major characters and events in this story are real and accurate re-creations based on Captain Jacob Roggeveen's log. Dialog and specific action have been invented to bring to life the wonder and experience of the crew on first discovering this tiny island and its giant statues.

## The Science

The mystery of the Easter Island statues was the subject of constant speculation through 1955, when Norwegian scientist Thor Heyerdahl theorized that Easter Island was populated by Myans from South America. He attempted to prove his theory by sailing a Myan-type ship, named *Kon-Tiki,* to Easter Island. His book of the same name was an instant best seller, and Easter Island skyrocketed to the top of everybody's interest charts. Archaeological excavations on Easter Island began the next year and have continued ever since. (The island is called Rapa Nui by its inhabitants, who believe that Jacob Roggeveen had no right to rename their island, which their ancestors discovered thirteen hundred years before the Dutch explorer found it.)

Forty years of detailed, painstaking study by research teams representing half a dozen different disciplines has created a complete and accurate picture of Easter Island's past and solved the Easter Island mysteries. Linguistic studies have matched the native dialect to early Hawaiian and Marquesan, both isolated from other Polynesian dialects by about A.D. 400. A 1997 DNA study of twelve Easter Island skeletons proved that the Easter Island population was Polynesian, not Myan, in origin. Easter Island crops—bananas, taro, sweet potatoes, sugar cane, paper mulberry—are all typical Polynesian crops. It is clear that the Easter Island settlers came from Polynesia, probably Tahiti.

When did they arrive? Radio carbon dating at various island archaeological sites has determined that the first humans arrived around A.D. 500. What sort of an island did they find? Core samples have been collected from a number of lagoons and marshes. Each layer of each sample was carbon-dated. In each layer, researchers examined tens of thousands of pollen grains to identify the plant species present on the island at that time. The first settlers found a subtropical rain forest paradise on Easter Island in A.D. 500. Towering trees— 90-foot-tall palms, hauhau (rope-yielding trees) and toromiro trees—lorded above a lush, dense underlayer of shrubs and ferns.

Archaeologists and biologists have studied bones excavated from archaeological digs and have been able to determine both the diet of early settlers and the animal species present on the island. In A.D. 500, Easter Island teamed with birds. Twenty-five species of nesting seabirds filled the skies around Easter Island—albatross, booby, frigates, fulmars, petrels, terns, tropical birds and gulls. Easter Island was the richest seabird-breeding site in all Polynesia.

The island also housed a large population of land birds—barn owls, herons, parrots and rails. The bones of every species were found in waste dumps after the birds had been caught and cooked in ovens fueled by the island's plentiful forest trees. Islanders also ate porpoise (almost a third of their diet), which they harpooned at sea from outrigger boats. They dined on turtle, seals, giant sea snails and fish. But without coral reefs on the island, fishing was relatively poor, and fish made up less than a quarter of the islanders' diet.

Life was good and easy for the early Easter Islanders, and they prospered and multiplied. Sociological and anthropological studies have shown that a complex governmental system emerged, allowing the islanders to produce, collect and distribute food more efficiently. Agriculture grew as forest land was cleared and made ready for sweet potatoes, taro and sugarcane. The population grew to greater than twelve thousand.

Then, around A.D. 1100, life began to change. Pride and vanity reared their ugly heads. Chiefs began building statue monuments to show their power and prestige. An escalating one-upmanship rivalry between clans followed, with each clan trying to erect more and bigger statues than any other clan.

Engineering studies have tested almost twenty schemes for transporting and erecting the giant statues, and have identified at least four viable schemes that could have been used—depending on how much human labor and timber were available. The most efficient and likely means of transportation was to build a canoe-shaped cradle around each statue and pull it over a highway of roller logs greased with a mixture of water and ground-up banana tree. Forty people (six to eight families) could easily transport an average-sized maoi, even uphill. The same group could also raise and erect the statue using ropes and levers. The resources and engineering knowledge available to the average Polynesian chief were sufficient to complete the task.

Trees—especially palms, with their long, straight trunks—were felled at an alarming rate to use as rollers for transporting the giant statues from rock quarry to a clan's "ahu," or ceremonial spot. The increased need for food forced islanders to clear more forest land for planting. Deforestation ran rampant across the island.

By A.D. 1400 the effects of the islanders' "jobs-over-trees" attitude and obsessive statue-building slammed home. By 1400 the last palm tree disappeared from the island, and grasslands dominated where once forest had stood. By 1500 the last tree—probably an overlooked, stunted species—was chopped for firewood. Because trees had been so scarce for more than a generation, their final passing was probably not even noticed.

With no trees, seaworthy boats disappeared. By 1450 porpoise disappeared from the islanders' diet. Birds became extinct by 1500, eaten, every one. Turtles, seals and sea snails were also driven to extinction.

With no trees and bushes for protection, soil erosion and depletion quickly left much of the island unfit for agriculture. Starvation set in. The government collapsed and was replaced by warrior groups (gangs) who started bloody clan wars. Statues were no longer built. Now they were torn down by enemy clans. By 1600 several of the clans resorted to cannibalism. Clans retreated to caves for safety.

Within two hundred years of the collapse of Easter Island society, no one was left who remembered anything about the statues. For generations, their focus had been on survival. Too many generations had lived without ever seeing a tree, and so couldn't relate to ancient stories of timber and forests. The population had crashed to less than 10 percent of its peak. By 1864 every statue on Easter Island had been pulled down and desecrated.

The collapse of this once happy and prosperous culture was a simple case of jobs and ego over environmental preservation and resource management. No one was willing to stop the work of destroying the island's trees and chiseling statues to consider the impact of this self-serving activity on the island's fragile ecosystem.

There have been theories that run counter to this historical scenario. There is a remarkable similarity between glyphs (script) on Easter Island statues and the Mohenjo Daro script from the Indus Valley. Neither script has been translated, but the symbols are almost identical. This has led some to propose a connection between these two places half a word apart. Most of these theories revolve around alien intervention, but no direct link has ever been identified.

Heyerdahl used two bits of evidence to theorize that Easter Island was populated from South America. Sweet potatoes originated in South America (but were present all over Polynesia by A.D. 600). The Easter Island stone platforms (upon which many of the statues were placed) show the same type and pattern of expert masonry developed by Myans in South America. Heyerdahl's theory, however, has been dismissed by the overwhelming evidence compiled over the past fifteen years.

# Fact or Fiction?

Were the Easter Island statues built by aliens as some have claimed? No. Were they built and moved by magic powers? No. Does the existence of the statues imply technology beyond primitive island civilization? No.

The results of the intensive, careful work over the past several decades have answered the mystery of Easter Island. Science has compiled a complete picture of the island's history. The islanders didn't properly shepherd and manage their essential natural resources (trees), and they devoted too much time to building monuments. Their society then collapsed as their environment radically altered for the worse.

There does remain one compelling mystery from Easter Island's chilling past: Will Easter Island fulfill its role as a prophecy for the fate of Earth, or will modern humanity learn the bitter lesson of Easter Island society in time to avoid a similar fate? Will the world one day look like Easter Island, or will we act to prevent the collapse of our supporting ecosystem? Here is a chilling mystery for the twenty-first century.

# Follow-On Questions to Explore

1. Why would people build statues as symbols of their wealth, power and prestige? Do people still build such statues to themselves today? What would be the modern equivalent of Easter Island's stone statues? Can you find such statues and monuments in your community? Do you think excessively big houses and expensive cars count as such monuments to wealth and prestige? Is that any different than stone statues? Are our modern versions of stone statues as costly to the environment and as self-serving as the Easter Island stone statues were?

2. The Easter Island civilization grew, flourished, advanced and then disappeared. It came and went. Why? Do you think the islanders knew their civilization was about to collapse? Why do civilizations collapse? Why don't they continue to expand and improve? Do all civilizations eventually collapse?

# Follow-On Activities

1. Make a list of all the cultures that have disappeared from the Western Hemisphere. Where did they live? When did they flourish? When did they disappear? See if you can find out what happened to each culture

and why it disappeared. Do you find any pattern in the rise and fall of Western Hemisphere cultures? Compare your findings to the history of Easter Island.

2. Pretend you are an adviser to the governmental council leader of Easter Island in the year 1300. If you could foresee the events of the next three hundred years, how would you advise the leader? How would you convince the clans to stop chopping trees, even though they thought it was their right to build statues. Write a letter to the leader, trying to convince him of the dangers, and suggest actions that he might take to protect the island and its human population. How should he convince the individual clans to go along?

# References

Bahn, Paul, and John Flenley. *Easter Island, Earth Island.* London: Thames and Hudson, 1992.

Clark, Liesl. *Secrets of Easter Island.* Boston: WGBH and NOVA, 1998. Videocassette.

Diamond, Jared. "Easter's End." *Discover,* August 1996, 63–69.

Heyerdahl, Thor. *Easter Island: The Mystery Solved.* Boston: Stoddard Publishing, 1989.

———. *Kon-Tiki: Across the Pacific by Raft.* New York: Pocket Books, 1966.

Lewis, David. *We the Navigators: The Ancient Art of Landfinding in the Pacific.* Honolulu: University of Hawaii Press, 1994.

Orliac, Catherine, and Michel Orliac. *Easter Island: Mystery of the Stone Giants.* New York: Harry Abrams, 1995.

Van Tilburg, Jo Anne, and John Mack. *Easter Island: Archaeology, Ecology, and Culture.* Washington, D.C.: Smithsonian Institution Press, 1995.

# Firewalks & Beds of Nails
## Mind Control or Self-Destruction?

## At a Glance

Firewalking was first mentioned in writing by the Greek playwright Euripides in his fifth-century B.C. play *Bacchae*. In the Middle Ages, court ladies accused of adultery had to walk on hot plow blades without burning their feet to prove their innocence.

*The Guinness Book of World Records* lists the hottest firewalk ever successfully completed as being over coals raised to 1,550 degrees Fahrenheit (almost hot enough to melt steel), the longest as being 120 feet. Both records were set by a Seattle, Washington, firewalking group. They are one of more than a dozen recreational firewalking groups in this country who hold monthly firewalkings where anyone can watch or participate.

More than half a million people now firewalk worldwide—some for sport, some for religious reasons, some to develop better control over mind and body. Several U.S. universities (the University of Wisconsin at Madison being the biggest) offer courses in firewalking. Firewalking ceremonies and groups exist on every continent except Antarctica. Several of the world's most popular religions (primarily Hinduism and Buddhism) have firewalking ceremonies as part of their religious practices. Bali, Africa, India, Cambodia, Spain, Hawaii, Canada, Argentina, the United States—it seems that everywhere people exist, they are walking on fire.

Firewalking is the best known of a group of seemingly deadly and self-destructive acts that mystics and New Age explorers regularly perform—and always survive. They walk across burning coals without being burned; they lie unharmed on beds of nails; they plunge their hands into vats of glowing, molten lead; they walk across beds of broken glass—all without any bodily damage. These feats seem to defy both common sense and the physical laws we all must live under. We naturally believe we would be fried to a crisp, punctured like a pin cushion and sliced to ribbons if we tried to do these things. We naturally suspect that practitioners of such acts must be cheating somehow to avoid similar self-destruction.

Is it a trick? Is it just an illusion? Do people really do these things? Are they protected by mystical powers, or could anyone do these things?

# The Mystery:
# Firewalks & Beds of Nails

The rickety tour bus ground to a halt, kicking up a cloud of dust in the dirt road. The doors squeaked open to the scorching, tropical heat of late afternoon. Some native Balinese and a dozen tourists— mostly wearing flowered aloha shirts and strapped with bulging camera bags—stretched in the aisle from the long, bumpy ride. One by one they stepped off the bus in front of the Hindu temple on the island of Bali, Indonesia, site of the Kechak Dance. After a flurry of preliminary events, the dance itself would feature young Hindu temple novices, who would walk unharmed through fire.

Jeff and Margo Chilters were among the tourists, on a vacation trip to Bali during Margo's summer break from teaching psychology at the university. Jeff, with his short, thick stature, rounded shoulders and bushy black hair and beard, looked as much like a bear as a human. Margo was tall and elegant-looking—even with a thick coating of road dust over her slacks and blouse.

They had decided at the last minute to watch the fire dance. Jeff, a skeptical mechanical engineer, thought it would be a waste of an evening and of the $56.00 they spent for tickets. Margo thought it would be an interesting experience.

After passing the ticket booth, they jostled with the crowd through the main gate of the temple and entered a wide, dirt court-yard. A simple dirt stage was lit with both floodlights and spotlights off to one side. U-shaped bleachers rose around it.

The growing crowd was hustled into the bleachers by red-robed monks. Oak logs and bamboo poles were stacked in a wide pit on one side of the stage. Jeff nodded. "Bamboo to burn hot and fast. Oak to develop a good bed of embers. I'm impressed."

A 6-foot bed of nails lay open on the other side of the stage. Jeff chuckled, "Boy, would I like to test those nails. Bet the ones in the middle are fakes."

Margo silently shook her head.

It started quietly. Chanting by a few voices back in the temple. The music barely drifting over the noisy bleachers. Slowly the crowd quieted as the voices grew. A lone figure in a red robe walked silently onto the stage. One spotlight followed him. "Before we begin, would anyone like to inspect the bed of nails?" He said it in four languages, English being the second.

Jeff's hand shot up and he was motioned to the stage.

"You are English?" the red-robed man asked.

"American."

The man gestured to the bed of nails. "Please satisfy yourself."

Jeff knelt next to the bed and reached in to tap his palm on the center nails. Then he grimaced and shook his hand. "Owww! They're sharp. They're *all* sharp."

"And would you like to light the fire?"

Jeff nodded and accepted a torch from a second robed figure, who had materialized from backstage. Drums began to beat from behind the backstage curtain. The chanting voices had increased and now bathed the viewers in a hypnotic and powerful melody that rose and fell in rhythmic waves.

Jeff could smell lighter fluid as he approached the fire pit. He tipped the torch forward. With a great "whoosh!" a ball of flame rolled into the sky. Waves of heat billowed out, forcing Jeff to protect his face and back away.

The Sun had set. The golds and reds of the western sky matched the golden glow of the raging fire pit. Jeff bulled his way through the thick crowd back up to his seat as a hundred bare-chested men of the Kechak chorus, each wearing black-and-white sarong-style pants and a thick red sash, filed onto the stage and sat facing the audience in a great circle. Their harmonic music rose and fell. A row of drums behind the curtain maintained a pounding beat.

At first dancers reenacted a few scenes from the Kechak myths. Margo appreciatively watched the graceful dancers. Jeff's eyes darted between the bed of nails and the roaring fire, which slowly crumpled in on itself to form a seething mass of red-hot embers.

As the dancers slipped into the shadows at the edges of the stage, the drums grew to a pounding crescendo and one of the circle of men rose and tossed off his sash. With slow, purposeful steps, his arms locked at his sides, he strode toward the bed of nails. Three spotlights poured radiant light onto the bed and glistened off the nail points.

A voice over the loudspeakers announced that the man had achieved a trance state and would be able to lie on the nails without harm. The drums pounded. His fellow monks' voices rose and fell with the pulsing rhythm.

For a moment the man stood with his back to the deadly bed. The audience inched forward and held their collective breath, every eye glued on the man's back. Slowly he lowered himself so that his hands touched the ground on either side of the bed. Crablike, he inched his hands farther up the sides of the bed until his body, from knee to shoulder, was almost completely horizontal, poised inches above the glistening nail points.

Slowly he lowered himself onto the spikes. He paused, and then raised hands and feet into the air, his entire weight supported only by sharp nails. The audience "Ooooh'ed." Some grimaced and sucked in a deep breath. Then the man lowered his hands to the ground, lifted himself off the nails and sprang to his feet. There was not a single mark on his back.

Margo murmured in amazement. Jeff's eyebrows scowled in skeptical doubt. "How could he ...?"

The drums and voices fell silent as the lone man jogged off-stage. Then five new dancers filed in and the dancing began again. The beat was demanding, frenzied this time. For several minutes the dancers leapt and spun while three attendants with long rakes smoothed the glowing coals of the fire pit into an even bed of glowing heat 10 feet across.

The attendants stepped back into the shadows. Slowly the dancers spun and pranced closer and closer to the fire. Spotlights flicked across each dancer as they twirled and jumped. One by one the lights dimmed out. The only light left came from the glowing fire. Waves of heat from the fire washed over the audience like a blast furnace.

One of the dancers stepped into the fire and began a shuffling dance through the embers. The crowd gasped.

Another dancer paused at the edge and began a slow measured walk straight across the coals. His sarong began to smolder before he had crossed to the far side, but his face showed no pain or discomfort.

The crowd cheered. Margo gasped and covered her mouth. Jeff glared hard, searching for some gimmick—hard soles glued onto the fire dancers' feet, a safe path through the middle that could not be seen from the bleachers—anything to explain what his eyes saw that his mind refused to accept.

Dancer after dancer entered the fire—from the sides, from the front—always moving gracefully, lightly, sometimes speeding straight through the coals, sometimes looping in lazy circles before exiting. The frenzied crowd roared for each one.

Suddenly an old man leapt from the bleachers, kicked off his leather sandals and sped past the seated monks. Arms spread wide, he jumped into the fire pit with the dancers. Instantly his face contorted in pain. His high-pitched screech rattled every person sitting fascinated and frozen in the bleachers.

The poor man managed three halting steps, all the while writhing in pain, before several dancers lifted him to safety. All the dancers stepped out of the fire pit. The lights came up. The music slowed. The man's feet were doused with water and he was rushed to a waiting ambulance that raced for Ubud, the nearest city.

The crowd sat in shocked silence, still staring at the fire pit, still hearing the old man's screams. A voice over the loudspeakers announced that the evening's ritual was over and said that the old man had been burned because he had not mentally prepared himself to be protected from the fire. The crowd began to shuffle toward the main gate, wrapped in low, awe-filled murmurs.

Jeff and Margo lingered behind. "I still say it has to be a clever trick," insisted Jeff. "The dancers didn't burn themselves because simple physics principles protected them. They chose types of wood whose embers don't conduct heat well."

Margo shook her head. "No. I could feel that something more than just physics was at play."

Jeff snorted. "Hooey. It's simple physics and all show."

"Then why was the old man burned?"

Jeff shrugged. "Probably part of the act. He probably wasn't burned at all. Probably anyone could do it."

Margo arched her eyebrows and gestured toward the glowing coals.

"All right. I will," Jeff huffed, stripping off his shoes. His heart pounded as he stepped, barefoot, onto the stage. He could feel waves of heat still pouring from the pit. Nervously he stretched one foot forward. The rising heat almost singed his skin.

A thick lump stuck in his throat. His palms sweated. "It's all simple physics … It's all simple physics …," he chanted to himself. "Walk briskly and evenly …"

One foot ground onto a large ember. He shifted his weight onto that foot and at first heard, more than he felt, the sizzle. Jeff panicked as he began to feel the searing pain.

He sprang back, a giant blister of charred flesh already forming on the ball of his foot. The scars didn't disappear for two months. And every day during that long period, Jeff wondered, How did they do it?

## About This Story

This story is based on the reported experience of one couple. The event—the Kechak Dance and firewalk at the Hindu temple outside Ubud on the island of Bali, Indonesia—is real and is regularly staged for tourists. The descriptions presented here are consistent with the official descriptions given by the promoter of this event, but are stated through the perspective of the American couple who reported their experience.

## The Science

Physicists say it is the application of well-known principles of physics and thermodynamics that protects firewalkers. Many knowledgeable practitioners say it is physics plus solid showmanship that makes it work. Believers say it is all mental preparation, the ability to enter a trance state and extend a protective aura about the body. Without the protection of sacred intervention through trance, say believers, a firewalker would be scarred for life. Who's right?

There is much evidence to support the notion that principles of physics and thermal conductivity are what protect the body—period. The only mental preparation needed is that done to talk yourself into doing the firewalk (even though you know physics will protect you). Still, this would be a considerable mental challenge for most people. And what about lying on a bed of nails? To find specific explanations, we must look separately at each of these supposedly mystical events.

### Bed of Nails

This one *is* pure physics. There is no mystery. Even the sharpest nail won't puncture your skin without some force behind it. Balance a nail, point down, on the palm of your hand. It won't hurt you because the nail's own weight isn't a great enough force to make it penetrate your skin.

If you sit on one nail, or even ten, your body's weight provides plenty of force to drive the nails deep into your behind. But what if you weighed 150 pounds and spread your weight evenly over 150 nails? Now there is only a force of 1 pound pushing down on each nail—not enough to make a nail break your skin.

Beds of nails are routinely made of a thousand nails or more. When someone lies on the bed, their weight is spread out over 200 to 300 of those nails. No one nail supports enough weight to leave more than a red mark. It's simple physics—and great care by performers to make sure they never concentrate their weight on too few nails. The time performers must be most careful is when they are easing down onto, and rising up off of, the bed, because if they slip and put their full body weight onto too few nails, they will pay a painful price.

## Firewalking

If there is a question, a lingering mystery, it is with firewalking. First, the physics of firewalking is far more complex than that of lying on a bed of nails. Second, physics doesn't quite explain everything.

Temperature doesn't burn anything. It is heat, transferred from one object to another, that does the burning. If you were to heat an oven to 450 degrees and place your hand momentarily inside, nothing would happen. But if you were to momentarily touch the metal side of that oven, you would be burned. Why? Two reasons. First, air can't hold very much heat (it has a low heat capacity). But metal can. So even when air is heated to 450 degrees, it doesn't hold as much heat as metal would at the same temperature. Second, air doesn't transfer its heat very quickly (it has a low thermal conductivity). But metal has a much higher thermal conductivity. Metal holds much more heat and passes it far more quickly to skin (or anything else). So hot metal will burn something much faster than hot air will.

What does this have to do with firewalking? Simple. To burn a foot, the embers, coals or hot rocks must transfer enough heat through the outer layers of the skin to burn the layers underneath. This takes a lot of heat. A foot, being mostly water, has a high heat capacity. If the material being walked across is porous rock or embers and has either a low heat capacity or a low thermal conductivity (many materials used for firewalking have both qualities), it will not deliver enough heat to a foot to burn it unless contact is maintained for an extended period of time. Walk briskly, but evenly, on the flat of the foot and the embers will not burn the skin. That's what physics says.

Three extenuating circumstances make the situation more complicated, and somewhat safer for firewalkers. First, calluses are excellent insulators, and many firewalkers have built up thick calluses on the soles of their feet. Second, many glowing coals are actually covered with a layer of ash. Ash is also an insulator and retards heat transfer. Third, feet perspire. Microscopic drops of water forming on the soles of the feet will vaporize into a layer of insulating steam (the Leidenfrost effect), absorbing much of the fire's heat and insulating the foot from direct contact with the fire.

Actually more dangerous than hot embers are hot, *burning* embers. If the embers are actively burning, the chemical process of fire continuously creates heat. That heat-producing chemical reaction is more likely to damage the foot than are the hot embers underneath. That is why firewalkers in San Pedro Manrique, Spain, advise walkers to stomp hard on the burning embers to block off all air and stop the burning. Without active burning, they claim that the hot embers will not harm the firewalker.

Firewalkers themselves say that all this physics is true, but that it is not what protects them. Many walkers do not use porous rocks, often heating their densely packed rocks to greater than 1,200 degrees Fahrenheit. Many do walk through burning embers. Some pause to stand still on the burning coals, allowing prolonged contact between coals and skin. Some have even stooped during a firewalk to handle the glowing coals by hand. In all too many firewalks, though, situations arise that are beyond the specific conditions under which the laws of physics will protect a walker.

Firewalkers consistently claim that extensive mental and spiritual preparation is required to protect the body. University experiments to test this hypothesis (at UCLA, in California) have shown that using meditative exercises to focus the mind and spirit on protecting the feet actually does seem to deaden pain receptors and helps prevent tissue damage.

There is some scientific support for this position. In 1980 a science team from the University of Tubingen (Germany) visited the St. Constantine firewalk in Greece. They attached thermocouples to firewalkers' feet and EEG electrodes to their scalps. In the fire pit—measured at 932 degrees Fahrenheit, the walkers' skin reached a temperature of 350 degrees with no damage. Spectator volunteers began to blister at skin temperatures slightly greater than 200 degrees. EEGs showed that successful firewalkers produced vastly increased amounts of theta brain waves during the walk. The presence of meditation-induced theta waves was the scientists' only available explanation for the walkers' feet being protected at such high temperatures. Other scientists suspect that the firewalkers had built up a very thick epidermal layer (skin and calluses) from walking barefoot much of the time (calluses are an excellent thermal insulator).

Often, those who attempt a firewalk without preparing themselves are injured—and often very badly. If it were a simple matter of applied physics, why wouldn't every firewalker be equally protected? Firewalkers say with great certainty that firewalking is far more a mental and spiritual activity than a physical one.

# Fact or Fiction?

Do they really do it? Yes, they do. But that's not the question. The question is: Is there anything beyond simple physics and showmanship that protects the participants? For lying on a bed of nails, the answer is definitely not.

For firewalking, though, the answer is not as certain. Nagging questions remain unanswered. Sweat on the bottom of the foot won't last beyond a few quick steps. If the steam layer those few drops create is what protects the foot, how can walkers survive walks across hundreds of feet of glowing coals? If it is the low thermal capacity and low thermal conductivity of porous embers that protects a walker's feet, how can walks over nonporous stones heated to 1,100–1,400 degrees Fahrenheit be successfully completed? The thermal conductivity of nonporous stones is substantially higher than that of wood embers.

How can walkers pause to stand still on the coals and not be burned? If it is fire more than hot coals that burns, how can walkers walk through *burning* coals? If it is simple physical laws that protect firewalkers, then why are so many spontaneous participants (who have not undergone extensive mental preparation) often badly burned when they leap from the audience to try their luck at a firewalk?

The principles of physics explain the vast majority of firewalking, and they *do* work—that is, they will protect a walker—so long as the conditions of the walk adhere to the conditions under which those physical principles apply. But walkers have gone beyond those particular sets of conditions without injury. What protects them? Clearly, there is a mind-body connection that comes to the fore during firewalking. It has not been quantified or extensively studied. It is not well understood. But it seems clear that firewalkers' minds can physically help protect their feet.

Exacting scientific studies and on-site measurements have not been conducted to entirely explain the phenomenon of firewalking. Rates of heat capacity and thermal conductivity have not been measured during an actual firewalk. Rates of thermal absorption through the epidermal layers also have not been measured. Until they are, there seems to be room left for mystical faith in pondering this ancient ritual.

# Follow-On Questions to Explore

1. Do you think the beliefs of the firewalker determine whether or not they get burned? Do you think that mental preparation is critical to their safety? Why or why not? Do you believe that you would be burned if you tried a firewalk? Why? What do you believe explains this phenomenon?

2. Have you ever been burned by fire, a burning marshmallow, hot summer pavement or barbecue charcoals? What burned you? How does that experience compare to firewalking and the physics principles presented above? Why didn't these principles protect you?

## Follow-On Activities

1. Carefully push (force) a sharp nail to penetrate a balloon, a wad of cotton, a rubber band and soft wood (such as balsa wood). How much force was required to make the nail penetrate these substances? Which substance or surface do you think is most like skin? Create a chart showing how much force is required to make a nail penetrate different materials, and showing how much force can be created in different ways (hammer blow, thumb push, simple gravity, etc.).

2. Research firewalking and firewalkers. Who does it? Why? What do they hope to get out of the experience? What do they walk on? Why? What mental/spiritual preparations (if any) do they undertake? Why? Is anyone ever burned? Why or why not? Explain your findings based on the physics principles described above.

## References

Constable, George, ed. *Mind over Matter.* New York: Time Life Books, 1988.

Gore, Rick. "Living on Fire." *National Geographic,* May 1998, 6–37.

White, Michael. *Weird Science.* New York: Avon Books, 1999.

Willey, David. "The Physics Behind Four Amazing Demonstrations." *Skeptical Inquirer,* November/December 1999, 44–46.

# Moans, Groans and Bumps in the Night

## Ghosts—Believe It or Not?

### At a Glance

Everyone enjoys a good ghost story. They've been a popular form of entertainment for millennia. Spirits and ghosts pop up to terrify story characters and delight listeners. Casper was a friendly ghost. Scrooge was beset by ghosts in Dickens's famous tale. Sleepy Hollow was beset by a headless, horse-riding ghost. Storytelling festivals feature whole sessions devoted to ghost tales. Every culture has stories of spirits that walk the earth. Then there are the ghosts of horror novels and horror movies—ghosts that populate grotesque, demonic nightmares and are made to slash, kill and destroy in an effort to create the most gruesome and disturbing story possible.

But what about *real* ghosts, spirits that walk around in your house, or in your neighbors' houses, and moan through the night. Gallup Poll and other surveys show that one in four Americans believes that ghosts really exist, and one in fourteen claim to have personally encountered a ghost. That's more than twenty million Americans who claim to have seen or heard a ghost!

But do we really believe in ghosts? Do you believe that ghosts walk (or float) freely around the earth? Most scoff at this idea. The very existence of real ghosts doesn't fit with the modern scientific view of the world. Science doesn't accept mysterious, unexplainable events.

But before you tell yourself that you don't believe in ghosts, think for a moment. Would you hesitate to spend a night in a "haunted" house or in a graveyard. Why? Because those places are scary and creepy. Why? Because those are places where ghosts are most likely to appear! A vague suspicion that ghosts might exist there is what makes such places feel scary and creepy. Doesn't that count as believing in ghosts?

There is, of course, a problem with believing in ghosts. For a ghost to exist, some part of a person—the spirit or soul—must have consciously survived after the death of the physical body and still be able to think and act like the person did when they were alive. That idea violates many belief systems, both religious and cultural. It runs counter to the beliefs of those who claim that there is no afterlife (that death is final), those who claim that the soul is whisked off to heaven immediately after death and those who claim that the soul begins a new life in a new body (reincarnation) after the death of its last body. None of these beliefs allows a place for souls to wander the world as ghosts, still acting like they did when they were alive.

Instantly, any scientific investigation is muddied by questions of fundamental belief and philosophy (*Who* are the ghosts? and *Why* are they here?). But to address this issue, science must focus first on *whether* ghosts exist. Are there physical entities (beings— ghosts) that exist and that can be seen and heard by human senses (and by machines that monitor the same electromagnetic spectrums)? That is one of the biggest and oldest mysteries of all.

# The Mystery: Moans, Groans and Bumps in the Night

The soggy, ovenlike heat of an August day in South Carolina was beginning to fade. The Sun had already sunk behind western trees by the time the moving van pulled away and Pam Cocker wearily closed the front door on the frantic activity of move-in day.

Odd, she thought. Lazy Bones stood rigidly in the hall, facing the arched doorway into the dining room, hairs bristled all along her spine, lips curled back in the first ferocious growl of the dog's life. A happy mutt who looked more like a collie than anything else, Lazy Bones was a perpetual tail-wagger, often doing so even in her sleep, as if even her dreams made her happy. The thought that flashed across Pam's mind was that the dog looked more frightened than angry.

Pam shrugged it off as the effect of a new house with new smells and clapped her hands to get the dog's attention. "Bones! Stop that!"

Reluctantly Bones turned and jogged toward her owner, tail wagging, tongue lolling out one side of her mouth in a doggy smile.

Pam Cocker had rented this modest house until she could find a place she wanted to buy. Pam was a teacher and had left a school and job she had grown tired of—not to mention the New Jersey urban grime—to make a fresh start together with her ten-year-old son, Tye, here in Spartanburg, South Carolina, the heart of the South. Everything she and her son owned had been crammed into a moving van and now was stuffed into this snug house with its grand sitting porch and beautiful shade trees.

Actually, only half of the load in the giant moving van had been Pam's. The other half belonged to a family moving from upstate New Jersey to somewhere in Alabama—not that Pam cared, as long as her load was delivered first and on-time. The New Jersey packers had marked every box and piece of furniture by room. Any box the South Carolina movers weren't certain about had been dumped in the dining room, which quickly grew into a sprawling "box central."

Odd, Pam thought again, after dinner, when the family cat, Withers—whom they called *Mr.* Withers, and who acted like the one true aristocrat in the family—slowly backed away from the dining room and flattened himself against a wall, hissing venomously. But then, Mr. Withers had had a long two days in the car and probably needed some time to adjust. Besides, it was late, the delivered pizza had all been eaten and Pam was too tired to care what had upset a cat.

Next morning Pam began the chore of unpacking kitchen boxes and deciding into which cupboards, drawers, shelves and nooks everything should go. Almost halfway through the project, she decided on a short break to sit on the back deck and watch Tye and Lazy Bones romp in the backyard.

She hadn't been outside thirty seconds when she heard a crash in the kitchen and then heard Mr. Withers spit and hiss in desperate fear and combat. She dashed inside to find every kitchen cupboard and drawer wide open and every item she had put away piled in a heap in the middle of the floor. Every packing box had been dragged back into the dining room. Mr. Withers crouched trembling in the back of the cabinet under the sink.

At first Pam stared blankly in shock and awe. Then her mind wondered—How …?—trying to calculate how long it would have taken her to create such a complete and total mess. She figured four minutes at least. How could this happen almost instantly? Then her mind wondered—Who …? and her heart began to pound.

She was alone in the house—at least, she thought she was alone. She glanced out a back window. Tye was climbing a tree. Lazy Bones happily barked and jumped, trying to climb after him.

Who did this?!

Pam screamed, "Who's there? Come out!"

She raced through the house carrying a carving knife. She heard not a sound and met not a soul. She couldn't think of anything to do but go back to unpacking.

Pam called Tye in to unpack boxes in his room and then help her in the living room. With a shrug, he started up the stairs, hardly noticing the shambles in the kitchen.

By dinnertime they had worked their way through three-quarters of their boxes and flopped onto the couch to watch TV and eat Chinese takeout. Lazy Bones and Mr. Withers lounged on the wall-to-wall carpet at their feet.

Bones's head snapped up. Then Mr. Withers sprang to his feet. Both animals growled at the empty, arched doorway into the dining room. As fiercely as they could, Bones and Withers hissed and barked at the doorway, slowly backing up as if being driven back by some great force. With wails of defeat, both animals bolted for the garage, tails tucked between their legs.

Pam was frozen with a forkful of sesame chicken halfway to her mouth. Tye blinked as if he had missed something, his head slowly turning between the empty dining room doorway and the garage door through which the animals had fled.

"What was *that*?" exclaimed Pam.

Tye shrugged and turned back to the TV, but a chilling breath of air blew across his arm and neck. He shuddered, but nothing was there in the room to worry about. "Must be the open garage door," he muttered and went back to dinner.

Pam wandered back downstairs before going to bed just to check the house and doors. Every packing box they had broken down had been reassembled and stood in a great wall across the dining room. She began to tremble. Her mind refused to accept that anything terrifyingly weird could happen—not to *her*. Not now.

Maybe, she thought, they hadn't broken those boxes down ... Maybe she had left all those kitchen drawers open and had stacked her kitchen items on the floor to better see what she had and where she should put it ...

Maybe ...

But as she trudged up to bed, she knew she hadn't. Something was very wrong in this house. But she also felt embarrassingly foolish as her mind flashed through pictures of ghosts and gremlins. She had a master's degree in science, for goodness' sake. She prided herself in her rational, problem-solving skills. Things didn't just happen by themselves. There must be a logical explanation. Maybe she was just too tired to see it now. She was suddenly sure that it would all become clear to her in the morning.

Tye woke up in the pitch-black night, his heart pounding, his face bathed in a cold sweat. He had heard footsteps and his door opening. Hadn't he? Or was it just a dream—a nightmare? He settled back into a fitful sleep.

Sometime later the same sounds wove their way into a new dream. So did a touch, a cold, soft nudge on his arm.

Again someone pushed on his arm trying to gain his attention.

No! That wasn't a dream. Tye jerked awake, gasping for breath. The room was empty. But the spot on his arm where he remembered being touched in his dream now burned as if it had been brushed by dry ice.

Pam couldn't sleep well that night either. She kept hearing creeks and groans from the house. Typical of an old house, she thought. But she also thought that several times she heard footsteps—soft, shuffling and distant. She woke with a start at 4:00 A.M. Now she *knew* she heard steps. She sprang out of bed to find Tye at the bottom of the stairs, sleepwalking, turning toward the dining room.

The dining room! Everything weird always happened around the dining room. That was it! There *was* something wrong in this house, and whatever it was was in, or connected to, the dining room. But … but what?

In the morning Pam found a slight burn—a red mark, like frostbite—on Tye's arm where he thought it had been touched. Other than for Lazy Bones and Mr. Withers being afraid to come out of the garage all day, that next day was uneventful. Pam unpacked more boxes and re–broke down the ones that had rebuilt themselves the night before. All the while she kept a wary watch on the dining room—not having any idea of what she was hoping, or dreading, to see.

During the darkest hours of the next night, Pam awoke, again hearing steps. She was about to check on Tye when her door opened. A vague, light-gray shadow shimmered in the doorway, the glowing outline of a man dressed in rags that once had been elegant clothes. It—he—took a step forward to stand at the foot of her bed. Both terrified and fascinated, Pam realized that the ghost looked sad, but with an edge of long-held, bitter frustration and anger.

Pam thought she heard the word "home," like a low moan, full of despair and grief. Both of his arms reached out toward her. Pam screamed for the thing to get out of her house and reached for her bedside light. The ghostly image was gone when light struck the room.

Downstairs all the packing boxes had been reassembled in the dining room.

Early the next morning Pam called her landlord. She knew it would be an awkward conversation, to say the least. How do you ask someone if they forgot to mention that the house they rented was haunted, without sounding like a crazy, undesirable tenant?

The landlord seemed totally innocent and unaware of any ghosts.

In a flash of insight, Pam realized it wasn't the dining room or the house, it was the *moving boxes* the ghost seemed to be attached to. On a whim, she called the moving company and, making up the excuse that she thought she had one of their boxes, got the phone number of the family in Alabama whose furniture had shared the moving van.

A woman about Pam's age answered the phone. Pam introduced herself and asked if they had "lost" anything during the move.

For a long, awkward moment all Pam heard was the soft hiss of static on the line. The woman's voice seemed older and more tired when she said, "Oh. That's where Jefferson went."

*"Jefferson?"* Pam blurted. "The ghost has a name?! He's *your* ghost?"

The Alabama woman explained. "Jefferson was in our New Jersey house when we bought it. He popped out every month or so to rattle drawers—he loved to mess up kitchen and clothes drawers. We had hoped to leave him behind in New Jersey. That's why my husband took a new job and we moved."

The stunning simplicity of it floored Pam. The ghost had wanted to stay with his old family and so had ridden with their furniture in the van. He had simply off-loaded at the wrong stop!

Pam and Tye left forty empty packing boxes lined up in the otherwise empty dining room. And they never saw or heard from Jefferson again. Lazy Bones and Mr. Withers, of course, still refused to go near that dining room.

Pam bought the first house she could find that she could move into right away. On move-out day, the landlord asked Pam if she wasn't going to take the moving boxes in the dining room.

"No," answered Pam. "They're extras. I thought the new tenant might want them."

She and Tye left and never dared go back, even though Pam always wondered who Jefferson was and what had happened to him. But more than curiosity, Pam was left with a deep, nagging doubt. It had felt that one night when she saw him, that Jefferson wanted—needed—help. What had he wanted? If she had asked, instead of screaming for him to leave, could she have done something to give his troubled soul some peace?

## About This Story

This story combines the separate experiences of two personal friends, both of whom have had very close and personal encounters with ghosts. Are the stories true? Both friends insist that they are. Both people are logical, rational beings with advanced degrees and a healthy dose of scientific skepticism. So, there would seem to be no basis for disbelieving their stories. Neither story, however, has been investigated or challenged by paranormal researchers.

## The Science

Like the Loch Ness monster and flying saucers, the question of whether or not ghosts exist pits an overwhelming mass of personal experience on the one hand against empirical, scientific research on the other. How can the millions of people who claim to have seen a ghost all be wrong? But if they're right, why hasn't anyone ever—even once—been able to prove the existence of their ghostly visitor? Why has no scientific instrument, experiment or measurement ever been able to detect or authenticate the presence of a ghost to the satisfaction of the scientific community?

Also like several other science mysteries, most scientists are afraid to study ghosts for fear that they probably won't be able to obtain any significant results (and therefore will lose whatever funding they were able to find), and for fear that their reputation as a serious researcher will be destroyed. Because of this lack of scientific attention, some claim that we know little more about ghosts now than we did a century ago.

But what can scientific investigators do the day after a houseful of people claim to have heard rattling chains and terrifying moans in the night? What can an investigator do to verify that someone saw a ghost or poltergeist drift through their bedroom? (Poltergeists are ghosts that actively interact with the human environment—throwing things, opening drawers, touching people, etc.)

Actually, there is a well-established scientific protocol (plan) for investigating paranormal phenomena (ghost sightings). Societies all over world have developed the process and trained their researchers to conduct these investigations. First, an investigator must establish that they haven't received a false report. There are six kinds of false reports researchers have learned that they must eliminate before they can hope to establish that a true encounter has happened:

1. **A hoax.** Most ghost reports are hoaxes—someone playing a joke or trying to get their name in the papers. Virtually ever photograph ever taken of a ghost (psychic photography) has been shown to be a fake. Dust gets on a lens and creates a ghostly white spot. Light refracts through the lens and creates a white blur. Double exposures place a ghostlike aberration in the scene. And so forth. Ghostly sounds are concocted, or simply made up. A hidden black string, rather than a ghostly hand, causes a book to leap off a shelf. The overwhelming abundance of hoaxes has given paranormal research a bad name.

2. **Natural phenomena.** Most of the remaining ghostly sounds and events are the result of very real and natural forces. Cats or rats in the basement, or small vermin in the walls, often sound like ghosts. Creaking foundations or clanging pipes sound like ghosts walking or dragging chains. A book crashes off a shelf—not because of a ghostly hand, but because the shelf wasn't quite level and gravity eventually pulled it off. And on and on.

3. **Misinterpretation or mistaken identity.** Humans are likely to err in their perceptions under the stress of thinking they have encountered a ghost. (Was it a ghost that moaned, or just the creak of an old house? Did the book move itself, or did I move it and forget that I had? etc.)

4. **Illusion or exaggeration.** The memory of emotionally stressful events always changes a little over time. Sounds grow a little creepier. If the mind can't make sense of events at the time they happen, it tends to shift them around slightly so they will make sense later.

5.  **Human expectation.** If someone expects to see or hear a ghost, that person will tend to interpret whatever happens as having been a ghost encounter.

6.  **Single or mass hallucination.** Seeing something that isn't there (hallucinating) happens far more frequently than most people might think. Hypnopompic visions are the most common form of such hallucinations. These visions happen in the moment between sleep and awakening and are typically interpreted by the brain as having been real. Seeing ghosts standing at the foot of the bed or women in long white dresses drifting through the bedroom—these are classic hypnopompic visions.

How does an investigator check for these false reports? The process is remarkably similar to a police inspector investigating a crime scene: Check the building and its foundation for signs of rats and other vermin (often the source of ghostly noises), for settling (another common source of noises), for pipes and washers that can make popping and rattling noises. Check whether each floor is level. Often objects that jump off shelves "all by themselves" actually move because of simple gravity. Use sound-detection equipment to see if noise from nearby neighbors, streets or construction activity can be erroneously interpreted within the "haunted" building.

Interview every occupant of the building and determine their background and personality type (imaginative, exaggerative, realistic, factual, etc.). Might any of the occupants be prone to creating a hoax? Is there anyone who might benefit from claiming to have seen a ghost, or who might need the profit that such a claim could generate? How reliable are the occupants as witnesses? Could they be easily fooled? Were there any trained observers? How objective were the observers?

Search for patterns in the sightings that might suggest an explanation. Are there any explanations discovered for past ghost reports fitting the same pattern that could explain the current ghostly appearance? Interview neighbors and officials to see if any activity at a nearby location could explain the sighting.

Try to duplicate the ghostly contact using conventional techniques. Magicians are often employed to conduct these tests and have been very effective in uncovering hoaxes by discovering how an apparent ghostly event was staged.

Once the common forms of false sightings have been eliminated, the researcher can begin to seriously consider the possibility of a ghost sighting. The observer must now record, measure and observe using thermometers, electromagnetic meters (for measuring the electric field), magnetometers (for measuring the magnetic field), compasses, infrared cameras and tape recorders. Psychics, psychologists and parapsychologists (mentalists) may also be helpful in gathering pertinent information. The goal of the researcher is always to search for physical, natural explanations. Only after all possible explanations have been eliminated can the existence of a real ghost be considered.

There exists a collection of hundreds of ghostly contacts that have survived through this extensive investigative process with no apparent physical explanation. They include reports of sight, sound, even the touch and smell of ghosts. What are these? Ghostly contacts? Maybe and maybe not. Supporters of the existence of ghosts say that, yes, these remaining reports are proof of ghosts. But scientists have never been convinced. They say that all that has been proved is that science can't explain the sightings. That is very different from proving what the sightings are.

Recently, a number of studies have begun to search for previously unconsidered natural explanations for ghost sightings. Several tantalizing possibilities have been uncovered by assuming that the visions people call ghosts are real and then searching for possible natural ways the images could have been projected in front of a viewer's eyes and ears.

If a sight is seen or a sound is heard, that sight or sound must have been created, recorded and then projected. Each of those steps requires some medium (equipment) and energy. We are all familiar with movie film and projectors, and with tape recorders, audio tape and speakers. These are the media we normally use for recording and projecting sights and sounds. Electricity provides the power to drive each of these processes.

If the recording and projecting media for ghostly images and the energy sources for their operation can be found, images that appear to be ghosts can be explained as real-world projected images, not as unknown mysteries. None of this research has been verified or substantiated. None has been independently tested. But it provides a fascinating glimpse into how scientific study could explain this major mystery.

First, how could an image or sound of a person be "recorded" without a camera or tape recorder? What would the image be recorded on? Research is under way to test the ability of various construction materials to record and later transmit images. Early results indicate that materials with higher levels of quartz might be induced to imprint, or hold, the basic information of an image—if enough energy were available to power the process.

Where would that energy come from? From the emotional energy of event. That's why only horrendous, traumatic events and images are imprinted. That's why people always see ghosts moaning in agony and death rather than happy, smiling ghosts on a picnic. Only the terrifyingly extreme events create enough emotional energy to force an image to be recorded by the surrounding walls and stones.

How is the image later projected into the air to appear as a ghost? One theory is that, if a person is highly excited and agitated, their mental and emotional energy could be strong enough to power the process of projecting an image stored in the surrounding material—if the vibrational frequency of that person's energy matched that of the material in which the image is stored. The emotional energy of the person who sees the vision actually drives and powers the process of projecting the image.

A second theory is that heat energy is used to project ghostly images. People who see ghosts almost always report that the room grew suddenly cold. If that is true, where did all that heat (thermal energy) go? It had to go some-where. Energy doesn't just disappear. It might have been converted into me-chanical energy to power the projection of an old image of a person into the air—which the viewer would call a ghost.

A third theory being explored is that the energy to create, record, store and project the image of a dead person might come from a very close loved one. At the moment that someone (whom we'll call the survivor) learns of the death of a loved one, a strong image of the loved one flashes through the survivor's mind. If the survivor's grief (emotional energy) is strong enough, and if the image in the survivor's mind is sharp and detailed enough, that image might be projected by the survivor's emotional energy to the site of the vision. That image would then reside there until either its energy completely dissipated or until some other person ran into the image and experienced it as a ghost.

There is also research under way indicating that severe mental stress and strain may create (or at least facilitate) psychokinesis (the moving of an object solely by a person's mind). A 1994 survey of ninety-two teenage victims of poltergeists (ghosts that moved objects around the victims' rooms) showed that 42 percent of victims had minor, seizurelike distur-bances in the brain (a percentage twenty times higher than in the normal population). These stress-related brain disturbances could be related to, could even be the driving force for, the events everyone attributed to mis-chievous ghosts.

Finally, two recent studies have indicated that high-intensity, low-frequency sound can be trapped in a building for extended periods of time and later heard as the moans, groans and clanks of a ghost. Ghosts could be nothing more than old broadcast energy rattling down the halls.

These theories, if proven true, could explain most, if not all, of the reported ghost sightings not previously explained by known phenomena. Do these theories provide the right answers? Maybe; maybe not. Only time and more research will tell.

Of course, there are two other possible explanations for ghost sightings. One is that science has not yet found the correct natural process to explain ghost sightings. The other is that there really are ghosts.

# Fact or Fiction?

Are ghosts real? Almost seventy million people in this country believe that they are real, and twenty million claim to have encountered one. Does that make them real? No scientifically valid evidence has ever been offered to establish that even one ghost really, physically exists. In other words, there is no scientifically valid evidence that humans can survive death in some form and return to interact with the physical world. Does that make ghosts pure fiction?

There are some intriguing theories on how ghostly images could be recorded, transmitted and projected. These theories could provide a logical explanation for what we call ghosts. None of these theories, however, has been tested or proved. None has been applied to well-documented sightings to see if it adequately explains the observed phenomena.

At this time, the best guess, based on available scientific information, is that there are no ghosts. Other, natural explanations will be found to account for the sightings we call ghosts. However, no such explanation for many of the documented ghost sightings has yet been found. Until someone can provide the proof to support one or more explanatory theories, ghosts are as real a possibility as any other theory.

Are ghosts replays of past energy? Creations of the viewer's mind? Misguided delusions and hallucinations? Physical entities? Much more research is needed by physicists, material engineers and biologists (three groups conspicuously absent from past paranormal research) before this age-old mystery can come to rest.

# Follow-On Questions to Explore

1. Do you believe in ghosts? Have you ever seen a ghost? Do you know anyone who has? What was your (or their) experience? What did the ghost do? What did you/they do? How did you/they finally get rid of the ghost? If you don't believe in ghosts, why do you think so many people do?

2. Do you find the reported behavior of ghosts odd? Why do they mostly show up at night? Why don't ghosts talk more and say what they want? Why do they make it so hard for us to understand and assist them? Why do you think they are here? What are they after? What do they want to do?

# Follow-On Activities

1. Find out about one ghost sighting that has happened in your community and research it as thoroughly as you can. Follow the investigative protocol described above to learn everything you can about the site and participants. Visit ghost researcher sites on the Internet and ask for advice on how to proceed. Seek as many possible explanations (other than real ghosts) as you can imagine. What do you think really happened?

2. Is there a so-called haunted house in your community? Is it open to the public? If so, visit it; study it; measure it. Investigate the history of the building and how it came to receive its "haunted" reputation. Is it just a creepy old house that looks scary? Did some disastrous event take place in the house? Have ghosts been reported in it? Does it feel haunted?

    Use a compass, a thermometer and a tape recorder to take readings in each room, especially in any rooms where major events or sightings happened. Did you find anything? What do you think that means? Do you think you would find a ghost if you had more time to study the house? Did you dare to stay there after dark?

# References

Ballinger, Erich. *Monster Manual: A Complete Guide to Your Favorite Creatures.* Minneapolis, Minn.: Lerner, 1994.

Carrington, Hereward. *Haunted People.* New York: Signet, 1978.

Cohen, Daniel. *Ghosts of the Deep.* New York: Putnam, 1993.

———. *In Search of Ghosts.* New York: Dodd, Mead, 1972.

———. *Raising the Dead.* New York: Dutton, 1997.

———. *Young Ghosts.* New York: Cobblehill Books, 1994.

Editors of USA Weekend. *I Never Believed in Ghosts Until ...* Chicago: Contemporary Books, 1992.

Garrett, Eileen. *Many Voices.* New York: G. P. Putnam's Sons, 1968.

Hansel, C. *ESP: A Scientific Evaluation.* New York: Charles Scribner's Sons, 1976.

Hines, Terence. *Pseudoscience and the Paranormal.* New York: Prometheus Books, 1992.

Landau, Elaine. *Ghosts.* Brookfield, Conn.: Millbrook Press, 1995.

Pratt, Joseph. *Parapsychology: An Insider's View of ESP.* New York: E. P. Dutton, 1976.

Randles, Jenny, and Peter Hough. *Encyclopedia of the Unexplained.* London: Michael O'Mara, 1995.

Siegel, Ronald. *Fire in the Brain: Clinical Tales of Hallucination.* New York: Plume Books, 1993.

Warren, Ed, and Lorraine Warren. *Ghost Hunters.* New York: St. Martin's Press, 1989.

White, Michael. *Weird Science.* New York: Avon Books, 1999.

Wilson, Colin. *Ghosts and the Supernatural.* New York: DK Publishing, 1995.

# Crackle, Snap, Pop
## Lightning—Deadly Danger or Remarkable Resource?

## At a Glance

Lightning strikes the earth at an amazing rate of more than a hundred times per second—every hour, every day. Most lightning bolts never reach the ground but flash between clouds (intercloud lightning) or zigzag between charged parts of the same cloud (intracloud lightning). Literally thousands of lightning bolts have crashed around the world in the time it took you to read this paragraph.

The average lightning bolt is less than 1 inch in diameter but is so bright it can be seen for miles. The bolt heats the air it streaks through to five times hotter than the surface of the Sun. These jagged, crackling ribbons of light are one of nature's most beautiful—and most deadly—spectacles. Almost 400 people are struck by lightning in the United States each year. On average, 150 of those will die. Lightning kills more people than tornadoes, floods and hurricanes combined. Most strikes happen to those caught in open fields—farmers and sports players.

Lightning causes two hundred million dollars in property damage each year in this country alone. It wreaks havoc on electrical power lines and systems, and destroys billions of dollars worth of trees consumed in forest fires. A single thunderhead can generate more instantaneous power than a nuclear power plant.

Humans have always feared, and been fascinated by, these thundering blasts from the heavens. Early Greeks were so in awe of lightning, they believed that Zeus, the king and most powerful of the gods, was the one who hurled lightning at the earth when he was angry. Similarly, the head Norse god, Oden, was the one who wielded lightning.

In medieval times, church bells were rung to drive lightning away from towns. Often the bell tower (the highest structure in town) was hit by a bolt. So people began to believe that lightning was the work of the devil. Up to the mid-1700s, even scientists thought lightning was a form of fire that rained down from the sky. Benjamin Franklin corrected that misunderstanding with his famous kite experiment in 1752. But in so doing, he opened the door to several other lightning mysteries that have not been completely answered even to this day: Why and how does lightning form in a cloud? How can it be controlled and harnessed? Public fear of lightning made lightning rods a popular addition to every fashionable house by the early 1800s, creating a very big and profitable industry in this country.

More than practical curiosity, though, we humans have always regarded this life-controlling force with awe. Lightning can and does kill. But it is also the creator of life. Mary Shelley, in her famous 1820s book, had Dr. Franken-stein use lightning bolts to bring his monster to life. In his famed 1956 experiment, Dr. Barry Commoner at Washington University in St. Louis, Missouri, used mini–lightning bolts to fuse inorganic chemicals into amino acids, the building blocks of life. He was the first scientist to actually use lightning to create life. Patients whose hearts have stopped are jolted back to life with electric pulses, like mini–lightning bolts.

Lightning can both destroy and create. It also defies our attempts to understand its structure and nature. In a vast sense, the power, control and potential of lightning are still a wondrous mystery.

# The Mystery: Crackle, Snap, Pop

The brilliant dabs of fall colors stood out like neon splotches across the mountain valley. The reds and glowing yellows seemed even more spectacular when set off against the surrounding gray granite cliffs. Birds sang. Tourists hiked and snapped pictures. Park Ranger Roy Sullivan was just beginning his afternoon guided tour of the meadow floor of Yosemite Valley, California, this third day of October 1992.

Roy loved fall in the valley and couldn't understand why so many tourists jammed into the park during the blazing hot summer, filled with afternoon thunder and lightning storms. He wondered why they didn't wait for fall, when a brisk and bracing breeze invigorated the soul. The Sun still felt gloriously warm, beating down past the towering cliffs that lined the valley.

Fall was the perfect time to visit Yosemite. Crowds were down. Parking was easy. There was space to walk in peace with nature. The tours he led, Roy believed, were also better in the fall. With smaller groups, he could ad-lib more, add in little extras, answer more questions and joke with the tourists.

This afternoon's valley walking tour had only twelve people: two young Japanese couples obviously on their honeymoons, four unattached adults who all looked like teachers to Roy (two even carried note-books) and one family, the Murrys, all the way from New Jersey. The Murry girl was seven and loved to skip and wander in her own imaginary world. The boy, who had three times introduced himself as Robert Myron, was twelve. Roy had already pegged him as an obnoxious know-it-all who could spoil an entire tour.

The magnificence of Yosemite was all about them. El Capitan's sheer face rose 3,500 feet straight up to their immediate north. Bridal Vale Falls to the south was barely flowing, now only a trickle down the cliff. Even Yosemite Falls, usually a thundering giant, was reduced to a quiet murmur by several years of drought.

After giving his group an appropriate moment to soak in the surrounding grandeur, Roy smiled and began to guide their focus back to the delicate flora of the meadow. Robert Myron had already proved himself to be a first-class pain, demanding in a loud voice to know the nine kinds of deciduous trees found in the valley. When Roy stumbled in his answer, Robert Myron scoffed, "Even *I* know that one. I read it at the ranger station." And he proceeded to complete the list without missing one. His parents smiled proudly and appreciatively.

Roy sighed. He was fifty-nine and could take early retirement in another three years. Too many more Robert Myrons and he would seriously consider it.

Then Roy tensed, hearing the rumble of distant thunder, feeling its soft vibration through his body. October thunderstorms were rare in the mountains. In October, Roy was just beginning to relax after surviving the summer lightning season.

Robert Myron continued to babble, demanding to know the frequency of lightning strikes in the valley. Roy sucked in a deep breath to calm himself, smiled as reassuringly as he could and began the canned talk about lightning safety in the park. "Lightning strikes start dozens of beneficial, natural fires in the mountains each summer. Lightning's greatest danger to hikers comes from the fires, not from lightning itself. There are relatively few lightning strikes here in the valley—even in the peak month of June—because lightning tends to strike the highest, most convenient point along its path. Climbers on El Capitan's cliff face, and hikers on the rim, are in far greater danger than we are here in the valley meadow."

Another gentle rumble drifted into the valley like the reverberation of a distant bowling ball. Roy nervously glanced at the crystal-blue sky above. He knew that thunderheads could be deceptively close and not be visible from the sheltered valley floor. Jabbing dread crept down his spine. It had been three years since he was last struck by lightning. He was the only ranger on staff to have been hit, and the only ranger in the whole park system to have survived four strikes. He had no desire to tempt his fate on a fifth.

Just half a mile away, the Yosemite High School football team was beginning afternoon practice in Curry Village, the housing area for staff and employees. The team counted cadence during calisthenics warm-ups. It sounded to Roy like they were softly counting the duration of each ominous rumble of thunder. Football players had helmets and shoulder pads to protect them. It made Roy feel all the more exposed out here in the wide-open meadow.

Again Roy Sullivan paused, feeling tiny prickles on his skin, sensing his short hair rising under his stiff, wide-brimmed ranger hat. He gazed up, frowning at the sky. There were no clouds overhead, but he could see the tops of dark, rolling clouds over the north rim.

He shook off the fearful feeling, realizing that everyone in his tour stared expectantly at him, waiting for him to say something and continue their walk. "I wouldn't want to be up on the top of El Capitan right now," Roy said. "It's an ominous place even on a clear day. But with those clouds ..."

He forced a smile. "Well ... Let's continue into the meadow to look at how marsh grass stabilizes the soil and begins the process of forestation."

He told himself it was just the jitters from being struck so often. Only twice had lightning done any real damage to him. Once it had landed him in the hospital with memory loss and severe burns. He still carried the scars down one arm. One leg had dragged for a month, as if the controlling nerves had been fried after another bolt had arced between the top of a nearby redwood and his head. His fingernails had all turned black and fallen off that time.

Otherwise, he had suffered no physical ill effects from his encounters with lightning. But the memory of those four moments of terror—as electric current sizzled through his body, violently shook every fiber of his being and blasted him into the air—the haunting memory never left him, not even for a day. A grinding nervous dread ate into the pit of his stomach, even at the ordinary sound of distant thunder in the mountains, even when it was many miles away.

One of the teacher types asked, "Has anyone been hit by lightning in the valley?"

Roy wanted to answer, "Me. Up by Mirror Lake." But park rangers are supposed to instill a sense of comfort and safety in tour members, not terrify them. "It's rare in the valley," he said instead. "Most strikes are on the rim high above."

That's where Roy had been hit twice by sizzling bolts, both times on rescue missions to save foolhardy hikers who had gotten themselves into trouble—so easy to do in the mountains. He wanted to add, "Of course, we don't understand lightning all that well. It so rarely does what it's supposed to do." But he held his tongue and started along the path toward the now creek-sized Merced River, which meandered through the valley.

Robert Myron broke into a whiny-sounding litany of facts about lightning bolts—their average temperature, the amount of light they produced (which he correctly called luminosity), their average length, that they strike the earth a hundred times every second. His parents glowed with pride at the brilliance of their son.

To shut the kid up, Roy began to talk about the ecology of a mountain meadow and how this one had changed over the past hundred years. But he sensed a thickness to the air, as if it were compressing itself for a mighty explosion. He detected a musty, burnt tinge to the crisp mountain atmosphere. He felt that his skin was beginning to crawl. His arm hairs lifted themselves up toward the sky.

In a sickening flash, Roy Sullivan recognized these sensations. They were not new to him. "Duck! Lightning!" he screamed.

As he crouched into a ball, trembling on the ground, Roy saw that everyone in his group stood, dumbfounded, staring at him. Several glanced at the clear sky and laughed as if it were a joke. Robert Myron whined, "But there's no clouds."

Roy was torn between an urgent calling for self-preservation and his duty as the ranger responsible for this tour group. Should he duck into a ball (the safest position in the open to minimize both height above the ground and direct contact with the ground) and protect himself, or stand back up and make these ignorant tourists see the danger they were in?

Stay safe or be a hero? His whole body felt electrically super-charged, as if an electric spotlight were shining on him, as if some curse made the gathering charge seek him out.

Muttering, Roy rose to a crouch. "We're in danger of lightning. Crouch down. Now!"

Most of his group still dumbly stared as if his warning made no sense. Roy took a step toward one of the honeymooners …

And … WHAM! Lightning bolt number five slammed into Ranger Roy Sullivan.

A curving ribbon of blinding heat and light arced out of the distant clouds, ignored the rocks and trees of the mountaintops, and descended an extra 4,000 feet to reach the valley floor. There it ig-nored hundred-foot-high trees and chose, instead, to link with the ground through Roy.

Roy was flung 15 feet off the trail as easily as if he were a piece of annoying trash. His ranger hat shot into the air in smoke and flame. His eyebrows were burned off and his fingernails turned black. Feath-ery burns covered his exposed skin. The buttons had been blown off his shirt and his boot soles still curled smoke into the air.

The deafening roar and blinding brilliance of the bolt struck each tour member simultaneously. The shock wave knocked the breath from them. The searing heat singed the hairs on their hands and faces. They smelled the strong odor of burnt ozone left in the fiery wake of the bolt.

The group crumbled into panic. The honeymoon couples screamed and pointed. The teachers argued amongst themselves: "Run for the trees and cover." "No. Stay in the open away from the trees." "No. Run for the cars." "No. Lie on the ground." "No. Crouch in a ball like the ranger said."

Mrs. Murry rushed to help the stricken ranger.

Robert Myron's eyes bulged big as golf balls. He seemed almost unable to breathe as the words tumbled out of his mouth. "Whoa! That sucker just—whamo!—blasted right into him. You could *see* it flowing down his body. He went flyin' through the air. I mean, it *really* hit him!"

Roy's legs were not working correctly as, dazed and disoriented, he tried to sit up. Mrs. Murry bent over him, testing to see if his heart, eyes and ears still worked.

WHAM! A second bolt split a nearby tree and blasted loud as a dynamite explosion. Boiling black clouds spilled, mean and angry, over from the top of El Capitan as if conjured out of an evil witch's brew. Swirling winds howled through the valley.

The Murry girl began to sob and scream. The honeymooners scattered. Mr. Murry snatched up his daughter and sprinted for their car a quarter mile away. Mrs. Murry and two of the teachers propped up struggling Roy Sullivan to help him limp toward the ranger station for medical attention.

They were stopped at the road by one of the rarest, least-understood and most bizarre of all kinds of lightning—ball lightning. A basketball-sized sphere of intensely bright lightning hovered like a glowing yellow-green minisun at the top of a power pole. The vibrating ball floated for a long ten seconds near the pole before zigzagging across the ground toward Curry Village whining like a New Year's Eve toy.

"Would you look at that …," muttered one awestruck teacher. "What *was* it?" asked another.

On the practice field, the entire Yosemite High football team had stopped in midscrimmage to watch the whining green ball dart onto the field and fizzle out in a final "poof!" near the 50-yard line.

WHAM!

A crisp, thin ribbon of lightning knifed out of the sky and tore through junior running back Tory Tice's helmet as he stood in the huddle waiting for his quarterback to call a play. It bubbled his plastic shoulder pads, burned a black streak down his jersey and blasted his cleats right off his feet. Tory felt himself arch back like a circus contortionist and fly through the air. As if he were inside a waterfall of purest-white electricity, he felt the surge, like countless tiny feet, fluttering over the surface of his sweaty body.

Tory landed in a crumpled heap like thrown-out rags as heavy drops of rain began to splat into the valley floor. The jolt of electricity stopped his heart until one of the coaches used CPR to start it again.

One side of Tory's helmet had melted into long drips of gooey plastic. The hair on that side of Tory's head had been burned off down to blistered skin.

One of the mothers, who had been watching practice, dashed into the school office to call for an ambulance. She had just finished dialing when—WHAM!—a lightning bolt found a utility pole a mile down the valley. The giant surge of electrical power raced through the phone line in a millisecond and exploded in a shower of sparks through the handset she held. She was shot back through the office double doors and slammed against the hall wall. Her chestnut hair had been turned instantly white. The telephone's plastic receiver— still in her hand—had melted into a sticky burning blob.

Outside, the sky cleared as quickly as it had darkened. Clouds retreated back over the rim of the valley. Birds sang and tourists continued their hikes, snapping countless pictures, marveling at the glorious fall colors and tranquil loveliness of the valley. Parking was easy, and it was another glorious day in this mountain paradise on Earth. No one even minded the intruding wail of the ambulance sirens as paramedics rushed to scoop up the scattered victims of these unpredictable lightning strikes.

## About This Story

The major characters and events of this story are real and well documented. However, the separate experiences of Park Ranger Roy Sullivan, football player Tory Tice and the woman (whose real name is unknown) have been combined to present the effects of more than one lightning strike in a single story. Most of the minor characters in Roy Sullivan's tour, and the specific dialog, have been created for dramatic effect. The portrayal of the lightning and its effects, however, is entirely real.

# The Science

Science over the years has wrestled with four big mysteries concerning lightning: What is it? Why does it form? How does it work? and Can it be controlled?

Benjamin Franklin answered the first of those four questions in 1752, when his kite experiment proved that the electric charges in clouds were the same as playful static electricity. It was just that clouds held a much bigger charge of electricity. But little more was discovered about the nature of lightning until the middle of the twentieth century, when improved technology and equipment allowed scientists to measure the changing electric field in the ground under a cloud. Helium balloons allowed scientists to float sensitive instruments into thunderheads to measure their winds and electric field.

Slowly a picture emerged of what happens inside a cloud to create electricity. Violent vertical winds (updrafts and downdrafts) jerk water droplets and ice crystals past each other inside a thunderhead. Just as happens when shoes are rubbed across a carpet, the collisions of these particles strip electrons away from rising ice crystals (which take on a positive charge) and attach the electrons to downward-flowing water droplets (which take on a negative charge). A negative charge builds up at the bottom of the cloud. Positively charged ice crystals congregate at the top of the cloud.

When the negative charge at the bottom of a thunderhead becomes strong enough, it literally pushes electrons in the ground away from the area below the cloud (like electric charges repel each other). The ground is left with a positive charge. Eventually a surge of electrons rushes to the ground to neutralize these two charged areas. We call this surge a lightning bolt.

Lightning bolts are simple electric circuits. They are flows of electrons trying to reach the positively charged ground. This electron flow will always flow along the path of least resistance. Air, however, is an insulator, a poor conductor of electricity. So, as bolts near the ground, they often strike buildings, pools of water and especially metal poles and power lines. Metal is an excellent conductor, so it is easy for the electrons to travel along metal wires and surfaces to reach the ground.

But scientists wondered why lightning bolts don't rush *straight* to the ground. Something else must be going on. High-speed photography and improved lab equipment allowed scientist to create and study simulated lightning in the lab. Now the picture became more complete. Invisible streams of electrons (called leaders) tentatively feel their way through the air toward the ground, following whatever convoluted path offers the least momentary resistance. When a long line of stepped leaders approaches the ground, a surge of current rises up from a spot of low resistance in the ground to meet it. A completed electrical pathway is created, and electric current surges from ground to cloud (called a return flow). That return, the lightning bolt, is what we see.

In recent years more sophisticated instruments have discovered that the electric fields in clouds are more complex than were first thought. Thunderhead clouds form sandwichlike layers of positive and negative charges. No one yet knows exactly why.

Medical sciences have carefully documented the injuries caused by lightning—primarily burns, hair loss, hearing loss, memory loss, nerve damage and finger- and toenail loss. What is not well known is why roughly a third of the people struck are killed, why just over half are injured and why almost an eighth are left completely unhurt. Surely every lightning bolt has enough current and voltage to kill. Yet most do not, and only educated guesses have been offered to explain why. More extensive research is needed to explain how lightning bolts interact with the human body.

Scientists have recently fired rockets with wires trailing behind them into clouds—much like Franklin launching his kite on a string into a cloud—and have discovered how much of an electric charge is needed at the bottom surface of a cloud to trigger a lightning bolt. They have also identified many more types of lightning than were previously thought to exist. Not just ribbon, sheet, heat, volcanic and ball lightning, but also the weaker and lesser-known Saint Elmo's fire, jets, sprites and elves (all forms of atmospheric electrical discharge).

Many of these forms of lightning are not well understood. Sprites, jets and elves are faint lightning discharges between the tops of clouds and the upper atmosphere and were not even identified until the early 1990s. Ball lightning fascinates researchers, but occurs so rarely that they have never been able to observe it closely enough and study it well enough to even know how it forms. They do know that ball lightning almost always forms near the top of a power or light pole, hovers for a few seconds and then zips across the land as it dissipates and fizzles out.

Now the rush is on to learn how to control lightning and prevent it from destroying property and life. The Canadian Electrical Authority, at their massive hydroelectric complex in Quebec, conducts continuous laboratory research. Universities in a dozen states conduct annual field programs using state-of-the-art equipment and research techniques. The National Lightning Detection Network records, monitors and studies every lightning strike in the country. And a hundred-acre lightning field built just outside Santa Fe, New Mexico, in the late 1980s—with metal poles every meter, a veritable forest of lightning rods—is being used to try to harness and understand this mighty force of nature.

# Fact or Fiction?

Science has learned what lightning is. Scientists have reached good agreement on how charged regions of a cloud are formed. Those charged regions are the energy source for lightning bolts. Science now understands how a lightning bolt acts. Through modern weather balloons and detection equipment, science is beginning to piece together a fair understanding of how electric fields act inside a thunderhead cloud. But there are important unanswered questions remaining: Can lightning be predicted, anticipated, controlled and harnessed for use as a power resource? Can humans be protected from its deadly effects? Those are remaining mysteries for the twenty-first century.

A second, minor mystery is the study and understanding of the rare and mysterious ball lightning. It occurs so rarely that few scientists have ever had a chance to observe it, much less conduct experiments to study it. Why does it form? What is a ball of lightning? What holds it together? These are lightning mysteries still to be unraveled.

## Follow-On Questions to Explore

1. Have you ever been close to a lightning strike? Do you know anyone who has been? What did the lightning bolt sound like, feel like, smell like, taste like and look like up close? What did you or that person think and feel when the lightning struck?

2. Why does some thunder seem to rumble for a long time, while a lightning bolt striking very close seems to produce only one sharp, loud clap? (Hint: A bolt of lightning produces sound claps all along its length. Are some parts of the lightning bolt closer to you than others? Will some of the sound from some parts of the lightning bolt reach you sooner than sound from other parts?) Do lightning bolts that travel horizontally between clouds usually produce a longer-lasting rumble of thunder than do bolts that travel vertically between cloud and ground? Why?

## Follow-On Activities

1. What is the truth about lightning safety? Develop a class Fact Sheet about lightning as an instructional brochure for elementary-aged children. Describe the different kinds of lightning and how electric charges form in a cloud. Include the amazing facts about lightning bolts (their temperature,

size, length, frequency, power, etc.) and describe when, where and how lightning is likely to strike. Finally, include safety tips for protecting one-self from lightning.

2. Make mini–lightning bolts. Sparks of static electricity are mini–lightning bolts. Create a bigger charge of static electricity and you will get a bigger mini–lightning bolt. In a dark room, pull a wool blanket slowly over your head from behind while holding one fist out in front of you. Pull the blanket forward so that it covers (is above but doesn't touch) your fist. Watch for purplish sparks (lightning) to jump from fist to blanket. Those are really tiny lightning bolts.

3. Make a list of all the forms and types of lightning. Research each and make a chart that compares their characteristics, frequency of occurrence, properties and so forth.

# References

Garmon, Linda. *Lightning!* Boston: WGBH and NOVA, 1995. Videocassette.
Harper, Suzanne. *Lightning.* New York: Franklin Watts, 1997.
Hopping, Lorraine. *Lightning!* New York: Scholastic, 1999.
Simon, Seymour. *Lightning.* New York: Morrow Junior Books, 1997.
———. *Storms.* New York: William Morrow, 1989.
Wagner, Ronald, and Bill Adler Jr. *The Weather Sourcebook.* Old Saybrook, Conn.: Adler & Robin Books, 1994.

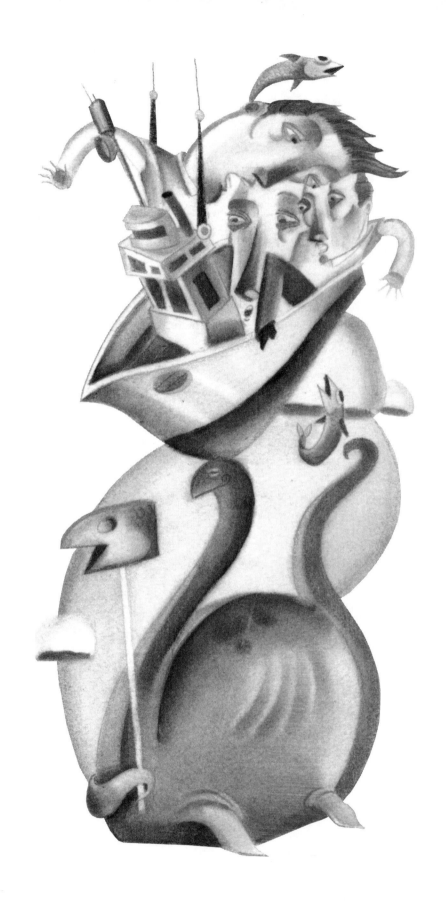

# Loch Ness Nessie
## Mammoth Monster
## or Mindless Myth?

### At a Glance

Steep hills tumble down through thick groves of trees and brilliant green meadows to the lake. Bright blotches of wildflowers and a crumbling fourteenth-century castle along the shore of Urquhart Bay make for a picture-perfect setting. Still, there is something eerie about Loch Ness, Scotland. Every visitor feels it like a chilling wind that nips through every protective layer to shiver your bones.

Loch Ness is not the only lake to claim a mysterious, sea serpent–like monster, but it is by far the most famous. "Champie" in Lake Champlain, New York, is the best-known American sea monster, but no monster can hold a candle to the intrigue of "Nessie" of Loch Ness.

Nessie was first officially sighted by Roman soldiers during their occupation of Britain around A.D. 200. However, local legend and story include mention of the so-called Monster of the Lake thousands of years before that time. St. Colomba's biography mentions an A.D. 565 encounter between the saint and a lake monster that roared and threatened to eat one of Colomba's men. In 1715 the men who built the first, crude road along the lake's south side mentioned seeing creatures "big as whales" swimming in the lake. In the 1800s, sailors and workmen building the canal system that connected Loch Ness to the Atlantic Ocean (on its south side) and to the North Sea (on its north side) also reported seeing huge monsters surfacing in the lake.

In 1933 a paved road was blasted into the steep hills skirting Loch Ness's northwest shore. Finally it was convenient for people to travel right next to the lake. Nessie was spotted more than eighty times that year. By 1990 more than four thousand sightings of the Loch Ness monster had been reported. However, not one of those who had seen the monster had touched it, had had any direct contact with it or had even taken a decent photograph of the creature. No one trapped it, caught it, shot it or even tagged it. No bones or skeletons have ever been found.

How could that be possible when four thousand people reported seeing the monster? If the monster were real, wouldn't at least one of all those people have been able to document their encounter convincingly? Hundreds of trained researchers with state-of-the-art equipment have spent years searching for the monster. None have ever been able to prove that it exists.

So, is the Loch Ness monster a hoax or a real biological being? In a lake like Loch Ness, the question has proved harder to answer than one might think. Loch Ness stretches 24 miles long and more than 1 mile wide, and reaches a maximum depth of more than 900 feet. Its average depth is more than 480 feet. Worse, the water has been turned a permanent yellow-brown by the thick tufts, scraps and flakes of peat that have washed down from the surrounding mountains. Even near the surface on a clear day, visibility is less than 40 feet. There's plenty of room in the deep, dark waters for a giant beast to glide like an unseen wraith past any detection effort.

# The Mystery:
# Loch Ness Nessie

Ping … Ping … Ping. The shipboard echo sounder seemed to tick off the minutes as it broadcast the audible pings that bounced back to let it trace the bottom contours of the Grand Canyon–like lake hiding beneath the blue-yellow water.

Wearing a faded red baseball cap over his short-cropped, snow-white hair, seventy-four-year-old Bob Rines, the lead investigator, called to his crew from the stern of the 35-foot boat. "Everything working? Have we got signals from all three sonars?"

Well-respected marine biologist Arnie Carr hunched over the stylus-pen printout from the sophisticated but temperamental sidescan sonar unit that traced every rock and bump along the lake bottom and marked every fish larger than a trout. Arnie's twenty-two-year-old graduate assistant, Judith Hinkly, monitored both the echolocation sonar and the fish sonar (which appeared as a series of green flashes that raced across an oscilloscope-like screen). She doubled as ship's pilot. Judith nodded to Arnie as her eyes scanned both of her instruments.

"A-OK," called Arnie. "We're ready to hunt."

Bob Rines glanced over the stern where the tow cables for their sidescan sonar disappeared into the murky water. The torpedo-like sidescan unit rested at the other end of the cables, 100 feet below and behind the boat. "Take her ahead slow—just above idle," he called. "Faster than that, we might miss something."

"Roger," Judith replied and eased the twin throttles one notch forward. The engines rumbled softly and the boat bobbed through the light chop on Loch Ness, barely leaving a wake to mark its path.

The redundant sets of sonar gear were designed to record proof that something large lived in Loch Ness. A second boat followed behind, dragging a metal array of lights with still and video cameras to capture positive photographic proof of whatever the sonar array found.

Tension was high in the crews on both boats. This was their last day with the sonar units. In the past three days of searching they had marked some tantalizingly promising targets, but had produced nothing on either sonar or video that proved the Loch Ness monster was real. If it was going to happen, it had to happen today.

Wind was beginning to stir as the boats puttered toward the northern third of Loch Ness and Urquhart Bay. The crews could hear the soft rumble of distant thunder, and see clouds building on the southwest horizon. A storm was brewing. In three or four hours they would have to turn back. Hopes dimmed. Time seemed to press against them. Everyone fidgeted nervously as they addressed their tasks.

Ping … Ping … Ping. The echo sounder ticked off the miles and the minutes as the boat eased past the crumbling ruins of a four-teenth-century castle that sat on the point of land marking the entrance to Urquhart Bay.

"Any contacts?" called Rines, still seated on a cushion in the stern.

"A few fish and a lot of rocks. A few tree stumps. That's it so far," came the reply from the cabin.

The four people seated in folding deck chairs in the stern made an odd-looking crew for a scientific research venture. All were older than seventy. Bob Rines, at seventy-four, was the youngest. Photographic inventor and MIT research scientist Charles Wycoff had just turned seventy-six. These two scientists had been searching for Nessie off and on for almost thirty years. They were credited with more than a dozen of the sonar contacts with "unidentified, moving objects over 10 meters long" in the lake. They had taken most of the underwater photographs of Nessie—all vague and blurry due to the dense underwater fog of floating peat. This trip they wanted proof the world could not dismiss. They were growing too old to organize another trip, not to mention the search for funding.

The other two people were older than eighty. They were locals who had seen Nessie on a number of occasions. Both appeared nervous and anxious to be on the lake they knew to contain a giant monster. Bob Rines had brought these two along because of their experiences with Nessie. Both agreed that Urquhart Bay was the best place to search. Both had met the monster in this section of the lake.

Ian Cameron, retired chief of detectives for the town of Inverness, Scotland, squinted his bushy eyebrows as he stared toward the castle ruins. Though almost completely bald, he still sprouted bushy, white sideburns. In his thick Scottish brogue, he muttered, "I hain't been on a boat in this lake fer near on twenty year. Not since the day I met Nessie face to face."

Ian paused briefly for effect, and then continued with his story. "It were a mild summer morn'. I was fishin' in a 12-foot wooden boat, motor off, drifting with the current and the breeze just there, out in the middle of Urquhart Bay. Suddenly the water began to boil. Thousands of tiny fish were jumping madly about, trying to escape.

"I almost dropped me pole, I was so fascinated, starin' at these wee critters so frantically trying to leap into the air." His voice lowered and a shudder rumbled through his body. "Then I saw why they were runnin'. A gray, snakelike head, more than 3 feet across, crept slowly out of the water. Beneath it, a thin, gray neck like an elephant's trunk rose more than 5 feet up. The head waved there a moment, starin' at me from cold, black eyes. Seemed for a full minute it just stared without blinking once. I could see two shiny humps in the water out behind the head, and two flipperlike legs treading water just under the surface.

"I could see its teeth and almost smell its breath. In a flash I knew I was about to die. I had seen Nessie afore. But always from the shore, always just a hump or two far out onto the lake. Now I was almost close enough to touch it. I had not been so terrified in all my years. I was too scared to breathe.

"Then with a storm of waves and a loud crash, the monster disappeared under the water. I was left alone, blinkin' in the sunlight, boat rocking over the monster's wake, fishin' pole still clutched in my fingers. I started the motor, sped straight for shore, and I hain't set foot back on this lake since that day."

Ian nodded once to indicate that his story was finished.

"And it happened right about here?" Rines asked.

Ian stretched in his chair to peer left and right at the available land markings. "Fifty yards to port, maybe. That'd be the spot."

"Swing 50 yards to port and go to idle!" Rines called to the cabin.

"Roger, 50 yards to port," Judith Hinkly replied as she swung the boat around.

The other local aboard, eighty-five-year-old Margaret Campbell, cackled her soft laugh in agreement with Ian's story.

"I seen him over by shore, next to that wee cove where the road dips near to lake level." She pointed at a thick clump of trees straight across the bay from the castle. "'Course there weren't a road back then. I was barely twelve. Me and Jenny McCullough were waitin' for friends, passin' time by skippin' stones into the lake. We heard an awful cracklin' in the trees at the head of the cove.

"More than frightened, we were intrigued. Our grandparents had told us there were wild horses in the loch, and we figured this must be them and we wanted a look see.

"The sound came nearer and seemed to grow bigger. Then this big … thing … waddled out of the trees and started across the rocky beach."

"He was on *land*?" Wycoff asked. "Not in the water?"

"We were less than 30 feet away when he broke through the trees and started toward us!" she answered. "His great, rounded body rocked side to side as he waddled on short flipperlike feet. I remember his head was too small for the body, but I don't remember how long his neck was.

"His great body just kept pouring out of the trees—20 feet long, 30 feet. More than 40 feet long he was if he was an inch! And his color was the dull gray of an elephant. As soon as he hit the water, he swam faster than dolphins out in the ocean."

She cackled her laugh and slowly shook her head before she continued. "When we girls burst into the house and spilled out our story, I remember my grandfather turnin' beet red and pounding his fist on the table. He shook his finger hard at us. 'Don't you *ever* tell anyone about this, ever!' And his face said that he meant it. So for fifty years, I didn't."

"I'm getting something on sidescan!" Arnie Carr called from the cabin.

Bob Rines bounded with surprising agility toward the cabin. The others followed, packing into the cramped cabin of Rines's boat.

"I see something on the fish sonar," Judith reported.

"Measures over 15 meters. Depth about 295 feet." Excitement rose in Arnie's voice as he spoke.

"I've even got it on the echo sounder," said Judith, shading her eyes as she stared at the tiny green blips on the sounder's screen.

"Fifteen meters? That's almost 50 feet!" repeated Rines. "It's the biggest contact I've ever made in this lake."

"Where is it?" Wycoff demanded.

"About 130 feet off the starboard bow."

Without glancing back from her instruments, Judith said, "That agrees with my reading."

"It's moving," Arnie called. "I have movement. It's not a tree. This is a 50-foot biological."

Electric tension filled the cabin. A 50-foot … something … swam less than 300 feet below them. Rines grabbed the radio mike to alert the boat carrying the cameras. "We have a target. A big one. Get up here now!"

A voice crackled over the radio speaker. "On the way."

Wycoff snatched a pair of binoculars off their hook next to the captain's console and focused first on the photo boat just swinging around the castle point, and then on the empty spot in the water directly above their giant contact.

Rines's voice sounded urgent as he called radio directions to the photo boat. "More speed, Dave. Forty meters off our starboard bow. Contact is moving …" Rines paused and turned his head away from the radio. "What direction is it moving?"

"Almost due east. Toward the center of the lake."

Rines nodded and turned back to the radio. "Dave. Swing wide to our starboard side. Sink the camera down to …" Again he leaned back. "What's the depth?"

"Still drifting just above 295 feet."

Again Rines nodded. "Drop the camera to 295 feet and start shooting."

A voice hissed and crackled over the tiny speaker. "Roger. Swinging 130 feet to your starboard. But 295 feet is pretty deep for these cameras. The housings are only guaranteed to 350 feet—"

"Just do it!" Rines interrupted. "And fast."

The pings of the echo sounder seemed to come hours apart to the anxious crew. The photo boat seemed to inch forward at a snail's pace. Arnie Carr continued to call off the position and depth of the hulking contact. "Moving away from us toward the deep part of the lake. Bearing 85 degrees. Depth now 312 feet."

"Faster!" Rines pleaded into the radio.

"Can't," came back the answer. "Not safe to accelerate with the photo housing tethered out on that much line."

Rines screamed back, "If you're not on-site in sixty seconds there won't be anything to photograph! Just get there!"

The bow wake of the photo boat began to churn as the captain jammed his throttles forward.

Ping … Ping … Ping.

"Depth 328 feet. Bearing 88 degrees. Horizontal distance almost 260 feet."

"Hurry!" bellowed Rines. "He's getting away!" To accent his urgency, a strong thunderclap rumbled across the lake. The storm was moving in fast. This would be their last chance for a positive contact.

"We're shooting. Stills and video," came the reply from the photo boat. "Video coming in now. Murky water. No sign of the target."

"Is the camera on-station and pointing correctly?" Rines asked into the mike.

"Orientation reads as correct. Cameras may be a bit high because we came in so fast. But they're where you told me to put 'em."

"What do you see?" demanded Rines.

"Water. Floating chunks of peat. Wait! Everything is swirling down there. Something just streaked by."

"Did you get it?"

"Uhhh, maybe," came the answer from the photo boat. "It happened so fast …"

"I've lost it," Arnie Carr announced with a sigh. "It accelerated and dove into a deep canyon."

All in the cramped cabin let out a slow sigh. In the excitement, they hadn't noticed that they were holding their breath.

"Uhhh, sorry boss," began the report from the photo boat. "We didn't get much. Video shows something like a big shadow that flicked by. I'm afraid still camera won't show much more."

Rines sank into a chair as the first raindrops began to fall. Deep weariness and frustration were etched into his voice. "Thank you, everyone. We better head back to port."

And so another mission would be officially logged as "Positive, but unidentified, sonar contact. Negative to indefinite photo contact. No visual sightings."

Loch Ness still refused to give up its secrets.

## About This Story

This story is real. The characters, equipment, expedition stories, descriptions and results are an accurate depiction of Bob Rines's final search of Loch Ness. Specific dialog has been created based on known events, outcomes and the general personalities of the characters aboard Bob Rines's boat.

# The Science

Is there really a giant monster in Loch Ness or not? Most scientists won't even seriously consider the question or the evidence before blurting out, "No!" Jacques Cousteau, famed underwater explorer, called Nessie "pure bull" and refused to take his crew and equipment to the lake even when the voyage would have been fully paid for. Many scientists are unwilling to even visit the lake for fear they will lose all credibility with their peers.

There have simply been too many hoaxes and mistaken sightings for most scientists to take the Loch Ness monster seriously. Several of the supposed photos of the monster have proven to be fakes. Most of the sightings have turned out to be the wake of a boat caught in front of the Sun, an orientation that causes the boat to cast a black shadow that looks like an animal's hump. Many sightings are of nothing more than an old tree trunk that has popped to the surface, or a large and tangled clump of peat that has risen as gasses collected in it on the lake bottom.

The hoaxes and faulty sightings are one of the four arguments against the existence of Nessie. The strongest argument is that no one has ever produced any proof of Nessie's existence. In the most studied, researched, observed and photographed lake in the world, no one has ever produced one scrap of positive proof. That is enough to make anyone skeptical—except for the four thousand who have seen the monster and the several hundred who have seen tantalizing hints of it while conducting scientific research.

The third argument against the existence of Nessie is that Loch Ness simply cannot support the monster. The water of Loch Ness is murky. Light doesn't penetrate very deeply into the water column. The water is near freezing and contains few of the nutrients aquatic plant life requires. As a result, there are virtually no bottom plants in the lake, and the population of plankton is scanty. Loch Ness more closely resembles a semiarid desert than a lush forest. There just aren't enough plants to support very many fish. And, therefore, not enough fish to support Nessie.

This is especially true because there can't be just one of whatever Nessie is. There must be enough of this type of creature to form a stable breeding population that could have survived for the fifteen thousand years that they would have been trapped in the lake since the last ice age. That would mean that there could be a dozen or more hungry monsters at any given time trying to live off of the meager stock of lake fish. It just couldn't happen. There aren't enough fish.

Finally, no skeleton—nor even a single bone—of one of the previous generations of monsters has ever been found. If a population of those creatures had been trapped in Loch Ness for fifteen thousand years, there would have been hundreds of generations of monsters, with a substantial number of individuals in each generation. How could so many monsters have lived and not left a single physical trace? Most scientists believe that they couldn't.

But there is also evidence to support the existence of the Loch Ness monster. Many of the four thousand reported sightings, of course, turn out to be honest mistakes—humplike shadows and thrashing tree trunks that can often look like a swimming or surfacing creature. Easily 95 percent of all sightings have been dismissed as such simple mistakes. But that leaves about two hundred other sightings. Some of these have been proven to be hoaxes. Some could be large eels, giant groupers (fish) or small whales. But a substantial number of these sightings, like the stories of Ian Cameron and Margaret Campbell, are so specific and detailed that they cannot be dismissed. Further, the creatures described in these sightings do not resemble any known living or extinct species.

There have also been photographs of the monster, thirty-eight taken above water and twelve taken underwater. Four of the surface photos have been proven to be intentional fakes. Two others, including the most famous picture of Nessie, taken in 1934 by London surgeon R. Kenneth Wilson, have been alleged to be fakes. All the photos show *something*. None, however, are clear enough, or were taken close enough, to allow for positive identification of what was photographed.

There have also been sonar contacts. Twenty-three search parties, dating from 1954 to 1997, have used sonar equipment in their efforts to find the Loch Ness monster. Seven search parties recorded nothing out of the ordinary. The results from five were inconclusive. The other eleven search efforts, including three trips by Rines and Wycoff (and including each of the six most recent trips, for which the most modern technology was available), reported positive contacts—that is, sonar contact with a large, solid, moving object that did not fit the description of any known animal species. That many positive contacts says that *something* has to be living and moving in Loch Ness.

What is to be made of these contradictory bodies of evidence? Some biologists have scoured the array of large aquatic species searching for those that have the humps and appendages of the reported sightings. The least likely answer—that Nessie is the dinosaur-age plesiosaur, which roamed England more than sixty million years ago—is the most popular with Nessie fans, partly because a plesiosaur's profile would exactly match the most commonly reported pattern of humps, neck and head.

Some have proposed that Nessie is a giant turtle or a giant sea snake, but no evidence for such a species can be located. Others say the reported profiles better indicate a small whale. Sea cows and basking sharks (which often reach 50 feet in length) could also create many of the profiles reported by observers. Biologists point out that most of the reported "sea-monster" skeletons that have washed up on small islands around Scotland have turned out to be the remains of giant basking sharks.

Many think the most likely answer is that Nessie is a giant eel (several species of which can reach more than 12 feet in length) that periodically swims in from the sea. However, though it is possible for such a creature to swim the shallow river connecting Loch Ness to the sea through the middle of the town of Inverness, it would be highly unlikely for this to happen regularly without townsfolk spotting the creature coming or going.

Others point out that fish and eels move by wiggling their bodies side to side, while mammals move their bodies up and down. Sighting reports more often mention that Nessie's body moves up and down through the water. Thus, some claim that Nessie must be a mammal and that the humps are schools of porpoises, sea lions or even giant otters that swim up the Ness River from the sea. Without additional evidence, no one can offer more than an educated guess.

## Fact or Fiction?

Although some scientists say that there is nothing unusual in Loch Ness at all, the vast majority of scientists who have looked at any of the available data agree that *something* lives in Loch Ness other than the commonly known populations of fish. What that thing is, is anybody's guess.

The only general agreement comes on what Nessie is not. Virtually all serious scientists who have studied Loch Ness agree that Nessie is not likely to be a dinosaur-age throwback such as the commonly mentioned plesiosaur, nor is Nessie likely to be one of a resident population of freshwater whales. Scientists also agree that it would be virtually impossible for a unique species of giant creatures, such as those described by Ian Cameron and Margaret Campbell, to exist in a confined lake without leaving positive, telltale evidence. After these general concessions, everyone digresses to their own pet theory—giant eels, porpoises, giant groupers, seals, snakes and so forth.

There is no species that fits with all the sightings, or even with all the photos and sonar contacts. It seems likely that Loch Ness will continue to hold tight to its secret until one of two things happens: The first is pure luck—the luck to have Nessie appear to an observer capable of recording some definitive, physical evidence. The second is for someone to scrape together the large amount of money required for a complete search of the lake by the most modern, high-tech locating and imaging equipment. Based on the past, neither of these two scenarios is very likely to happen soon.

## Follow-On Questions to Explore

1. How would you compare the weight of four thousand eyewitness accounts to that of a single photo? Which do you think is a more reliable source? Which would you believe? Why?

2. Why do you think everyone has heard of the Loch Ness monster, but not of America's own Lake Champlain monster, Champie? Why haven't we heard about the monsters people have claimed to have seen in more than twenty other lakes worldwide? In your opinion, what about the Loch Ness monster has made it so famous and popular compared to the other lake monsters left in relative obscurity?

3. Many scientists say they are afraid to study Loch Ness for fear they will lose credibility with their peers. What does that mean? What do they fear will happen? Are there other topics that scientists should study, but that scientists are afraid to tackle for fear of looking foolish to the rest of the scientific community? Do you think scientists have to be careful in picking what they will research in order to protect their reputation and their career? Why?

# Follow-On Activities

1. Conduct your own test of eyewitness reliability. Stage an event at school and then question other students who were eyewitnesses to see how accurately they remember what they saw. Any quick event will do. For example, have twelve students run across the school playground in a tight pack, in costume, screaming and yelling and carrying signs. They must burst into view from a closed room, race at full speed, making as much of a disturbance as possible, and disappear behind a building or into another room as quickly as possible.

   After an interval of time—between a minimum of an hour and a maximum of a couple of days—interview other students and ask them to describe in detail what they saw. Have them describe the number of runners, what they wore, their ages, what they were doing and what they carried. Did different students remember seeing different events? How accurate were they descriptions? What does that imply about the accuracy of the reported Loch Ness monster sightings?

2. Nessie is only one of the many lake monsters that have been reported. America's one, well-documented monster lives in Lake Champlain, New York. Research Lake Champlain and its monster, Champie. Compare Lake Champlain and Loch Ness. How many sightings have been reported? In what years were they made? How many photographs have been taken? Have any sonar scans been made? What have local and national officials said about the reported sightings? Why hasn't Champie been more thoroughly investigated?

# References

Bendick, Jeanne. *The Mystery of Loch Ness.* New York: McGraw-Hill, 1986.

Berke, Sally. *Monster at Loch Ness.* Milwaukee, Wis.: Raintree Books, 1987.

Campbell, Elizabeth, and David Solomon. *The Search for Morag.* New York: Walker, 1983.

Campbell, Steven. *The Loch Ness Monster: The Evidence.* New York: Prometheus Books, 1996.

Ellis, Richard. *Monsters of the Sea.* New York: Alfred A. Knopf, 1994.

Lyons, Stephen, and Lisa Wolfinger. *The Beast of Loch Ness.* Boston: WGBH and NOVA, 1999. Videocassette.

Meredith, Dennis. *Search at Loch Ness.* New York: New York Times Book, 1977.

# Martian Mania
## Parched Planet or Fountain of Life?

## At a Glance

**M**any claim that early Roman scholars named the planet Mars because it was stained blood-red, the color of war and the province of the war god Mars. But astronomers claim it was named Mars because, more than any other object in the night sky viewed from the perspective of Earth, that planet wanders forward and back, up and down, visiting virtually every constellation in the heavens. It is as if, like a marauding army, Mars is trying to invade and claim the entire heavens for its own.

Mars is Earth's closest neighbor, and is a small planet—only Mercury and Pluto are smaller. Mars is only twice the size of our Moon. Mars's diameter is less than half of Earth's. Its mass is only 10 percent of our home planet's. Yet Mars, more than any other planet, feels like a companion to Earth.

White polar ice caps cover both the north and the south poles, expanding toward the equator during the winter and shrinking back during the summer. Dark-green belts expand during the summer as the frozen caps retreat, looking very much like blooming summer vegetation. It all looks very much like the annual cycle on Earth. The Martian year is almost exactly twice as long as Earth's, and the Martian day is only thirty-seven minutes longer than Earth's. Martian gravity is only 38 percent of Earth's, but that is still comfortably within the range humans can tolerate.

Mars feels like a comrade in our spinning voyage through space, like a spot where humanoids could survive—could thrive. If we weren't here, we think, we'd want to be on Mars, home of the highest single mountain in the solar system (Olympus Mons, more than 16 miles high), and home of the solar system's longest, deepest canyon (Valles Mirineris, more than 2,500 miles long and 6 miles deep). For more than a century, the words *alien* and *Martian* have been virtually synonymous. When we think of life beyond Earth, our eyes and thoughts often stray first to our neighbor Mars.

But Mars is actually a barren, inhospitably cold desert of sand and iron-rich rocks. It is pounded relentlessly by ultraviolet radiation from the Sun and has a surface atmosphere similar in density to that present on Earth at an altitude of 75,000 feet. On Earth, there isn't enough oxygen above 30,000 feet for humans to survive. At 75,000 feet, there isn't enough air to suck in even one sustaining breath. Worse, Mars's thin atmosphere is almost pure carbon dioxide, with only traces of nitrogen, argon, oxygen and water. Even if the Martian atmosphere were as dense as Earth's, you still couldn't breathe it.

Current theory says that a planet must have a liquid, molten-metal core (as does Earth) to be a vital, livable planet. Liquid cores are detected by measuring the telltale magnetic field they produce around a planet (as happens on Earth). But Mars has virtually no magnetic field, which means that it lacks the molten core necessary to support a vital planet. Mars also possesses a pitifully weak gravitational field—one that has proved too weak to even hold the planet's own atmosphere tight against its surface, so that most of the atmosphere and water it once claimed have escaped into space over the eons.

Worst of all, Mars shows no signs of surface water. The polar ice caps are predominantly frozen carbon dioxide—dry ice. Water and oxygen, the essentials for life as we know it, are both conspicuously absent on Mars.

Still, when humans think of life beyond our own cozy planet, our eyes, dreams and hopes turn unfailingly to Mars. Over the past forty years, the United States and the former Soviet Union have launched more than forty probes to the Red Planet. Twenty-six of these have successfully reached Mars—sixteen were orbiters designed to take pictures and conduct remote sensing operations, and ten were Martian landers. Only three of the landers, though, have successfully landed and returned data to Earth—*Viking I* and *II* (1976) and *Pathfinder* (1997).

Collectively, those probes have returned more than thirty thousand pictures of Mars, have sampled the atmosphere, have tested and analyzed Martian surface soil and have measured every facet of the Martian landscape. The two things Earth's unmanned voyagers have not found on the Red Planet are water and life. Scientists were ready to write off Mars as a totally barren chunk of rock.

Then, in 1996, scientists discovered a meteorite in Antarctica that came from Mars several billion years ago and that, when closely analyzed, seemed to contain the remnants of microscopic Martian life. What looked like the now fossilized shells of tiny microbes were embedded in the rock. The search for life and water on Mars once again became NASA's top priority.

The *Martian Polar Lander* was launched, designed to search for water lurking deep beneath the Martian surface and to search for proof of present or past Martian life. Unfortunately, contact with the lander was lost after it entered the Martian atmosphere. We humans are left to wonder: Did life exist on Mars? Does it still cling to protected nooks and crannies? Could an underground Martian ecosystem support life? Did life develop on Mars before it developed on Earth? Did life on Earth originate on Mars? These are the greatest mysteries of the solar system as humanity continues to probe its way into space.

# The Mystery:
# Martian Mania

"Have you seen them?!" The question was shouted from the crowd of reporters that pressed forward as tall, confident Percival Lowell swept into the briefing room on this late October evening of 1894 and marched to the podium. A commanding man dressed in a fashionable three-piece suit, Lowell beamed radiant enthusiasm and confident power as he waved his hands for quiet. Others involved in the project had advised Lowell to wait until their astronomical research and analysis were complete and verified. Lowell had smiled as a father does to a small child and said, "Nonsense. The world deserves to know what glorious findings we have discovered."

The press conference had been announced with only two weeks' notice for reporters to make the trek from the major cities to this 10,000-foot-high mountaintop, a five-hour ride outside the tiny town of Flagstaff, Arizona. Reporters grumbled that Lowell had scheduled the conference for 8:00 P.M., well after their deadlines, should he have the "grand, sensational scoop" he promised.

Again, one of the reporters shouted, "Have you seen them?!"

"Pardon?" Lowell cupped one hand to his ear to hear above the din of other questions being shouted by other reporters, their pencils poised above note pads.

"Have you seen any Martians yet through your telescope? Can you see them walking around on Mars?"

Lowell smoothed his thick mustache with one hand as he chuckled. Then he raised both hands to signal for quiet. "Gentlemen. Please."

The room buzzed with electric excitement. "Martians? Lowell has discovered Martians?!" That *was* a world-class scoop! Pencils scribbled at a lightning blur across pages.

"Gentlemen! Please!" The throng of almost sixty reporters quieted to a dull rumble. Lowell continued, "A Martian would have to be hundreds of feet tall to be detectable through my 24-inch telescope. What I have seen is their engineering and their agriculture."

Flashpans exploded with loud "poofs!" as newspaper photographers snapped their pictures. A thick, sulfurous haze drifted through the room from the row of photographers and their flashpowder. Some began to cough.

"But there *are* Martians? You *have* proved it?"

At the mention of proof, William Pickering and Andrew Douglas, Lowell's research partners, both winced as they stood unnoticed in the shadows at the back of the room.

Lowell, however, beamed with unshakable confidence and continued his scholarly, and yet fatherly, talk for the gathered press conference. "First, thank you all for coming all the way out here to this mountaintop in the wilderness of northern Arizona—not easy to get to, but the perfect spot for my telescope." He cleared his throat and continued. "The Martians live on an inhospitable, harsh world. But they have learned to adapt, to mold their environment to ensure their survival. They have built a great system of canals to channel what little water they have, to produce their wide belts of agriculture—"

"The Martians can build canals and cities?" the reporters interrupted in a dazed mumble. "There really *are* Martians! And Percival Lowell has seen them!"

"What crops do they grow?" interrupted another of the reporters.

Lowell scowled. "I can't see individual plants, man!" he barked. "I just see the wide bands of green that *indicate* the seasonal presence of fertile agriculture."

Reporters nodded and scribbled notes. More pans of flashpowder exploded as a new round of photographs were snapped.

One reporter in the front row raised his hand. "If you can't *see* the Martians, how do you know they're there?"

Lowell tweaked his graying mustache and tried to laugh. "Gentlemen. Gentlemen. I have seen their canals. Hundreds of miles of expertly engineered canals. Think those canals built themselves?"

Most of the reporters chuckled along with Lowell. But the reporter in the front row still thoughtfully tapped the end of his pencil on his pad. "Wasn't it the Italian astronomer Giovanni Schiaparelli who first saw the Martian canals?"

"Yes, in 1877," Lowell snapped. "Mars and Earth were even closer together that year than they are this year. Schiaparelli *saw* them. But *I* have mapped the entire Martian system of—"

"Wasn't Schiaparelli the one who described them using the Italian word *canali*?" interrupted the reporter.

"Also true," Lowell grunted. "What's your point?"

"*Canali* translates to English as 'channel' not 'canal.' Couldn't they be natural channels rather than man—er, Martian-made—canals?"

Many reporters chuckled. Lowell scowled and drummed his fingers on the podium. "Natural?!" Lowell's face reddened and his voice rose like rumbling thunder. "Natural?! Have you ever seen 'natural channels' with vertical sides that run straight as an arrow for hundreds of miles across the landscape? Have you? Does that sound natural to you?

The great canals the Martians have built allow them to survive on their cold, parched planet. Without their canals, the Martians would perish."

The reporter shrugged and lowered his eyes in defeat. Lowell beamed and breathed deep to regain his fatherly composure. "No, my boy, there are intelligent Martians up there who are undoubtedly jealous of this garden paradise we live on and wish they were down here."

The reporters all dutifully chuckled at Lowell's attempted humor.

The front-row reporter looked up again with one last question. "You don't have any academic training in astronomy, or even very much astronomical experience, Mr. Lowell. Couldn't you be in error?"

The crowd of reporters hushed and prepared to record every word of this answer.

Lowell's cheeks reddened and his eyebrows scrunched into a fierce scowl. "I may not have a degree in astronomy, young man. But I know what I have seen! William Pickering and Andrew Douglas, both prominent astronomers from Harvard University, are here to assist me, and they agree with my every finding."

Again Pickering and Douglas winced. "Shouldn't we say that he's overstating his case?" Douglas asked Pickering in a whisper. "We don't have enough data to prove anything."

Pickering, the senior astronomy professor, shook his head and whispered, "No. It would only give the reporters a bigger story to write about. Besides, Lowell could be right. We probably will have enough evidence in a few more years. Better not to say anything now. And if he's wrong, let it only be Lowell who opened his mouth."

Douglas shook his head and muttered in disgust.

In a booming voice, Lowell announced, "And now, gentlemen, if you would follow me, I'll lead you to the observatory and allow you to see the work of the Martians!"

A buzz of excitement swept through the reporters. With giddy "Ooooh's" and "Ahhhh's" they rushed for the door, jamming and elbowing to force their way to the front of the line. They acted as if they had been promised a close-up view of a miracle.

The nighttime mountain cold slapped the reporters hard enough to take their breath away as they left the heated briefing room and walked the open-air path to the domed observatory. Their breath hissed out in shining clouds. Their fingers tingled and grew stiff in the subfreezing cold.

The round observatory building was unheated, even though they could hear the hum of electric generators outside. Lowell typically wore a heavy coat, even in midsummer, as he consumed the night-time hours staring at his beloved Mars. The pack of reporters stomped their feet on the wood floor and blew on their fingers as they huddled in the bitter cold of the wood-paneled dome.

Lowell pushed a button and noisy electric motors ground open the telescope doors. The reporters gazed through the 8-foot-wide slit at a stunning splash of stars that seemingly twinkled close enough to touch. The telescope itself was a black, metal tube 30 feet long and scarcely more than 3 feet across. Rods, cranks, clamps and brackets ran the length of the tube, making it look like a giant clarinet.

At the bottom end of the telescope, an ordinary, wooden, straight-backed chair sat on a small, metal platform that had been bolted onto an angled stepladder. The ladder rested on four metal wheels. Its top attached to a metal rail that ran all the way around the circular wall of the observatory. Once the telescope had been positioned to focus on a selected star, the ladder was wheeled around the wall, and the chair's platform was raised or lowered on the ladder by an electric motor, so that the eye of an observer sitting in the chair would be per-fectly aligned with the telescope's eyepiece.

Lowell took his seat and reached out with practiced hands to make final positioning and focus adjustments so that Mars filled his entire field of vision. He leaned back and gently patted the end of the telescope. "Twenty-four inches of perfectly ground glass focuses the distant image of the Red Planet on this eyepiece." He gestured along, and then past, his telescope. "There, gentlemen. Behold the home of the Martians!"

As one body, the reporters turned to gaze with solemn awe at the tiny white dot in an endless blanket of stars. As one body, they wondered if, in a Martian observatory right this very moment, a pack of Martian reporters were perhaps gazing through a telescope of their own, looking at the dot in their own sky that was Earth and searching for signs of life.

One reporter waved and called, "Hello up there!" Another waved and yelled, "We're here!" The moment seemed magically solemn and reverent.

Lowell chuckled and gestured at the eyepiece. "You can look at Martian life if you want."

There was a great scramble as the reporters struggled into line. One by one they slid into Lowell's seat, blinked and then gingerly, tentatively eased up to the eyepiece. "What am I looking at?"

"Search for the canal—I have focused on one I named Trans Verdi."

"The black wavy line? Is that it?"

"Distortions in our own atmosphere create the wiggle, man," snapped Lowell. "My calculations show that, once you correct for the distortions created by our swirling atmosphere, that line is perfectly straight on Mars."

Douglas hissed in Pickering's ear. "We don't know that. They don't always look straight or even always the same to me. Shouldn't we say that we're not at all sure?"

Pickering patted his assistant's arm and softly shook his head.

The reporter at the telescope said, "All I see is a green blotch next to a fuzzy black line."

"That's what your inexperienced eye may see," explained Lowell. "But mine sees proof of Martian civilization, engineering and culture."

The reporter shrugged and scratched his head as he slid out to give the next in line a turn.

"Can we signal them somehow?" asked one reporter.

Lowell nodded. "They have most likely already received radio signals broadcast on Earth. I am sure they are aware of our presence down here."

All gazed again in wonder at the white dot.

"I think we should wrap it up for tonight, gentlemen," announced Lowell, noticing the shivering bodies around him. "Thank you all for coming. Please send any further questions you have by letter and I will gladly respond."

The reporters soaked up a final gaze at Mars and broke into vigorous applause. Then they raced for their carriages and blankets for the long ride back to town.

Two days later the headlines broke all across the country: "Life on Mars!" "Martians Are Engineering Wonders." "Scientists Make Contact with Martians."

The country went wild for Mars and Martians. Telescope sales took a hundredfold jump and Martians were instantly enshrined as an integral part of American culture. The terrible errors in Lowell's presentation did not gain public notice for more than sixty years.

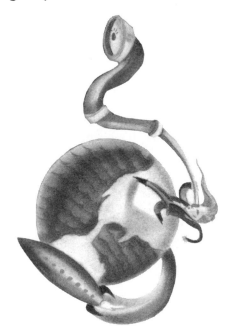

## About This Story

The characters and events in this story are real. Percival Lowell created an international sensation in the fall of 1894 with his grandiose proclamations about Mars. Some of the story's dialog is taken from newspaper reports. The rest has been inferred based on known personality traits and reported events.

## The Science

Early astronomers were aware of Mars. But no one was able to study features on the planet in any detail until sufficiently powerful telescopes were developed in the late eighteenth century. Italian astronomer Giovanni Schiaparelli, in 1877, was the first to study any surface detail on the Red Planet. It was he who noted the meandering black lines he termed *canali*. He never ruled out the existence of Martians, but he never claimed to have found supporting evidence for their existence.

American Lowell Percival, who first took up astronomy in 1892, was able to talk Harvard University into lending him the equipment, assistance (Professors Pickering and Douglas) and construction money he needed for his Arizona observatory. Lowell set up shop in 1894 and, during a three-month period that summer when Earth and Mars were in their closest proximity to each other, made all of his famous observations establishing the notion that there were Martians, engineered canals and agriculture on the Red Planet.

The theory gained instant popular success and spawned dozens of science fiction stories. However, Lowell's evidence never gained any support in the scientific community. Scientists pointed out that a canal would have to be 30 miles wide to be seen by Lowell's 24-inch telescope. Positively *no one* would build a canal 30 miles wide!

Lowell countered that he hadn't actually seen the canals. They were far to narrow. What he had seen, he said, were the 30-mile-wide bands of dense agriculture along the length of the canals. The canals themselves, he said, must run down the middle of the bands. Still, no one accepted his explanation and Mars was dropped as a topic of significant interest by the scientific community.

By the mid-1950s, more powerful telescopes established beyond any doubt that there were no canals on Mars and that it was only meandering shadows off ridge lines and cliff faces that Lowell had mapped. Lowell's greenbelts of agriculture were far more likely some form of rock than vegetation, with the seasonal appearance being caused by the retreating of the polar ice caps. There was no life on Mars, the scientific community concluded. Mars was, however, our nearest neighbor, and so would remain an interesting target to study for discoveries that might reveal new information about the history of the solar system and of Earth.

In the 1960s, the United States launched a series of unmanned *Mariner* spacecraft, each designed to streak past Mars and send back new close-up photographs. The former Soviet Union launched its *Mars* and *Zond* series of probes with the same objective. By 1970 almost six hundred photos of Mars had been transmitted back to Earth, some from as close as 1,000 miles above the Martian surface. Those photos showed dried streambeds, hills and mountains eroded by countless years of rain and running water as well as by the ever-present Martian wind. Some photos showed evidence of ancient oceanic shorelines. Though every photo confirmed that there was no measurable surface water on Mars, they also seemed to prove that Mars used to have proportionately as much water as Earth does today.

Most shockingly of all, several of the photos seemed to show a giant, humanlike stone face pointing up to the sky, as if early Martians had constructed an immense, Sphinx-like monument. Other photos showed regular-sided pyramids sprinkled across the Martian landscape. Had Martian civilization developed long before Earth civilization? And had Martians abandoned their dying planet and flown to Earth to build the pyramids in Egypt, Mexico and South America?

NASA scientists claimed it wasn't a face at all—just a trick of light and shadow over an ancient, weathered hill of barren rock. More photos were taken by orbiting space probes. Believers insisted that each new photo proved it was a huge monument carved by intelligent life-forms. Skeptics scoffed that it was just a rock mountain, nothing more. Interest in Mars was rekindled.

Landing missions were planned to search for water and signs of life. The Soviets aimed two unmanned landers at Mars. Both were apparently destroyed on impact. The United States successfully landed *Viking I* and *II* on Mars in 1976, and used them to measure the atmosphere, take photographs and probe the dusty, sandy surface.

No evidence of life or water was found. The surface was desolate—dust, sand and iron-rich rocks (which created the dominant red color). Polar caps were almost pure dry ice (carbon dioxide). The atmosphere would not support life and was mostly gaseous carbon dioxide with trace smatterings of nitrogen, argon and oxygen. But the existence of extensive surface water six billion years ago was confirmed, as was the notion that the ancient Martian atmosphere used to be much more dense and carried more oxygen. Ancient Mars *could* have supported life.

Interestingly, the structure of several riverbeds indicated that they were created not by a gathering and funneling of rainwater, but by gushing eruptions of groundwater—vast springs where underground rivers burst onto the surface. Could Mars's water still be on the planet and locked underground? Could life be hiding there with it? What happened to the surface water and atmosphere?

Additional orbiting probes were launched through the 1980s. Thousands more photos were radioed back to Earth, more samples were collected and analyzed. Slowly a picture of the ancient fate of Mars emerged. Ancient Mars looked much like ancient Earth (though much smaller). It had a dense, carbon-based atmosphere, spewing volcanoes, abundant water (one of the byproducts of volcanic eruptions) and a warm surface. Slowly the planet and its tiny core cooled. The crust solidified. Volcanic activity ceased. The Martian surface used to shift and fracture like the surface of Earth with its tectonic plates. But no more. The core of Mars had cooled too much to drive the process.

All might still have been well, except that Mars was too small. Its gravitational pull was too weak to keep its atmosphere from slowly drifting away. Surface water evaporated and escaped with the gasses spinning off into space. As the core hardened, Mars's magnetic field collapsed and ultraviolet rays bombarded into the planet's surface, sterilizing the surface layers.

Just at the time when life might have been able to form on Mars, the planet's small size doomed it to early destruction. The remaining questions were: Did life *ever* form? Was there still microscopic life on Mars? and Was there still groundwater under the Martian surface? Most scientists felt that the answers to all these questions were no, but their answers were only educated guesses.

Then, in late 1996, scientists found a meteorite in Antarctica and were able to date it as being several billion years old. More importantly, they were able to match the composition of the meteorite to that of Martian rocks. The meteorite broke away from Mars several billion years ago. The scientists cracked open the rock, studied it under a microscope and sent shock waves around the world by announcing that they had found fossilized signs of ancient Martian life!

But many scientists doubted these conclusions. Yet another Martian expedition, *Polar Lander,* was planned to probe the Martian south pole during the Martian summer for that part of the planet. *Polar Lander's* mission would be to search for groundwater and subsurface life to learn how far Martian life had developed before it had been doomed by the planet's loss of atmosphere and surface water.

Unfortunately, all contact with *Polar Lander* was lost when it entered the Martian atmosphere in December 1999. With the failure of this mission, scientists are no closer to assembling the final pieces of the Martian puzzle. The answers will now have to wait until the next scheduled NASA launch in 2003.

# Fact or Fiction?

Are there Martian-built canals on Mars? No. Definitely not. Are there giant faces and pyramids? No. Recent orbiters have established that they are just naturally occurring rocks and mountains. Did there used to be life on Mars? Probably. Scientists lack final proof, but all available evidence points toward life having begun on Mars.

Did there used to be intelligent life on Mars? Almost certainly not. The Martian ecosystem collapsed long before intelligent beings could have evolved. There never were any little green Martians.

Is there still life on Mars? Quite possibly. It would have to be microscopic and subterranean though. Its existence depends on the availability of groundwater. Jim Head, a noted biologist from Brown University who studies life in extreme environments, said, "Once life gets started, you have one heck of a time eradicating it." There probably is still some life on Mars—somewhere—if there ever was.

Did life on Earth come from Mars? That is, are we humans really Martians? It is possible. Microscopic life could have clung to rock fragments flung into space many billions of years ago and found their way to Earth. But it is very unlikely. Far more likely, early life developed in both places at about the same time. But while life flourished on Earth, life on Mars died out as the atmosphere thinned and water evaporated. The best-guess answer is that life on Earth did not come from Mars.

Two final thoughts emerge from studying the tragic fate of Martian life. First, if Earth's core cools in another billion years or so, will Earth suffer the same fate that befell Mars? Is life on every planetary body doomed as soon as the seething fires burning deep beneath the planet's surface cool in the near–absolute zero deep freeze of space?

Second, it seems that Mars should have developed abundant life. Six billion years ago it seemed poised to flourish into radiant life. But it didn't. It turns out the planet was a bit too small. What does this mean? Life is hearty—almost unstoppable. But a planet must possess an exacting and very specific set of characteristics for the life force to blossom. Earth is the anomaly, the perfectly designed and placed exception. It is just the right distance from our Sun, just the right size, has experienced just the right progression of developmental events, has maintained just the right temperature and composition of its core. Planets able to develop and support life are the rarity. Mars-type failures would seem to be the norm.

# Follow-On Questions to Explore

1. What is required to support life as we know it? Certainly water and air. But what else must a planet provide to allow life to develop and flourish? How abundant are those elements on Earth? Are any in short supply? Are any becoming in shorter supply and in danger of running out?

2. As the core of Mars cooled, the surface stopped shifting and volcanoes stopped erupting and spewing new oxygen into the atmosphere. The atmosphere slowly escaped into space. Surface water evaporated and was flung out into space. Life disappeared on the surface. Do you think the same thing could happen on Earth? Could Earth become a barren chunk of space rock in another billion years? Why or why not? What could people do to survive if it did?

# Follow-On Activities

1. If life still exists on Mars, it exists under extreme conditions: underground with no light, within barren soil with no plant life, without oxygen, under constant bombardment from deadly ultraviolet radiation and extreme cold. Those are pretty extreme conditions for life to exist. Still, life flourishes on our own planet under adverse and extreme conditions.

   Research extreme life on Earth—life that survives in acidic water, under caustic conditions, with no light, with no oxygen, in extreme temperatures. What lives under these conditions? How? Why? Mark on a map the places where extreme life-forms have been discovered. Make lists of the characteristics of these life-forms and of the advantages those species have given that they can withstand conditions other species cannot. Do you think any species alive on Earth could survive on Mars?

2. Suppose you have just completed your first day on Mars at a colony settlement. Write a letter back home describing what you see and do. What is it like outside? What do you eat? How do you get water and oxygen? What does the reduced gravity feel like?

3. No scientists have ever set foot on Mars to study the planet. All of our knowledge about the planet has been gained through observation, sample collection and analysis, remote measurements and data interpretation.

   Find a dry streambed or similar site near your school. Collect samples of the surface soil, and of soil 2 feet down. Compare them. Which has more water content? (Weigh the samples as soon as they are collected, then oven-dry them and weigh again. The lost weight was water.) Search both samples for signs of life. Observe rocks and vegetation patterns. How high does the water get during the flood season? What information led you to that conclusion? Do your observations give you an accurate picture of that streambed? Why or why not? How much harder would it be if the streambed were located on another planet?

# References

Arvidson, Raymond, and K. C. Jones. "The Surface of Mars." *Scientific American,* May 1978, 217–224.

Baker, Victor. *The Channels of Mars.* Austin: University of Texas Press, 1982.

Burges, Eric. *To The Red Planet.* New York: Columbia University Press, 1978.

———. *Return to the Red Planet.* New York: Columbia University Press, 1990.

DiPietro, Vincent, and Gregory Molenaar. *Unusual Mars Surface Features.* Glenn Dale, Md.: Mars Research, 1988.

French, Bevan. *Mars: The Viking Discoveries.* Washington, D.C.: NASA, 1977.

Horowitz, Norman. "The Search for Life on Mars." *Scientific American,* November 1977, 86–91.

Kelch, Joseph. *Millions of Miles of Mars.* New York: Norton, 1997.

Landau, Elaine. *Mars.* New York: Franklin Watts, 1999.

Leovy, Conway. "The Atmosphere of Mars." *Scientific American,* July 1977, 110–118.

Reaburn, Paul. *Uncovering the Secrets of the Red Planet.* Washington, D.C.: National Geographic Society, 1998.

Sheehan, William. *The Planet Mars.* Tucson: University of Arizona Press, 1996.

Spitzer, Cary, ed. *Viking Orbiter Views of Mars.* Washington, D.C.: NASA, 1980.

Wilford, John. *Mars Beckons.* New York: Knopf, 1990.

# Birth of a Universe
## Big Bang or Big Bust?

### At a Glance

We must gaze out from our tiny planet across seemingly endless stretches of emptiness just to find another tiny spinning rock, the Moon. From there it's millions of miles to the next tiny rock, Mars. Earth is 93 million miles from the nearest star, the Sun, and more than 30 trillion miles (30,000,000,000,000) from the next nearest star, Alpha Centari. Those are vast distances of nothingness between solid objects—just in our tiny corner of our galaxy.

Our galaxy has not just two stars, but tens of billions, spread over billions of trillions of miles. The universe contains not just our Milky Way, but millions of galaxies, each with billions of stars, spread over billions of trillions of miles, with trillions of trillions of miles of emptiness between galaxies. In fact, galaxies are clumped into clusters—thousands of clusters—each with thousands of galaxies, each separated by millions of trillions of trillions of miles. The universe is more vast than the human mind can clearly comprehend.

Worse, there is no way for humans stuck on Earth to be sure how big the universe actually is. All we can know of the universe is that which we can detect. There is no way to see beyond the farthest star that we can see to find out if there is any more of the universe out there.

If the universe began 16 billion years ago (as scientists now believe), then a gamma ray or photon of light emitted at the moment of universal creation could have traveled only 16 billion light-years since then. (A light-year is the distance light travels in a year, almost 6 trillion miles.) But if the universe were (for example) 100 billion light-years across, rays of radiation from a very distant object might take 70 or 80 billion years to reach the spot where Earth now sits. The universe would have to be 70 billion years old before that light could reach us to let us know that those objects and that part of the universe existed. We would have to wait another 54 billion years before we would detect those rays emitted so long ago.

Of course, even then, we would not see what that part of the universe currently looks like, but only what it looked like 70 billion years ago when the rays were released. It is all quite mind-boggling. Worse, by that time, Earth will have moved and could be millions of light-years farther away, so we still wouldn't be able to detect the light emissions from that very distant object.

Earth spins on its axis once a day. If a person stood in the middle of the United States, they would actually be moving through space at about 800 miles per hour to complete that daily spin. Earth also orbits around the Sun once a year, moving at more than 5,500 miles per hour to do so.

But the Sun also moves because our galaxy spins on its axis. The Sun races through space at more than 500 miles per *second* just to keep its position as our great, spiral giant of a galaxy spins around its central axis. Earth, of course, races along at that same speed to keep up with the Sun—in addition to orbiting around the Sun, in addition to spinning on its own axis.

But our entire galaxy is also moving through space. The Milky Way rockets along at almost 20,000 miles per second. And, yes, Earth speeds along at the same pace with it, in addition to completing all of its other movements. You are blasting through space at almost one-tenth the speed of light—even while you sit still in a chair!

Yes, the universe is a wondrous and mysterious place. Scientists have struggled for centuries to comprehend and understand its wonders. More myths and stories have been fabricated about the creation of Earth, the stars and the universe than about any other aspect of human existence. In all those centuries of human pondering and wondering, only very recently has the scientific community begun to ask itself this most basic question: How, and when, did this crazy and wondrous universe begin?

Until the early twentieth century, scientists (and everyone else) assumed that the universe had always been just as it was. Then the world was rocked by the discovery that our universe is expanding. Other galaxies are speeding away from our own, moving ever outward into the void. Instantly scientists realized that, if the universe is expanding, then it used to be smaller. What did it look like when it was half its current size? When it was one one-thousandth its current size? In a blink they were asking, How did the universe begin? and What did it look like when it began? The next question, of course, was, How can we possibly know anything about something that happened so long before Earth even existed? Scientists had no idea what to look for, how to measure it or even how to look for it.

But science does not give up easily. Scientists began to search for clues, hints, tiny shreds of evidence and theoretical concepts that could point the way ever closer to our universal birth. What greater thrill and mystery could there be than to crack open the door and peer at the birth of our universe, at the very beginnings of space and time?

# The Mystery:
# Birth of a Universe

It was a typical southern California spring day in March 1925, with its balmy breezes and brilliant blue skies, when Edwin Hubble paused in the main entrance of the Mt. Wilson Observatory and glared up at the ceiling. The observatory sat at just above the 8,000-foot level in the mountains above Pasadena, up where the crisp air still held a chilly bite.

Hubble was a tall, broad-shouldered, physically powerful astronomer of thirty-five years who, ten years earlier, had almost chosen a career as a professional boxer over academic studies. Hubble had been hired by observatory director George Hale in 1920 to complete and operate Mt. Wilson's mammoth 100-inch telescope, then the largest in the world. Hubble's eyebrows bunched in such a way that he appeared to have a permanent, ferocious scowl. When he paced the observatory halls, he looked to be contemplating some deep and dreadful secret of the cosmos.

This day he paused to scowl at the painted image of the universe spread across the wide ceiling 30 feet above him. The painting showed the Milky Way, with a few odd nebulae dotting the edges beyond its spiral—the known universe.

Hubble sighed and shook his head.

Sixty-two-year-old, bushy white–haired George Hale passed by carrying a stack of papers toward his office, his steps echoing off the polished floor. "What's wrong, Edwin?"

Without looking down, Hubble answered, "The universe is changing."

Hale stopped next to Hubble and also gazed up. "Changing? How so? Is our ceiling cracked?"

"No," huffed Hubble. "*We* are changing—No, *I* am changing the universe. And I'm not sure I like it."

Hale leaned back, questioningly. "How can *you* change the universe?"

"Before Copernicus, everyone believed that Earth lay at the center of the universe, with eight neat rings around it that contained the planets and stars," answered Hubble, finally lowering his eyes to his boss. "The universe was simple, easy. Then Copernicus and Galileo put the Sun at the center, with the planets and stars in vast spheres around it. Earth was demoted out of the middle, but it was still symmetrical and simple.

"Late in the last century, astronomers realized that the stars are not in a perfect, ball-like sphere around our Sun, but are spread across a thin, spiral, disklike shape with a few odd nebulae like Andromeda and those in the Virgo cluster hanging at the outside fringes of the disk. Our Sun—and we ourselves—were demoted from the center to an unnoticeable corner off near one edge of the universe." Hubble again looked and pointed up. "That universe."

"Yes," agreed Hale. "So what?"

"Every time we change our view of the universe, Earth and humankind grow smaller and more insignificant."

"But as we learn more," said Hale, "the universe becomes more exciting and wondrous!" He patted Hubble's back in a fatherly way. "Speaking of wondrous, what have you seen with that 100-inch telescope?"

Again Hubble sighed and pointed at the ceiling. "That we have to change *that* view of the universe and make humankind smaller."

Hale scowled. "Really?"

Hubble nodded. "I'll get my calculations and some of the images we have recorded and I'll show you."

Ten minutes later, Hubble spread three photos onto Hale's desk, all of which had been taken by the giant telescope. "The Andromeda Nebula," Hubble announced as he jabbed one photo with his finger. "I wanted to use the 100-inch telescope to study nebulae because these clouds of gas seem so different from ordinary stars. But look! Andromeda isn't a cloud of gas at all. See here? It's really a tightly-packed cluster of a million stars."

"Really?" gasped Hale, peering at the wash of photographed white dots on a black background. "Are you sure?"

"Positive."

"Fascinating," Hale murmured. "A million stars hanging on the edge of our galaxy?"

"No."

"No?" repeated Hale.

Hubble's finger shifted to the second photo. "Here and here, I was able to locate Cepheid stars in Andromeda."

Cepheid stars pulse. Earlier work at other observatories had shown that the beat of a Cepheid star's pulse was always a direct measure of the absolute amount of light (luminosity) given off by the star.

"Excellent work," said Hale. "Now we can calculate the distance to Andromeda by comparing their apparent luminosity [how much light we see] to their actual luminosity [how much light they actually produce] by measuring the rate at which they pulse."

"I already have."

"And ...?" asked Hale.

Hubble sighed. "Andromeda is 900,000 light-years away."

"What?!" Hale exploded. "That can't be!"

"I have checked my calculations and measurements a dozen times."

"But … but that would put Andromeda far out in space and far away from our galaxy."

"Andromeda *is* a galaxy—a separate galaxy—just like the Milky Way," answered Hubble.

"There are *two* galaxies?" demanded Hale, slumping into his chair with the enormity of this revelation.

"No."

"No?"

Hubble tossed pages of calculations onto his director's desk. "I have measured eighteen other nebulae, mostly in the Virgo cluster."

"And …?" insisted Hale.

"And they are *all* separate galaxies ranging from 5 million to 100 million light-years away."

Hale's jaw dropped. He shook his head as if trying to grasp this incredible news. "There are twenty separate galaxies? Spread over 100 million light-years of space?"

"More likely, we'll find that there are thousands," answered Hubble, "once we finish searching."

Hale finally stammered, "An hour ago I thought I understood the universe. But now you tell me that everything that I knew is just one small corner of a vast network of galaxies spread over countless millions of light-years of space?"

Hubble shrugged and nodded. "And humankind is knocked down another peg toward insignificance, and our ceiling map of the universe is wrong."

Hubble paused, trying to decide how best to say the next part. "Something now bothers me."

"You're afraid you have made an error?" Hale asked hopefully. "Afraid that your methodology could be wrong?"

"No."

"No?" Hale sounded deflated.

"I couldn't figure out what was nagging at me," Hubble answered, "until I remembered reading an article by Melvin Slipher of the Lowell Observatory. He detected a red-shift from one of the nebulae in Virgo."

"A red-shift?" repeated Hale.

Scientists had discovered that each element (helium, hydrogen, argon, oxygen, etc.) always emitted energy in a specific set of wavelengths (frequencies characteristic for that element). If scientists made a spectrograph (a chart of the energy radiated at each separate frequency and wavelength) of the light being emitted from a star, the lines on the spectrograph would tell them which elements were present in the star and in what relative quantities. When Slipher looked at one nebula in the Virgo cluster, he found all the common spectrograph lines for helium, hydrogen and so forth, that were normally found in a star. But all the lines on his graph were at slightly lower frequencies than normal. It was called a red-shift because when visible-light frequencies decrease, their color shifts toward red. If their frequency is increased, their color shifts toward blue (a blue-shift).

"What would cause a red-shift?" asked Hale.

"It might be that elements act differently in different galaxies," said Hubble. "It might be a different mix of isotopes. It might be that the other galaxies are moving."

"Moving, you say?" repeated Hale. "Moving through space?"

"I'd like to buy new test equipment to run spectral analyses on all of the nebulae I have studied."

Hale thought for a moment, rubbing the stubble on his chin. "Do it. This is important."

Over the next two years, Edwin Hubble conducted exhaustive tests of the twenty galaxies he had identified. He concluded that they each had the normal mix of elements scientists saw in nearby stars, and that those elements behaved as normally as elements in our own Sun. But still the pesky red-shifts continued to show up on every spectrograph. The mournful whistle of a train rumbling toward Los Angeles reminded Hubble of the only other possible answer—a Doppler shift. The galaxies were all moving.

Most people have heard the pitch of the siren from a passing ambulance or police car drop lower as the vehicle passes. Because the ambulance itself is moving, the speed at which the siren's sound waves travel through the air while the ambulance is approaching equals the speed of sound plus the speed of the vehicle. The sound arrives at a higher frequency and is heard as a higher tone. After the vehicle passes, sound reaches your ear at the speed of sound minus the speed of the vehicle—creating a lower frequency and tone. That change in the apparent pitch of sound is called a Doppler shift. If a Doppler shift happened to light, it would shift light toward red for objects traveling away from Earth, and toward blue for objects traveling toward Earth.

Hubble realized that, if the galaxies he was studying were moving away from our own galaxy, the Doppler shift could account for the red-shift in the spectrograph lines of the various elements in the nebulae's stars. So he carefully measured the amount of the red-shift (or blue-shift) for each galaxy. And from that he calculated its speed toward, or away from, Earth (the greater the shift, the greater the relative speed).

Hubble's hands must have trembled as he looked at his results. With his one telescope, he had completely shattered science's view of the universe. First he had proved that the universe was made up of many galaxies, of which the Milky Way was only one. And now this!

Hubble's results showed that every galaxy was moving away from the Milky Way (except our closest neighbor, Andromeda, which was moving toward the Milky Way at 300 kilometers per second). More startling, the galaxies were moving away from the Milky Way *and* away from one another. Every galaxy he studied was speeding straight out into open space at speeds of between 800 and 50,000 kilometers per second!

The universe was expanding, growing larger every second as the galaxies raced outward! The universe was not a static thing that had remained unchanged since the beginning of time. It was a moving, dynamic, changing thing that was growing at an incredible rate. In every moment the universe was different than it had ever been before.

A few scientists refused to accept Hubble's theory of an expanding universe, claiming that the red-shift could be due to some other cause than galactic motion. Fifteen years were spent checking, testing and confirming his experiments before all resistance to an expanding universe was swept away.

By showing that the universe was changing and growing, Hubble created an image of the universe that allowed others to wonder about what the universe *used* to look like. In so doing, Hubble unlocked the door that led to the two greatest remaining mysteries of the universe: How did it begin? and How will it end?

## About This Story

The characters and events in this story are real and accurate, though almost four years of Hubble's work has been compressed into a single story. Much of the detail of his daily work and slow discovery has been omitted. Still, all the revelations, events and discoveries presented here are historical record.

## The Science

In the 1930s, when the idea first emerged that the universe had a beginning, scientists had little idea of even how to investigate it. Scientists had to find a way to trace the universe backward and see if their description could accurately account for how the particles, elements, matter and galaxies of our universe were created. Lifetimes of effort by thousands of astronomers, cosmologists, physicists and mathematicians have been dedicated to uncovering hints and clues that could shed light on our universe's distant past.

Hubble established that the universe was expanding at a known rate. Scientists immediately reasoned that, if the universe has always expanded at that same rate, then they could rewind it backward through time and see how long it would take to collapse the universe back to a single point. That would give them the age of the universe. They arrived at an age of twenty million years.

But no one knew if that estimate made sense. They didn't know if it was correct—or even plausible—to assume that the universe had a beginning, as the expanding-universe scenario implied. And if the universe truly had a beginning, scientists didn't know what it would have looked like, or even where the universe would have come from to arrive at its beginning. There was no way to test the age they had arrived at, and no way to test the growing process they had assumed.

Then scientists began to reason that if the universe started in a giant explosion, the explosive force would propel all matter outward, but gravity would constantly act to draw it back in. This model for the universe's beginning as a giant explosion would later be named the Big Bang theory (1967). Scientists used Newtonian gravitation equations to conclude that the universe would expand more and more slowly over time as gravity tugged on and slowed all matter, just as gravity tugs on a ball thrown into the air and stops its upward motion.

But how fast did the material of the universe speed outward just after the moment of the big explosion? How much had it slowed? Einstein's relativity theory provided a new model to help more accurately describe the expanding universe and improve the picture scientists held of an early expanding universe. From this strenuous effort, they concluded that the universe was more likely only sixteen billion years old.

From this study, the first of three troubling "miracles" of the universe came to light. If our early universe expanded too fast, atoms would never condense into matter, and galaxies and stars would never be created. If it initially expanded too slowly, all matter would collapse back to a single point (representing the end of the universe, called the Big Crunch) before stars and galaxies could develop. Calculations showed that only a very specific initial expansion velocity would create a viable universe. Ours, apparently, had that exact velocity. But no one could explain why.

Still, no one knew if the emerging picture of a cosmic explosion and rapid expansion was reasonable. Would a massive explosion at infinite temperature and density push matter out in the way predicted by this model of the universe's development? Would it create the types of elements and matter present? Would it create the amount of matter present?

In the early 1970s, new and highly sensitive antenna arrays detected a faint, low-frequency background radiation seemingly coming from every direction in space. Although the team members who discovered this faint radiation weren't sure what it was, cosmologists were able to calculate that, if there had been a Big Bang, it would have sent out a high-energy radiation pulse that, after sixteen billion years, could look exactly like this cosmic background radiation. The discovery of cosmic background radiation was the first independent physical evidence to support the Big Bang. Instantly the theory gained great popularity and became the central focus of worldwide cosmological work.

The fact that the background radiation was the same in all directions bumped scientists up against the second apparent miracle of our universe's creation. Matter could have been sprayed out of the Big Bang explosion in virtually any pattern. However, any pattern except a perfectly even and spherical one would have badly hampered the development of elements, matter and galaxies. Ours was perfectly even and spherical. Why? No one knew. They could only say it was a lucky happenstance for our universe and a baffling mystery.

With the physical evidence of the cosmic background radiation to support the Big Bang theory, the hunt for further evidence grew more intensive. Beginning in the 1960s, physicists at universities all across the country used high-energy accelerators to conduct experiments with elementary particles—electrons, protons, neutrons, muons, gluons, quarks and so forth. From this research, scientists gained a picture of how these particles act and interact under different temperatures and pressures, of the conditions required to tear them apart and to create them and of the conditions required for them to combine to form elemental atoms and molecules.

Simultaneously, vastly improved telescopes and radio telescopes as well as orbiting radiation receivers and cameras were able to probe farther into the distant corners of the universe, and thus farther into the universe's past. Scientists were able to record radiation emissions in all of the frequency and energy bands—high-energy gamma rays, ultraviolet, visible, infrared, all the way down to low-frequency radio waves—and to study the patterns of the radiation in these frequency and energy bands.

This flood of new information gave scientists new ways to test the Big Bang theory. Scientists were not able to describe the Big Bang explosion it-self, because their calculations showed that it would be a place of infinite temperature and density (called a singularity). Normal physics and math do not work in a singularity. Scientists cannot mathematically describe what happens in a singularity, or even what a singularity looks like.

However, knowing that they must start with a singularity, scientists were able to predict physical conditions just after the explosion of the sin-gularity. Temperatures, pressures and velocities at one hour after, at one minute after, at one second after, at one one-hundredth of a second after, at one one-thousandth of a second after the explosion, were calculated. Scientists were able to show that the conditions their calculations predicted at each moment after the Big Bang would match the conditions needed to create the kind and amount of elementary particles, elements and galaxies we have today. In other words, scientists were able to show that, if there had been a Big Bang sixteen billion years ago, it would have created a universe that looks like what we see around us today. The Big Bang was both possible and plausible.

In early February 2000, European scientists announced that they had been able to re-create in the CERN lab the conditions immediately following the Big Bang. They had mimicked the natural process that created the dense soup of gluons, muons and quarks that preceded the creation of the more common elementary particles. If confirmed, this achievement will be a star-tling feat of high-energy physics—creating a space of explosive energy in an environment of almost infinite pressure and temperature!

During these calculations, scientists bumped up against the third miracle of our universe's creation. They realized that our universe produced just the right amount of matter in its earliest minutes to create just the right amount of gravity, to in turn slow the expansion of the universe just the right amount to allow matter to clump into galaxies and stars, all at just the right moment in the universe's development. Again, why did our universe happen to form so perfectly when the laws of physics say it could have formed in any of an infi-nite variety of ways? No one knew.

Recent studies in the 1990s using the Hubble telescope and other space probes have allowed scientists to gather far more detailed information and to make new observations farther out into space. Scientists are studying the composition and movement of stars and galaxies, and the temperature and radiation patterns being emitted from different bodies and regions of space. All the information they have gathered supports the Big Bang theory. That is, if the Big Bang happened as currently described, it would have created what we see around us in space today.

The picture of our universe's beginning predicted by the Big Bang theory is now complex and compelling. But it is not complete. Scientists have been able to describe what would have happened after the first thousandth of a second, and from then on up to the present. They have been able to determine when quarks, electrons and muons formed, when matter condensed into protons and electrons, when nuclei and atoms formed. They have been able to determine at what moment the universal temperature dropped to a billion degrees, to a million degrees, to a thousand degrees and so forth. But the Big Bang theory has not yet explained everything it needs to explain. Questions remain to be answered before the theory can be universally accepted.

Why did our universe start so perfectly with the perfect velocity, perfect mass, perfect distribution of matter, perfect evolution and perfect expansion pattern to create a complex universe? Many scientists have said that it seems to have started too perfectly to be pure chance, as if the universe had been set purposely into motion. Others disagree and say that the way our universe began is as probable and likely as any other. They claim it is all just chance and physics.

What created the slight density fluctuations in the expanding matter of the universe that started the process of matter gathering into clumps, which then turned into galaxies and stars? Why didn't matter continue to be spread evenly, like a pudding, rather than clump together in dense knots?

Where is the anti-matter? At the first tiny fraction of a second after the Big Bang explosion, when high-energy gamma rays first cooled and formed into matter, they should have also created an equal amount of the opposite of matter, anti-matter. Matter and anti-matter should have been created in equal portions (one anti-electron—a positively charged electron, called a positron—for every electron; one anti-proton—a negatively charged proton, called a negatron—for every proton; etc.). Why did we wind up only with matter? What happened to the anti-matter?

Where is the rest of the necessary mass of the universe? Scientists are able to calculate the gravitational forces that must be acting in the universe by measuring the movements of the galaxies. However, the known mass of the universe is insufficient to create that necessary gravity. In fact, 90 percent of the necessary mass is missing. Scientists call this missing mass dark matter, because they can't see it or find it. What and where is it? And if it isn't there, how does that affect and alter the Big Bang theory?

What happened in the first thousandth of a second of the universe? Science can't describe the singularity that erupted into the Big Bang. But they can inch ever closer to it. Soon scientists hope to be able to accurately describe even the first billion-trillionth of a second after the Big Bang. They hope that, by accurately describing earlier and earlier moments in time, they will be able to address many of the remaining questions, doubts and uncertainties surrounding the Big Bang theory.

Finally, recent studies of black holes point not only to a fascinating possibility of how the universe was created, but also to the possibility of multiple universes. A black hole is a singularity, a place of virtually infinite density and temperature. Could a black hole have been the singularity that created the Big Bang, by exploding and tearing a hole in the space-time continuum? Could black holes start new universes? Did our universe begin as a black hole in some other universe? Will the black holes scientists have found in our universe eventually explode into new universes of their own? Are there multiple universes, each started by the explosion of a singularity in another universe and linked to all other universes through black holes?

# Fact or Fiction?

Does science know for sure that the universe started in the explosion of a massive singularity (the Big Bang)? No. It is still a theory, not a fact. However, all available evidence supports the theory and is compatible with it.

Does the Big Bang theory answer all the questions science must answer to turn theory into fact and natural law? No. Several important questions remain as mysteries to be unraveled in the twenty-first century. Most importantly, scientists must answer these questions: How did density variations form in the early universe's matter to begin the process of forming galaxies? What happened to the early anti-matter? What happened in the first trillionth of a second of the universe? and Where is the missing dark matter?

Did our universe begin in the explosion of a black hole in some other universe? Quite possibly. Black holes form singularities and suck in light, matter and energy. Possibly, when one grows too large, it explodes in a cosmic fireball, spraying out its collected matter through a rupture in the space-time continuum to form a new universe in a parallel dimension.

Is ours the only universe? Not likely. There probably have been, and currently are, many universes, linked to one another by the black holes through which they were created. However, we have no way at present to explore this mind-boggling possibility. The true nature of space and the universe remains a fascinating mystery for twenty-first-century scientists.

## Follow-On Questions to Explore

1. Most scientists say that there is nothing outside the universe. Do you believe that? Do you think something exists beyond our universe? If the universe began as a point, where is that point? What did space look like before the universe began? What will it look like after the universe ends?

   These questions fascinate the general population. But scientists say they are meaningless questions that cannot be addressed or answered. Can you imagine why they say that? Do you think it has to do with the idea that science says that the Big Bang was the beginning of space and time as we know it? Do you agree? Do you think something was out there before the universe began? What?

2. Every generation of scientists, from Aristotle to Galileo, to Stephen Hawking and his Big Bang theory, have claimed to have finally developed the definitive, true model of the universe. Do you think the Big Bang will turn out to be correct? Will scientists one hundred years from now laugh and wonder how we could be so ignorant as to believe in the Big Bang? Does it make sense to you? What discoveries about the true nature of the universe can you imagine will be made during your lifetime? During the next century?

## Follow-On Activities

1. Hubble used the principle of Doppler shift to determine that the universe was expanding. First, listen to passing cars at different speeds to hear common examples of Doppler shifts. Record several car's sounds as they pass. Back in the classroom, try to match sounds to musical tones, or notes. Decide how many notes (tones) the sound dropped as each car passed. Did the tone start higher and drop lower for cars going faster?

Now show yourself what a Doppler shift looks like. Bob your finger lightly up and down in one spot in the middle of a bowl of calm water. Your finger creates waves that radiate out in perfect circles in all directions.

Now *move* your finger as you lift it up and down to see how that affects the way waves radiate out across the bowl of water. Dip your fingertip into the middle of the water and push it (flick it) toward one side of the bowl. Lift your finger out and dip it again in the same, original spot, flicking it again toward the same side of the bowl. Again and again, dip and flick your finger toward the same side of the bowl. Don't flick your finger back and forth in the water; while in the water, your finger must always move in the same direction.

While you create this series of waves, have other students count how many waves arrive in a twenty-second period at the side of the bowl you are flicking toward, and how many arrive at the opposite side. Did the fact that your finger was moving increase the speed of the waves in one direction and reduce it in the opposite direction? If those waves were a sound, then the greater the number of waves arriving during each time period (that is, the greater the frequency), the higher the tone; the fewer the number of waves (that is, the lower the frequency), the lower the tone. Shifting your perspective from the high-frequency side of the bowl to the low-frequency side of the bowl creates a Doppler shift.

2. The universe is expanding, with all galaxy clusters pulling away from one another. To see what this looks like, and to see the difficulties of mapping an expanding universe, mark dots on a balloon to represent galaxy clusters. As you blow up the balloon, watch how all of your marks (galaxy clusters) move away from one another as the balloon (universe) expands. Also notice that the only way you can describe the position of these dots is by using a grid system outside the balloon. If you had to describe the position of these dots only by using reference points inside the balloon, it would be much harder. A point on the edge of the balloon stays exactly where it is on the edge as the balloon expands. It's harder to create a reference point when every point inside the balloon is expanding along with the balloon.

# References

Barrow, John. *The Origin of the Universe.* New York: Basic Books, 1994.

Burns, Ruth Ann. *Stephen Hawking's Universe.* New York: Thirteen: WNET, 1997. Videocassette.

Gribbin, John. *In Search of the Big Bang.* London: Heinemann, 1986.

Haven, Kendall, and Donna Clark. *100 Most Popular Scientists for Young Adults.* Englewood, Colo.: Libraries Unlimited, 1999.

Hawking, Stephen. *A Brief History of Time.* New York: Bantam Books, 1988.

Longair, Malcolm. *The Origins of the Universe.* New York: Cambridge University Press, 1990.

Munitz, Milton, ed. *Theories of the Universe: From Babylonian Myths to Modern Science.* New York: Free Press, 1977.

Rees, Martin. *Before the Beginning: Our Universe and Others.* Reading, Mass.: Addison-Wesley, 1997.

———. "Exploring Our Universe and Others." *Scientific American,* December 1999, 78–83.

Sharov, Alexander, and Igor Novikov. *Edwin Hubble: The Discoverer of the Big Bang Universe.* New York: Cambridge University Press, 1993.

Silk, Joseph. *The Big Bang.* 2d ed. San Francisco: W. H. Freeman, 1989.

Weinberg, Steven. *The First Three Minutes.* New York: Basic Books, 1987.

Wilson, Robert. *Astronomy Through the Ages.* Princeton, N.J.: Princeton University Press, 1998.

# Cold, Dark and Deadly
## Sea Serpents—Deep-Sea Tales or Deadly Demons?

## At a Glance

Virtually every ancient map of the seas shows evil, monstrous sea serpents lurking near the fringes. Every seafaring culture has a trove of stories of giant sea creatures—some like snakes, some like giant dragons, some like slithering tentacled squid, some like dinosaur-era oceanic reptiles, some described as looking like bigger cousins of the Loch Ness monster, a few even described as monster turtles.

Every seafaring nation boasts a hoard of mariners who claim to have seen and encountered giant and ferocious beasts in the sea and lived to tell the tale. Every nation possesses a long list of their stout ships lost to the vicious attacks of these creatures. Literally thousands of sightings and attacks by giant sea serpents have been well documented through the ages.

Ancient Greeks feared Scylla, a horrible monster that waited along the Strait of Messina to snatch seafarers from their ships. Aristotle, the world's first scientist/zoologist, described several species of sea serpents in great detail. Roman soldiers along the British coast described constant encounters with sea serpents.

These monsters have been given fearful-sounding names such as Leviathan and Kraken. Sometimes they are said to attack ships; sometimes they swim by. Sometimes the ships escape; sometimes they are sunk. Movies and fiction stories have often used monstrous sea serpents. In *20,000 Leagues Under the Sea,* the *Nautilus* submarine was attacked by a giant squid. Moby Dick was a monstrous sperm whale with a chip on its shoulder. These stories resonate with audiences because we believe that they have a core of truth. Anthropologists and psychologists say that humans create sea monsters because we need to put physical form to our unnamed fears and anxieties. Certainly, the sea already possesses plenty of "monsters" for sailors to dread: cold, dark and deadly waters, treacherous currents, razor-sharp coral reefs and raging storms.

Some of the claimed sightings and attacks are easy to dismiss as fanciful exaggeration. Many, however, are not. The Glouster Harbor, Massachusetts, sea serpent was seen by more than two hundred people during its ten-day stay near shore. In the twentieth century, two British Navy ships and one U.S. Navy ship have been attacked by monstrous sea serpents, which were seen by more than a hundred sailors in each instance. Two of these monsters appeared to be giant squid more than 100 feet long. One was described as looking more like a giant whale with a long neck and long front flippers.

Are there really giant creatures lurking in the sea lanes waiting to attack hapless ships? Are there mysterious, oversized creatures in the deep oceans that humans have never seen? Or are they merely sea stories invented to entertain bored sailors on long and idle voyages?

# The Mystery:
# Cold, Dark and Deadly

The *Carolyn* was classed as a merchant ship sailing full out of Halifax, Nova Scotia, in August 1888 and bound for Baltimore, Maryland. A trim schooner, the ship struggled through unusually calm seas for the North Atlantic with both masts rigged fore and aft, trying to catch any puff of breeze that might wander by. The ship rode deep in the water, carrying 190 tons of cargo and a crew of eighteen.

As the Sun set in a great orange ball, leaving the cloudless sky to the stars, the ship's bell clanged eight times, the tones floating across an empty ocean. Eight bells was the universal signal for a crew change.

Johnny Longden, ship's mate, stood at the helm. "New deck crew up the rigging. Tighten all ratlines." His voice always sounded thin and whiny. But rat-faced Johnny Longden was as mean as a ferret and as tough as a wolverine.

"What's the point?" grumbled Jefferson Kitlers, a short, powerful black man the crew called Kit. "There's no wind to catch no matter how tight we trim the sails."

"You arguing with the mate?" snapped Longden.

"No, Mr. Longden."

"You're on report, Kit! Now get movin' afore I throw you in chains. I want to make some headway here."

With a deep sigh, Kit scrambled into the rigging beside Samuel Withers, a red-headed Canadian who had been working flatboats on the St. Lawrence until he signed onto the *Carolyn*.

Longden muttered, "I don't like a sea with no wind. Gives me the creeps. Evil things happen on a flat sea at night."

The four crewmen coming off-duty massaged rope coils into comfortable chairs and lounged on the deck. It was still too stuffy down below from the heat of the day.

Ned Billings slid his harmonica out of a pocket and began to play. Ned was only twenty-five, but had been called Old Ned since he first joined the *Carolyn* four years ago. Everyone—except Johnny Longden—loved it when Ned settled into his harmonica. The music seemed to calm the seas and floated every ache and care far away. Longden hated anything that pulled the crew's mind away from sailing.

Jerimiah Coglin, the cook, and Billy Wolf, ship's cabin boy, both hustled up onto deck, wiping their hands on aprons, to listen. Jerimiah was a lousy cook, but always got the food served on time. Billy was a thin, graceful boy of fourteen. Most on the crew believed he could carry a tray of brimming soup bowls in one hand across a pitching deck in a violent storm and not spill a drop.

Like a magnet, Old Ned's music drew every free crewman to the decks. Even the hands high in the rigging paused in their work to lean on the spars and listen, letting the harmonica carry their emotions far off across the darkening waters.

Henry, ship's carpenter and the only white-haired member of the crew, leaned dreamily against the rail. His head snapped to the left. Something had caught the corner of his eye. There! A hump rising slightly out of the water 100 yards off the port bow. He rubbed his old eyes, straining to see past the dusky twilight.

There it was again. A dark-gray mound gliding through the calm waters. "Lookie there!" he cried. "Somethin's out there."

The music stopped. Most dashed to the rail and squinted into the darkness, following Henry's pointing finger.

"I don't see nothing."

"It was there, I tell, ya! A big hump … well, a *something*."

Most of the crewmen laughed and shook their heads.

"You're gettin' too old, Henry. Your eyes are playing tricks on you."

Jerimiah Coglin chided, "Maybe the hump you saw, Henry, was a bloody *wave*." The sailors burst into a new round of laughter. "A wave in the ocean would be worth pointin' out, all right!"

"It's calm as a millpond out there, I tell ya!" Henry snapped. "I saw something." He leaned back and called up into the rigging. "You see anything, Kit? How 'bout you, Samuel?"

Both men shook their heads. "Sorry, Henry."

Old Ned blew life back into his harmonica and the crew forgot Henry's hump in the water.

As he slid back down the ropes to the deck, Kit eased over to Henry and said in a low voice, "I didn't see it, Henry, but I believe it. Nights such as this, with a hot, calm sea and not a breath of air, it drives some things crazy and turns them mean."

"What sorts of things?" asked Jerimiah. "Like first mates?"

The crew laughed—but not too loudly for fear that Johnny Longden back at the helm would hear.

"I mean sea serpents!" Kit hissed. His eyes glowed in his shining black face.

"You trying to conjure up some voodoo magic on us, Kit?" Old Ned asked, still lounging in his coil of rope.

"I've *seen* them!" Kit insisted. "Twice. Both like monster snakes over 60 feet long. Jaws big enough to swallow a man whole. I watched one pull down a longboat and I heard the screams of all six men as the monster ate them, one by one."

Jerimiah broke the long, ominous silence that followed with a forced laugh. "You sound bloody crazy, Kit. Get outta here with yer wild stories."

"I've seen 'em, too," said Samuel Withers, the Canadian, in a soft, solemn voice. "On the St. Lawrence. Something big and black glided up next to our ship. It was longer than I could see. Then it darted off. Our whole ship pitched and rolled in its wake."

A rumbling vibration ran through the ship, sounding like the keel scraping over an uncharted mud shoal. Every sailor froze, bracing himself against deck and rail for another shock wave.

Captain James Blanchard stormed onto the deck wearing only the red long johns he slept in and carrying his cutlass. "What in blazes did you run us into, Mr. Longden?" demanded the captain. He was a giant bear of a man who could outwrestle any two of his crew put together. He growled and snarled like a bear, but every man who served under him knew him to be fair and kind, and to possess a flawless "fifth sense" about the sea.

"We're in open sea a hundred miles from shore," Mr. Longden protested. "There's nothing out here to hit."

"Well, *something* bumped against my ship!" snarled the captain.

The *Carolyn* lifted slightly higher in the water and rolled ominously to starboard.

"By thunder!" Captain Blanchard roared. "No sea monster is taking *my* ship!" He clanged the ship's bell. "All hands to deck! Prepare for battle!"

"Against what, Cap'n?" Old Ned asked.

The *Carolyn* stopped dead in the water, as if a giant hand suddenly held it back. Timbers creaked. Spars and ropes groaned. The deck shuttered.

The captain clasped his hands behind his back. In a fatherly tone he asked, "And why aren't we moving, Mr. Longden?"

"I ... I don't know, Captain."

"Well, I do, by thunder!" bellowed the captain. "Break out the ship's arms. Grab pikes and axes. Man the rails!"

"Against *what,* Cap'n?" repeated Ned.

"We gots ourselves a first-rate sea monster attack, and I aims to live to tell about it!"

Henry muttered, "I *knew* I saw something."

Kit trembled. "I *knew* it was a bad night ... I'm going to die! I *knew* it."

Except for the gentle lapping of tiny waves, not a sound broke the eerie silence for several long minutes. Mr. Longden stood at the helm. Captain Blanchard stood nearby, twisting his cutlass, chuckling like a prizefighter eager to enter the arena. The other sixteen in the crew were spread evenly around the ship, staring into black, empty waters.

Hearts pounded. Mouths turned desert-dry. Kit nervously kneaded the handle of his long gaffing spike. "I *knew* monsters would come out tonight ... I *knew* it."

Old Ned tried to play his harmonica, but he found his mouth too dry to blow, and his hands trembled too much to play a clear note. Even sailors who had been at sea for twenty years felt pangs of fear and suddenly longed for the safety of land so very far away.

Jerimiah Coglin swallowed hard to ease the throbbing lump in his throat and started for the hatch leading down to the kitchen.

"And where do you think you're goin', Cookie?" growled the captain.

Coglin's voice answered small and tight. "Thought everyone would be bloody hungry after the fight, Cap'n."

"Get back to the rail, you bilge rat."

The *Carolyn*'s bow dipped as if starting down a hill. The crew wailed a collective "Whooooooa!" and grabbed tight to whatever was near.

"I see arms, Cap'n!" called young Billy Wolf, hanging over the bow rail. "They've grabbed the bow."

"Well, shoot the arms, by thunder!" roared the reply.

"Cap'n, I see a giant eye. Bigger'n my whole head!" called Henry. "It's lookin' at me."

"Well, shoot it, man!"

Henry raised his single-shot pistol. But before he could steady himself, aim and fire, a thick tentacle whipped over the rail and wrapped around Henry's waist. Thick as a mast and long as a coiled rope, the tentacle hoisted him high in the air as if he weighed no more than a feather.

Henry screamed and dropped his gun. The crew stared in frozen shock. "That monster's bigger than the whole bloody ship!"

Stout Samuel Withers dove at the wiggling appendage, sinking his knife deep into its flesh. The tentacle recoiled, snapping back across the rail. Samuel was thrown overboard. Still wrapped tight, Henry disappeared with a final scream into the black sea.

"Man overboard!" cried the captain. "Throw him a line!"

Samuel didn't make it halfway up the side of the ship before two thick tentacles locked onto his legs. As if he had no more strength than a child's doll, he was sucked underwater faster than he could cry out for help.

Again all was calm and quiet on the sea. Aboard the *Carolyn*, all was terrified panic and pandemonium. Cries of "We're doomed!" and "The monster will get us!" echoed across the deck.

"Silence!" bellowed the captain. "I will not have my crew disintegrate into a bunch of blubbering children! Man your stations. Fire or stab at anything that moves! You savvy?"

A long, terrifying minute of silence followed.

Faster than men could cry the alarm, three tentacles rose over the starboard rail. Two men fired shots into the water at the tentacle's base. One tentacle wrapped around a crewman's neck and snapped him into the water. One man hacked at a slithering tentacle with an ax until he was flung far out to sea. Jerimiah Coglin raced across the deck and finished the job, severing the tentacle with his long cleaver.

The monster withdrew. But two more in the crew were gone. Thirty feet of rubbery, severed tentacle flailed about on the deck. Ned reached out to touch it. In a final spasm, the thing snapped around his legs, locking him tight. It took three men to pry him free of the appendage.

"I think he's gone, Captain!" cried Johnny Longden.

"You blockhead!" grumbled the captain. "He'll be gone when we kill him!"

Five thick and deadly tentacles curled up to lock onto the ship's side and rail. The *Carolyn* rolled hard to port. Ropes, men and supplies tumbled across the deck. Heavy cargo crates crashed across the hold, smashing into the wooden hull and springing several leaks.

Five men were flung into the sea as the grotesque monster tightened its grip on the *Carolyn.* One mast collapsed under the violent strain, crashing to the deck. Ropes and sheets fluttered down to trap the remaining crew.

Enraged, Captain Blanchard struggled to his feet and lurched across the deck toward the slimy tentacles, his cutlass in one hand, a long pike in the other. Jamming his sword clear through one tentacle to pin it to the rail, he snatched an ax from terrified Billy Wolf, who cowered in the main hatchway, and hacked off the limb.

The monster refused to release its prize and pulled harder, dipping the rail almost to waterline.

"That does it, by thunder!" yelled the captain. "You'll not get my ship!"

Razor-sharp pike in hand, the captain dove overboard into the heart of the frothing mass of tentacles to attack the beast. Sharks appeared and began to circle, hoping to feed on the scraps.

The rail dipped below waterline. Seawater rushed into open hatchways and sloshed into the cargo hold. Clinging to the broken mast stub, Ned could clearly see past the seething tentacles to a sharp and metal-hard beak that clicked and churned the water, eager to devour every living creature on the ship. He saw no sight of the captain, only his pike jammed into the side of the monster's gaping mouth.

The *Carolyn* was sinking. There was no longer any way to save the ship. Old Ned and Kit tore at the main hatch cover to loosen it from its hinges. Ned grabbed Billy Wolf by the collar and dove onto this makeshift raft as the deck sank below the rippling waves. Johnny Longden flung himself on just before the raft drifted clear of the wreck.

The four sailors huddled together, adrift in a sea of circling sharks, as ship and monster both disappeared with a final swirling gurgle into the deep.

Three days later, two men and a cabin boy were plucked from the ocean by a passing ship. First Mate Johnny Longden had mysteriously disappeared in the night. The three survivors all agreed on every detail of their frightful encounter with the Kraken—except on how Mr. Longden had disappeared, which remained, forever, an unsolved mystery.

## About This Story

This story of the sinking of the *Carolyn* was discovered among old naval records. A board of inquiry was called, partly for insurance purposes, partly, it seems, to determine whether or not Johnny Longden was murdered on the makeshift life raft. The account presented here is based on the statements by the three survivors of the wreck. Specific dialog had to be created, as it wasn't included in the naval report.

## The Science

Science cannot study what it cannot see, measure or directly detect. Sighting reports unaccompanied by hard evidence could contain subtle mistakes of size, color or markings by a biologically untrained observer, which would lead to incorrect identification. Reports could be wildly exaggerated or even totally falsified. Most scientists dismiss the very notion of sea serpents and sea monsters as ridiculous folly saying, "Show me some evidence, some proof, and then I'll study it." It is certainly true that, as knowledge of ocean species has increased during the past century, reports of sea monster sightings have markedly decreased. It is therefore likely, say many scientists, that virtually all early sea serpent sightings—if they weren't the product of overactive imaginations—were encounters with ordinary ocean species we now know about.

Most scientists, however, believe that most sighting reports are laced with a healthy dose of intentional or unintentional exaggeration and storytelling and are therefore unusable for serious study. To support this notion, they point out that reported sea monster behavior over the centuries has matched societal expectations and views on sea monsters rather than biological reality. In early sightings, sea monsters were all ferocious, violent and aggressive. That's how people expected sea serpents to act. Late-nineteenth- and twentieth-century sightings all report shy, harmless and lonely-looking beasts. Those descriptions match what human society thought about sea monsters, not how real species act in the wild.

However, the descriptions and size of the reported monsters are intriguing, and many sightings are too well documented to dismiss. Typical of the many reported and verified sightings are the following seven.

1. In August 1817 and again in 1819, more than two hundred Glouster Harbor, Massachusetts, citizens reported seeing a giant serpentlike creature between 50 and 80 feet long lolling in the harbor. Its head rose 8 feet out of

the water. It remained in the harbor for ten days before disappearing back out to sea. How could two hundred people making multiple sightings over a ten-day period all be wrong? Yet there is no known species that fits the consistent description of the monster.

2. On November 30, 1861, the 100-foot French gunboat *Alecton* was attacked by a giant squid. The crew decided to rope and capture it. However, it was so large that they couldn't secure it to the ship, even using all available ropes. The ship would have been dragged down and sunk if they hadn't cut the squid loose. That had to be one big squid!

3. In March 1896 a large blob of jellylike tissue was found on the St. Augustine, Florida, beach. It weighed 6 tons and measured 92 feet from tentacle to tentacle. It was identified by Professor Verrill as being a species of octopus, "but far larger than any octopus on record." Other sightings have hinted that deep-sea octopuses might be as large as 200 feet across, but no species larger than 35 feet across has ever been brought in whole.

4. In November 1958 eleven Brazilian fishermen fled from a sea serpent that threatened to capsize their boat. They each claimed that the dinosaurlike monster was more than 65 feet long. The picture each drew closely matched the Jurassic-age *Plesiosaurus*.

5. In June 1956 three fishermen off Nova Scotia reported meeting a 45-foot turtle, more than four times the size of any known to exist.

6. In October 1971, Robert Le Serrec photographed what looked like a 50-foot-long snake-shaped sea monster just under the water near Hook Island in Australia. The photo has been studied and authenticated, but the creature does not match any known species.

7. On April 25, 1977, off the coast of New Zealand, the Japanese fishing trawler *Zuiyo Maru* hauled aboard a huge, decaying carcass more than 22 feet long and weighing 3 tons. It had a long neck, developed spine, fins and flippers. Japanese scientists studied photos and tissue samples and concluded that it looked like a plesiosaur—the same species many think lives in Loch Ness.

What are we to make of these reports? Are they wild stories? Intriguing yet factual accounts? What does science make of them?

In 1968, Dr. Bernard Heuvelmans, an eminent zoologist, published the results of his detailed study of more than six hundred reported sea serpent sightings over a period of 150 years. Every legitimate sighting, he concluded, fit the description of one of nine different types of large, known sea creatures. Other researchers who have studied sea monsters agree with his findings.

Tops on this list are contacts with giant squid, the Kraken, the most elusive and least-known of all marine species. *Karken* is a Swedish word for "uprooted tree," which is what a squid looks like with all those tentacles snaking around like roots. A 60-foot-long giant squid (the longest ever caught and studied) leaves sucker marks from the tiny teeth and curved claws in the suckers on its two longest tentacles, which are about 8 inches across. However, sperm whales have been caught with the scars of squid sucker marks measuring more than 18 inches across. The "monster" that made those marks would have to be more than 150 feet long, plenty big enough to account for even the most outlandish sighting reports.

Sharks are the species second most often identified as sea monsters. Large great-white sharks can top 28 feet in length and act every bit the terrifying monster. More often identified as sea monsters, however, are whale sharks and basking sharks (both harmless), which can grow to more than 60 feet in length. In 1972 a new species of shark (the megamouth) was discovered off the coast of Hawaii. This 15-foot-long shark-find gave hope to sea serpent lovers around the globe (if a 15-foot-long species of shark can go undetected, then why not a plesiosaur or some other prehistoric monster?).

Third most often identified are octopuses. Pacific octopuses can grow to more than 35 feet across and have 240 suckers on each arm. Samples of larger octopuses have been found, though, hinting that deep-sea monsters 200 feet across probably exist. Certainly an encounter with one of these would make anyone think they had seen a sea monster, and such a giant would fit nicely with many sighting descriptions.

Fourth most often identified are whales, the Leviathan. Sperm whales historically have had a habit of beaching themselves. These 65-foot-long giants are probably the origins of many sea monster myths and legends. Narwhals are native only to Arctic waters and grow a long, straight tusk (a pointed horn that looks like a unicorn's horn) that stretches more than 10 feet in length. Seeing this pointed spear rise up on a whale's head for the first time could conjure many a vision of sea serpents. Blue whales grow to more than 100 feet in length and weigh as much as 200 tons: the biggest (heaviest) creature to ever live on Earth (*Seismosaurus* and *Ultrasaurus* were both a bit longer, but not as heavy). Though not aggressive by nature, a frightened or wounded blue whale could easily smash a wooden ship and start a sea monster legend or two.

Other existing species match fewer sighting reports. Saltwater crocodiles (Southeast Asia) reach almost 30 feet in length and are exceptionally aggressive. Manta rays can also reach almost 30 feet across and, while floating on the surface, would appear to be as big as a ship. Oarfish (also called ribbonfish) are harmless snakelike fish that can grow to almost 40 feet in length. They swim with a vertical undulation that creates a series of humps visible on the water (a frequently reported sighting), and they possess a red crest along their row of spiny fins (also frequently reported).

Larval eels are usually very small. However, babies for one particular subspecies of larval eel have been caught that are 6 feet long. If their growth was proportionate to other larval eels, those babies would grow into 60- to 90-foot-long monsters looking very much like sea serpents. Finally, giant seals can raise their heads 4 or 5 feet out of the water (a frequently reported sighting).

These known oceanic species can account for almost all of the known sea monster sightings. It is still possible (but very unlikely) that some large prehistoric creatures or other unknown giant sea creatures have survived undetected. None, however, have ever been caught, captured, killed or filmed.

# Fact or Fiction?

Do sea serpents exist? No. Not as a separate group of unknown species. Are there monstrous, prehistoric, dinosaur-era creatures lurking in the seas? It is impossible to prove that they don't exist. But in the absence of any concrete evidence to support the notion that such creatures still exist, the answer is as definitely negative as an unproved answer can be.

Do sea monsters exist? Yes. The sea is full of giant creatures that would appear terrifying to sailors in small wooden ships—creatures that adequately match virtually all reported sea serpent sightings over the past two hundred years. The most probable candidates are listed above. Sea monsters are one of the best examples of how honest ignorance can, without the rigid and strenuous controls that science has created for scientific study, lead to wildly erroneous and damaging conclusions. The scientific process is not glamorous and does not typically lead to great stories, but it does lead to reliable knowledge and truth.

# Follow-On Questions to Explore

1. Why do you think people have always wanted to—almost needed to—believe in sea serpents and sea monsters? Even people who have never been to sea or seen anything strange often insist that sea serpents are out there. Why? Is believing in sea monsters any different than children believing that monsters exist under their bed, or any different than believing in the boogeyman or in demons? What good do such beliefs do for humans who believe in them?

2. Usually, stories of encounters with sea monsters grow considerably bigger with each telling. The size of the monster increases. The danger to the seafarers increases. The sailors and their ship seem to come closer to disaster with each telling. Why does this tend to happen? Does it happen to you with your stories? Is this bragging, or is this what naturally happens to stories?

# Follow-On Activities

1. How big is "big"? Make scale-model silhouettes of a 100-foot-long blue whale, an octopus that stretches 200 feet from tentacle tip to tentacle tip, a giant squid that extends 150 feet from the top of its head to the tips of its longest tentacles, a 60-foot-long whale shark, a 65-foot-long sperm whale, a 28-foot-long saltwater crocodile and a human standing 6 feet tall. Use the library and the Internet to find the body shapes and proportions for each of these species. What would you, the human, feel like if you met one of these monsters?

2. Collect stories of sea monsters and sea disasters. From which cultures and countries could you find them? Which stories seem believable? Why? Which sound like wild exaggeration? Why? Which do you think make for better stories? Why?

# References

Abrahamson, David. "Elusive Behemoth: Giant Squid." *Rodale's Scuba Diving,* October 1992, 106–118.

Baker, Robert. "Jurassic Sea Monsters." *Discover,* September 1993, 78–85.

Bright, Michael. *There Are Giants in the Sea.* London: Robson Books, 1989.

Ellis, Richard. *The Book of Whales.* New York: Knopf, 1985.

———. *Monsters of the Sea.* New York: Alfred Knopf, 1994.

Garinger, Alan. *Water Monsters*. San Diego, Calif.: Greenhaven Press, 1991.

Gleman, Rita. *Monsters of the Sea*. Boston: Little, Brown, 1990.

Haven, Kendall. *Close Encounters with Deadly Dangers*. Englewood, Colo.: Libraries Unlimited, 1998.

Heuvelmans, Bernard. *In the Wake of the Sea-Serpents*. New York: Hill and Wang, 1978.

McGowan, Christopher. *Dinosaurs, Spitfires and Sea Dragons*. Cambridge, Mass.: Harvard University Press, 1991.

Pirotta, Saviour. *Monsters of the Deep*. New York: Thomson Learning, 1995.

Rabin, Staton. *Monster Myths: The Truth About Water Monsters*. New York: Franklin Watts, 1992.

Steele, Philip, and Martin Camm. *Sharks and Other Monsters of the Deep*. New York: Dorling Kindersley, 1991.

Sweeney, James. *A Pictorial History of Sea Monsters*. New York: Crown Books, 1977.

Waters, John. *Giant Sea Creatures*. Chicago: Follett, 1983.

# Stonehenge Secrets
## Mystical Monoliths or Mysterious Map?

## At a Glance

The ancient stone circle sits on a slight rise in the rolling, grassy Salisbury Plain of southern England. Fifty oblong sarsen stones (a kind of dense sandstone) have been raised on their ends and formed into a circle almost 200 feet across. These stones rise 15 feet out of the ground. Along their tops lie horizontal capstones called lintels, forming a perfect circle except for the few that have fallen over the centuries. Even though the ground slopes, the circle of lintels is (was) perfectly horizontal.

Far outside the stone circle is a circular ditch and evidence of a much older circular dirt wall 2 or 3 feet high. Inside the stone circle rise five towering trilithons forming the shape of a horseshoe (a trilithon is a monument of two vertical stones with one lintel cap across them). The tallest, central trilithon rises 28 feet into the air. The bases of its vertical sarsen stones are buried 8 feet in the ground.

This is Stonehenge. Stone circles on a plain surrounded by roads and agricultural fields, overrun by tourists and tour busses. But every visitor senses the power, solemnity and spirit of the place. It feels alive and full of energy.

Stonehenge is also a place of mystery. For millennia no one knew who built it. Some said the Romans did, around A.D. 200. Some claimed it was Druid priests, around A.D. 1000. One popular story said that Merlin, the magician, built it with the wave of a single hand. In recent years, many have given aliens the credit, saying they built it to gather and channel cosmic energy. But who really built it? And when?

Neither could anyone agree on why the Stonehenge circle was built. Some said it was a calendar to help farmers plan their planting seasons. Some said it was built as a calculator to predict eclipses. Some said it was a cathedral. Some claimed it was a burial ground for the rich and mighty. Some insisted it was an ancient observatory and astronomy lab. One early researcher claimed it was an election and inaugural site for ancient kings. Many at the time agreed with him. But why was it really built?

Researchers also wondered how the great stone circle and trilithons were built. The closest sarsen stones lie more than 20 miles away, near Avery. Early estimates claimed that it would require the brute muscle of hundreds of workers toiling for a month to carve, drag and erect just one of the giant stones. Stonehenge has more than eighty stones. That would require more than five years of full-time, dedicated work by hundreds of people. But did that kind of available labor pool exist? Who did the farming, the hunting, the cooking, the housebuilding and the protecting while these hundreds dedicated their lives to building a monument? Why sink so much effort into a stone circle that doesn't even have a roof? Why not build better houses instead? But how was it really built, whoever built it?

Is Stonehenge unique? Yes and no. There are thousands of stone circles across England, Ireland and Scotland. There are, or were, tens of thousands spread across Europe. Stonehenge is far from being the only preserved stone circle. But the inner horseshoe of trilithons at Stonehenge contains the biggest, tallest and heaviest stones ever used by the builders of ancient stone monuments. Stonehenge is also one of the best-preserved stone monuments. Many others became camps, castles, forts, garbage dumps, quarries for later building materials or sites for amphitheaters. Many were torn down by the Catholic Church to stop the local masses from worshipping at those sites.

Somehow Stonehenge survived, remaining intact through the ages. Theories about Stonehenge abound, but the mysteries remain: Who? When? Why? and How?

# The Mystery: Stonehenge Secrets

"One … two … three … Pull!" Twenty-four-year-old Elise Markley groaned and dug in her heels as she tugged. She and twenty-eight other volunteers strained on this inch-thick rope, trying to budge a 40-ton, 28-foot-tall cement monolith. Their group was assigned one of the four rope lines snaking up the gentle English hill trying to see if it was possible to pull a 40-ton giant stone uphill over a bed of smoothed, rolling logs.

"One … two … three … Pull!"

Elise gritted her teeth and yanked. Her weary arm and leg muscles knotted in their effort to move the cement stone.

"Why did I volunteer for this?" Elise hissed between pants.

"One … two … three … Pull!"

"Why did I throw away two weeks of vacation to work like a slave?"

"Halt!" yelled Mark Whitney, the project engineer. "Hold it. It's not working."

"Halt! Drop the ropes!" yelled volunteer leader Mike O'Rorke, an Irishman with flame-red hair and sparkling green eyes. Elise collapsed to the dirt, deciding that O'Rorke was far to chipper, considering *they* were the ones pulling and *he* was the one yelling out the commands to pull.

Elise was a graduate student in archaeology at the University of North Carolina, where she had heard about this project. The plan was to use ancient methods to reconstruct one of Stonehenge's giant trilithons (a monument of two vertical stones with a smaller, horizontal stone—called a lintel—balanced along their tops). She had volunteered to fly over and help, having expected sunrise ceremonies, drumming, sacred chanting and a spiritual link with the mystical—not backbreaking work better suited for a bulldozer.

Worst of all, she had been in England for three days already and still hadn't seen Stonehenge. They began their work on Marlboro Down near Avery, the most likely source of the giant sarsens used at Stonehenge. A sarsen, she found out, was not a shape of rock, but a kind of rock, an incredibly dense form of sandstone used to build the Stonehenge monoliths.

"The stone's too heavy," announced Mark Whitney, sadly shaking his head. He wore a white shirt with rolled up sleeves and a tie. "It's crushing the wood rollers."

"*I* could have told him it was too heavy," grumbled Elise. Two volunteers sitting next to her nodded and chuckled.

Whitney, clipboard in hand, huddled with Julian Richards, the senior archaeologist, and Roger Hopkins, a stonemason from New Hampshire who had experience moving and working with large, heavy stones.

The volunteers flopped back to soak in a little Sun. Sandwiches and water were passed around while the project leaders argued about a new plan. Several rope-pulling volunteers dashed off to do errands or run home. Most of the volunteers were locals. Some came and went as their jobs and chores permitted. Some were here for the duration. About twenty-five, like Elise, were Americans.

At least the weather was good, thought Elise—hazy Sun, no rain. All in all, as good as you could expect for southern England in this late May of 1995.

O'Rorke called the volunteers down to the bottom of the hill and gathered them around the stone. "How many carpenters do we have?" he called. A dozen hands went up.

"We're going to build a wooden rail line," explained Whitney, sketching a picture on his clipboard pad. "Two parallel tracks with a gap between. Then we'll build a sled for the stone with a keel that rides along that gap. If we grease the tracks, it should ride much better."

The carpenters went to work with saw and hammer. The rest grabbed picks and shovels to dig out a shallow trench for the rails. By late afternoon the sled and 200 yards of rail had been built, enough to get the giant stone to the top of the hill. Three people dragged 5-gallon tubs along the rail line, slathering thick grease across the wood.

"Isn't this a lot of work just to move one stone?" Elise asked one of the other volunteers.

"Think it would have been less work *forty-five hundred years ago*?" he answered.

"It's *still* a lot of work," Elise muttered.

O'Rorke yelled at them to get back onto the ropes. Whitney and Richards, the archaeologist, eagerly rubbed their hands.

"Why do we have to pull it uphill?" Elise asked the stocky woman beside her. "Why don't we go around?"

The woman smiled back with a big gap in her front teeth. She reached out to shake hands before she wrapped her gloved hands around the rope. "Bess Dougharty, love. I have a small farm just down the road. And this is a test, love, to see if 130 people can pull a 40-ton stone uphill."

"Who cares?" asked Elise.

"They would have had to pull uphill forty-five hundred years ago, love."

Elise asked, "But don't we want to try to re-create the feel and purpose of the ancient builders?"

The gap in Bess's front teeth seemed to grow as she grinned. "This is an *engineering* study, love. We aim to find out *how* they most likely built Stonehenge. *Why* is a question for another study."

Elise tensed and took up the slack in her thick rope as Mike O'Rorke raised his hands to signal the pullers to get ready. "But why do you think they built it, Bess?"

"I've lived within 8 miles of Stonehenge all my life, love. You walk over there and you'll agree. It's a sacred place now, no matter what the original builders intended."

Elise was going to ask more, but O'Rorke yelled from the head of the lines. "One ... two ... three ... Pull! One ... two ... three ... Pull!"

Ten times they struggled to inch the stone forward. Ten times it seemed to laugh at them, refusing to budge from the bottom of the hill.

"Halt!" yelled Whitney and O'Rorke.

Gasping for breath, the volunteers flopped to the ground or leaned on their knees.

"It's stuck," said Whitney.

"*I* could have told them that!" Elise called out. Many of the pullers laughed. Elise's short, auburn hair was tucked under a baseball cap sporting the logo from her hometown Chicago Cubs. She wore hiking boots, jeans and a light work shirt. I'll have to bring a sweater tomorrow, she decided. The breeze was cold during long sits. And there was more sitting than pulling while they waited for the project staff to settle arguments and devise new plans.

Stonemason Hopkins, wearing a broad Panama hat and a smugly superior smile, suggested using levers. A dozen pullers were brought down to the stone to use long poles as wedges to try to lift the stone while the rest continued to pull.

"One … two … three …Pull! One … two … three … Pull!"

The stone broke free and scooted forward along the greased rails. Many pullers were caught off-guard by the sudden lack of resistance and toppled to the ground. They all cheered and laughed. Ten minutes later the giant slab rested at the hilltop. The pullers shook off their gloves and stretched cramped fingers. Some rubbed sore feet where others had accidentally stomped on them, struggling for footing as they scrambled up the hill.

They were tired. Still, all smiled broadly with a deep sense of accomplishment. Using five-thousand-year-old technology, they had accomplished what many of them had thought impossible.

"Don't get too comfortable, love," said Bess Dougharty. "We still have to lug this thing all the way to Stonehenge."

"Can't they truck it?" asked Elise.

"Did they truck it forty-five hundred years ago?"

Elise answered, "But had their volunteer pullers forty-five hundred years ago spent the last four years at desk jobs? This is hard work!" Many of the pullers laughed and applauded in agreement.

At day's end most hopped into cars and drove home. Some nonlocals were driven to a hotel. Elise and six other college students had been offered tents set up behind a farmer's house. Two meals and the shower came with the offer.

Elise had volunteered because she wanted to experience Stonehenge and see if she could feel the magic of the place, see if it was real. So far she had only experienced sore feet and muscle strain. Each night her back, legs and arms, too used to a life of classrooms and library study, ached as she collapsed into her sleeping bag.

It took six days to build the rails and drag their monstrous stone the 20 miles to Salisbury Plain. Progress was slowed by mud from two days of rain. By now Elise felt like part of a team, almost as if the other pullers on her rope were family. She knew everyone's name and much of their history. No one stomped on others' toes anymore. Automatically they pulled and stepped in unison.

They stopped half a mile from Stonehenge. O'Rorke called for a long break while the engineer, the stonemason and the lead archaeologist debated how to erect the monster slab. Under low, swirling clouds, Elise got her first look at the legendary circle of stones. Cars and tour busses lined the road that ran just outside the ancient earthen ditch and berm that surrounded the site. Tourists snapped pictures, laughed and chatted. Children romped in and out, playing tag and hide-and-seek.

Still, the mighty stone circle was an awe-inspiring sight for Elise and the other American volunteers gaining their first look at this wonder of the world. They talked in whispers, like in a library or a church. The circle seemed infused with great spiritual energy—a raw and powerful energy. Elise could almost feel the humming vibrations of long-departed spirits. It felt like an ancient and mighty place, as if a bit of the soul and strength of each person who ever stood there was still locked in the stone circle, a place far bigger and more important than an individual. The giant stones humbled Elise with a sense of awe and majesty.

Having seen Stonehenge, the work of raising a new trilithon took on new meaning and purpose for Elise. She resented Mike O'Rorke's "One … two … three … Pull!" commands less (which had begun to infest her dreams). She felt closer to her fellow volunteers. She felt more attached to their test cement stone itself.

Julian Richards, the archaeologist, gathered the volunteers around a scrawny wooden shovel, which looked more like an oar than a shovel, and some kind of antlers.

"Elk," whispered Bess Dougharty, pointing at the antlers. "Use to be very plentiful in these parts."

Richards held both tools high over his head. "We think these are the types of tools stone-builders used for digging. I'd like two volunteers to do a thirty-minute timed dig with these to see how far they get."

Elise shrugged and raised her hand. So did a young college man from Cornell. Everyone else cheered and crowed around to watch as Elise held the antlers at their base and began to furiously claw at the ground. The Cornell man used the shovel to scoop up whatever she clawed loose.

Elise began to pant.

"Pace yourself," called Richards. "Twenty-seven minutes to go."

Eight minutes later they switched implements. Elise liked the shovel better. Let him kill himself scraping into rock-infested clay with dull elk antlers, she thought with a slight chuckle.

Her shoulders and back ached. Her arms felt like lead. She would have stopped, except all ninety volunteers still on the project had begun to chant, "Go! Go! Go! Go!"

Richards blew a whistle. "Time's up!" The crowd cheered. Elise dropped to the gummy dirt, gasping for breath. Mark Whitney leaned into their shallow hole with his tape and began to measure their progress. He scratched out numbers on his clipboard and consulted with Richards. Both men nodded enthusiastically. "Two diggers could easily dig even the biggest of the holes in two and one-half days ... Very doable."

A dozen people congratulated Elise and patted her on the back as she crawled out of the hole. O'Rorke bellowed that now anyone who wanted could help dig the hole with modern picks and shovels.

"As long as we're going modern," said Elise, "how about using a backhoe?"

The volunteers laughed and cheered.

Whitney constantly checked the width, shape and depth of the hole. "More in this corner ... Straighter over here ..."

When the hole was big enough, deep enough and properly sloped on one side, Whitney shifted the diggers to building a low, sloping dirt ramp that led up to the sloped side of the hole.

"To the ropes!" called O'Rorke with a wide smile. It was second nature now for the teams to space themselves along the four great ropes. "One ... two ... three ... Pull!" They dragged their mighty stone, still on its sled, up the ramp, so that one end dangled off the end of the ramp in midair over the hole.

Next they slid a pile of smaller rocks along the top of the giant rock past its center of gravity. The giant stone began to tip.

"Why are we doing this?" asked Elise.

"Leverage, love," said Bess. "The small stones will weigh down the bottom end of the monolith and flip it vertical without us having to lift it." Then she giggled. "Perfectly clever, I think."

"One … two … three … Pull!" One last pull did the trick. The end of the monolith swung down, crashing into the hole. The back end flipped up. The monolith now rested at a 70-degree angle along the hole's sloping side.

"It worked!" Whitney cried.

Everyone cheered.

The next day they used ropes and wooden wedges to raise it to vertical. It was no longer a mere slab of concrete to Elise. Now it felt like a great monument. It seemed to take on power and purpose.

A second cement slab was trucked in and raised next to the first with a crane. O'Rorke said that they didn't need to drag the second—they had already proved it was possible to do by hand.

The volunteers all cheered.

The next three days were spent building a long, sloping earth mound up to the side of the two monoliths to enable the volunteers to drag the lintel up to the top. (Actually, British safety officers made them use an elaborate metal scaffold system instead of a dirt mound like the ancient builders would have used. Each person had to *imagine* an ancient dirt mound.)

The next day was to be the final time the eighty remaining volunteers would pick up the ropes. It was their final chance to work with those who had become close friends.

Elise said, "This is the last time we'll ever hear 'One … two … three … Pull!'"

All the volunteers cheered, and then laughed as Mike O'Rorke turned an embarrassed beet-red.

There was a somber, sad feeling during final raising of the lintel. Everyone hated to see it end. For two weeks this trilithon had occupied their every waking minute.

With the lintel dragged into place and the scaffolding torn down, Richards and Whitney threw up their hands, yelling, "It's finished! We did it!"

The volunteers cheered and repeated, "We did it!"

Just then, the late afternoon Sun broke through the soggy overhead clouds. Golden rays lit up the trilithon. The stones sparkled and glowed. For just that brief moment, the trilithon looked magical, like something out of a fairy tale, like a gateway to the lands of enchantment and cosmic power.

To Elise, their long hours of sweat, strain and blisters now seemed like a mighty statement in stone that would survive for all time. Standing before their massive trilithon, she understood how the ancient builders must have felt—pride, wonder, reverence. Each volunteer shared a glorious sense that they had accomplished a miracle.

The next day, with the rain streaking car windows and dulling the ground, Elise packed for her return to the university classrooms and library studies. She left knowing that the magical place called Stonehenge had forever captured a part of her heart and her soul during the two greatest weeks of her life.

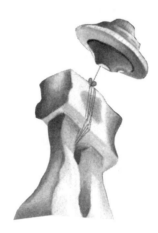

## About This Story

This story is true. The May 1995 effort to reconstruct one of the Stonehenge trilithons was well documented in a number of articles and was filmed for the NOVA series *Secrets of Lost Empires*. The characters and events are taken from the accounts of that effort. Most of the dialog between Bess and Elise has been inferred.

## The Science

Stonehenge is the most studied of all stone circle sites in the world. The first written research on Stonehenge dates from A.D. 1200. Detailed scholarly studies written in 1550 and 1630 are still available.

Extensive, modern archaeological, anthropological and engineering studies began at the site in the 1950s and continued through the mid-1990s. These studies have produced an excellent picture of the history, construction process and development of Stonehenge. That history is significantly different from the myth and legend surrounding Stonehenge.

A henge is a circular earthen enclosure with a bank and inner ditch. Stonehenge was probably so named because the famed circle of stones is surrounded by an outer, circular earthen ditch and bank. There is virtually no part of the British Isles that does not feature these earthen and stone circles.

Archaeologists have been able to carbon-date the various constructions at the Stonehenge site by excavating sample holes in and around the circles, by dating artifacts and by dating timbers and fossils. Simultaneously, anthropologists have pieced together a picture of the evolving local population— size, lifestyles, structure, organization, food sources and stresses. This picture has included social habits and changing beliefs.

Combining these studies creates the following best-guess history of Stonehenge: Almost five thousand years ago, probably in the spring, local farmers gathered at this spot with long sticks and ropes to map out a large circle in the ground. They dug a ditch along this circle and built up a smooth mound, or berm, along the inner bank. In this simple enclosure they conducted their ceremonies, festivals and celebrations (harvest, seasonal, religious, etc.). Some three to five hundred years later, a circular ring of fifty-six wooden posts was added to the site, just inside the ditch. There is some conjecture that the number of posts relates to the multiyear cycle of lunar eclipses. There is recent, independent evidence that the Moon was very important to the lives of this farmer population. But it has not been proved.

Around four thousand years ago, a wooden, oval structure with a thatched roof was built in the middle of the circle, slightly smaller than the current stone circle. It apparently was a ceremonial and religious building. But, again, there is no proof that it wasn't really a communal granary. About this same time, four small stones (just over 4 feet high above the ground) were placed between some of the existing wooden posts to form a perfect rectangle. The short sides of the rectangle point toward sunrise on the summer solstice. The long sides point to the spot on the horizon where the Moon rises during the full Moon closest to the summer solstice. Interestingly, Stonehenge is exactly on the one and only latitude in the Northern Hemisphere where these two sight lines cross at right angles.

Some claim that the stone-builders wouldn't have dragged giant sarsen stones 20 miles if they hadn't know this, and if astronomy hadn't been the primary purpose of the site. However, the site was first developed twenty-five hundred years before the great stone circle was constructed. The four "station" stones were erected fifteen hundred years before the stone circle. It is far more likely that the stone-builders dragged stones to Stonehenge because the site was already well established as an important religious and ceremonial site.

Between twenty-five and twenty-six hundred years ago, the giant stone circle was created during the height of the Stone Age (that period of early human history characterized by the predominance of stone tools). All traces of the wooden structure were apparently long gone by this time. Four hundred to five hundred years later, the horseshoe of five giant trilithons was added. The central axis of the trilithons points to sunrise on the summer solstice.

The period between 500 B.C. and A.D. 100 represented peak activity all across Europe for the builders of stone monuments. Several thousands of stone monuments were raised each century. Then, about A.D. 500, they stopped. The Stone Age ended and they built no more. Druid priests first arrived at Stonehenge around A.D. 1000, fifteen hundred years after the circle had been built.

Engineering studies have confirmed that Stone Age technology was sufficient to shape, move and erect even the largest of the Stonehenge stones. Stone Age tools and ropes were quite adequate for the task, and the effort would not have excessively burdened the community or destabilized the agrarian economy or social structure.

Anthropological studies have tried to discover why this simple farming society built the stone circles and why they stopped. One key to understanding Stonehenge's purpose has been a detailed study of burial mounds across Europe. Group burial mounds were massive and well constructed, and have endured far better than houses and barns from the period. This means that death and burial were important parts of communal activity.

Individual burial mounds for the wealthy and nobles first appear around 1000 B.C. The most elaborate, most extensive individual burial mounds in southern England (those of the wealthiest and most powerful people) are all clustered around Stonehenge. More than three hundred are dotted across the landscape within 2 miles of Stonehenge. The site was obviously an important religious center.

The theory that Stonehenge was built, expanded and maintained as a site of worship is supported by other studies of Stone Age Europe. The great stone circle and trilithons were a cathedral, a central and important place of worship for the region. This structure was built by a culture that habitually erected stone monuments and circles as part of their religious ceremonies.

Why did they build it? Why does any society build great cathedrals? The final evidence for Stonehenge being purely a center of worship comes from the archives of the Vatican. Between A.D. 600 and 1000, orders went out to northern bishops to have all stone circles torn down and the stones removed to prevent local populations from gathering there to worship. The circles were places of worship, not places for astronomical study or monumental calendars to mark astronomical dates.

Why did builders stop building? No one knows for sure. The Bronze and Iron Ages dawned as the Stone Age faded. The new metals gave people new weapons, new mobility (raids and warfare increased, creating a more uncertain life) and new tools. Agricultural systems improved. Farming expanded. Livestock herds grew. Life turned away from communal monuments. A true upper class emerged. With new nobility came a new serf class. Most people were demoted to subsistence living and to greatly increased labor just to survive. Society changed. Stone monuments lost their central role. Castles, forts and armies took center stage.

Of course, there are no written records from the period to confirm these theories, and there are those who disagree with this picture of Stonehenge. Some still claim that, above all, Stonehenge was a calendar and astronomical observatory. Although there is some evidence to suggest that the number of wood poles is linked to a lunar calendar, and that the original number of stones in the circle (fifty-nine) equals the number of days in two lunar months, there is no evidence to show that this is why those numbers of poles and stones were chosen. There are (and were) far easier ways to construct a more accurate calendar with far less labor and less room for error and misinterpretation.

Similarly, proponents claim that sight lines between various stones within the stone circle align with many important celestial sightings through the course of a year. However, critics say that, with so many stones to draw lines between, and with so many celestial sightings to choose from, they were bound to hit some by pure chance. There is no indication that celestial alignment played any part in the design and layout of the site. There are only 360 degrees in a circle. With more than eighty stones and markers to use for alignments, it would be almost impossible to not align with many celestial phenomena.

Whether or not there is any astronomical purpose in the arrangement of the Stonehenge stones, it is abundantly clear that the builders, simple farmers from an age of quiet communal life, were ingenious and talented engineers and excellent stonemasons. They crafted and set their stones with a precision that would not be surpassed in Europe for almost two thousand years. Their open-air stone cathedrals deserve as much respect and admiration as any of the great Middle Age cathedrals that dot the European landscape.

# Fact or Fiction?

Who built the circles at Stonehenge? Not Druids, not Romans, not aliens. Stonehenge was built by the Stone Age local culture that thrived for more than a thousand years across Europe.

Why did they build it? Was Stonehenge a mystical conduit for communicating with space? No. A place for channeling mystical energy? No. An advanced calendar? No. An astronomy lab? Partly. Possibly. The main entrance points toward sunrise on summer solstice. There is strong linkage between the Stonehenge design and the lunar calendar. Beyond that, there is virtually no evidence that the placement of the poles or stones were intended to line up with other astronomical events and dates marked and measured in the stone circles. Stonehenge was a place of worship, a temple, a sacred place, a mighty religious cathedral, the greatest and most majestic of its time in that region—just as cathedrals have been for European communities during the past thousand years. Stone circles were how that culture worshipped and celebrated.

Why was it built at that particular spot? Scientists will probably never know if there was a special significance to the site. Lunar and solar alignments are unique at that site, but there is no indication that the first builders on the site in 3000 B.C. used that fact in their selection. After the site was begun, later builders simply added on.

There seem to be few mysteries remaining at the Stonehenge site. Maybe it is time then to simply appreciate the effort, precision, grandeur and majesty of this ancient work of art and engineering.

# Follow-On Questions to Explore

1. Why do you think an ancient culture would go to all the trouble and bother to build something like Stonehenge? Why not relax and work on their own houses? Why not use that labor to stock up a better food store before winter? Why not build a library or a hospital? Why did they insist on building stone monuments?

   Have European cultures done the same thing since? What about African, Asian and other cultures? Do modern cultures still do it? What do we get out of building great stone monuments in public places? Towering medieval cathedrals in Europe, community and national monuments in Washington, D.C.—what purpose do they serve? Do you think they are a good idea?

2. Do you think there is value in collective, community efforts and struggles for a common project—any common project? Have you ever been a part of such a project? Do you know anyone who has? How did it make you/ them feel?

## Follow-On Activities

1. Design a stone monument of your own. What would its purpose be? What would you make it out of? What would it look like? Why? How would you build it? Where would you build it? Why? What would happen at this monument?

2. Write a letter describing an imagined one-day visit to Stonehenge. What did you do? What did it feel like? What was the weather like and how did that affect your visit? What would you want to take away from this one-day experience? What was your impression of the stones? Were they bigger or smaller than you thought they would be?

## References

Balfour, Michael. *Stonehenge and Its Mysteries.* New York: Scribner, 1980.

Branley, Franklin. *The Mystery of Stonehenge.* New York: Crowell, 1989.

Burl, Aubrey. *The Stone Circles of the British Isles.* New Haven, Conn.: Yale University Press, 1986.

Capt, Raymond. *Stonehenge and Druidism.* Thousand Oaks, Calif.: Artisan Sales, 1989.

Chippendale, Christopher. *Stonehenge Complete.* Ithica, N.Y.: Cornell University Press, 1983.

Fowles, John. *The Enigma of Stonehenge.* New York: Summit, 1980.

Lyon, Nancy. *The Mystery of Stonehenge.* New York: Raintree/Steck-Vaughn, 1997.

Mass, Wendy. *Stonehenge.* San Diego, Calif.: Lucent Books, 1998.

Page, Cynthia. *Secrets of Lost Empires: Stonehenge.* Boston: WGBH and NOVA, 1997. Videocassette.

Roop, Peter. *Stonehenge: Opposing Viewpoints.* San Diego, Calif.: Greenhaven, 1989.

Stover, Leon, and Bruce Kraig. *Stonehenge: The Indo-European Heritage.* Chicago: Nelson Hall, 1978.

Wernick, Robert. *The Monument Builders.* New York: Time-Life Books, 1993.

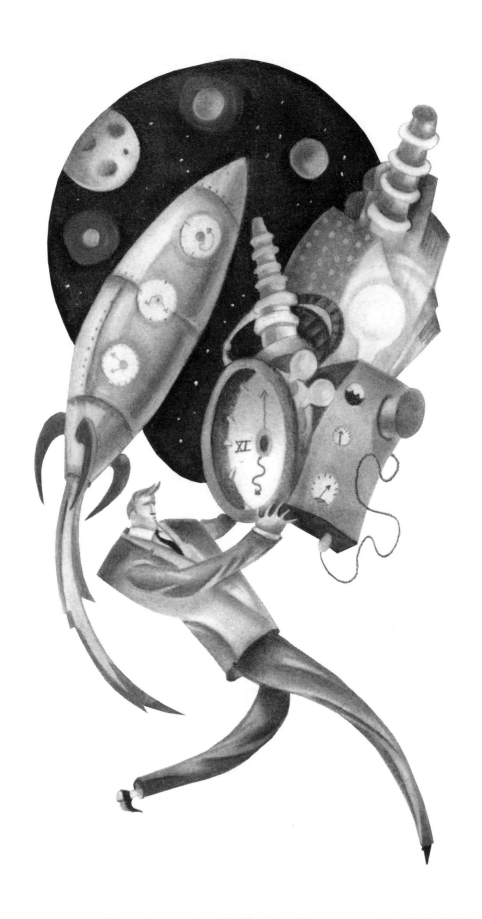

# Time Travel
## Science Fiction
## or Science Prediction?

## At a Glance

**M**any think that Albert Einstein started all serious talk about time travel when he showed in his theory of relativity that time could speed up and slow down. But H. G. Wells wrote his book *The Time Machine* when Einstein had barely turned sixteen. Actually, even ancient cultures used to dream about travel through time, the fourth dimension. Shamans and priests took herbs and drugs to induce trances they hoped would propel them beyond the time barrier into the past and future. What Einstein did was to draw serious scientists into the discussion of time travel, giving them mathematical equations and theoretical tools to use to visualize travel through time.

Time travel itself is not an oddity, a farfetched dream. It is the ordinary reality of your everyday life. We already do travel through time. We march through time in one direction, forward, all together, at the same uniform, linear rate—one hour per hour, one day per day. The real question is not: Can we travel through time? We already do and can't stop ourselves. The question is: Can we travel *at will* forward or backward to any point along the timeline? That is the great question.

There are, however, several problems created by freely bounding about into the future and past. First, time travel eliminates the past. The past is what happened before. If you can visit yesterday as easily as tomorrow, yesterday is no longer the past. It can be as much a part of your future as tomorrow is. Eliminating the concept of a past also eliminates history. If you can jump to 1776 tomorrow and argue the Pennsylvania delegates out of voting for the Declaration of Independence, no events can ever be completed and concluded. Everything is still ongoing in the present.

In the same way, time travel eliminates the future. If time travel is possible, all of time becomes one continuous blurred present—a continuously changing present as different people flip into the past and alter past events, which changes the timeline between that past and the present, which then changes the present itself. Time travel would seem to create unmanageable chaos in the present. That is a problem.

Second, time travel creates time paradoxes—impossible events. If I travel into the past and accidentally kill my grandfather before he meets my grandmother, I will never be born. But if I am never born, I can't travel back and kill my grandfather. I will have prevented my birth from happening after I was already born. That's impossible. It's a paradox. But time travel makes it appear to be possible, and that's a problem.

Without worrying about these bothersome glitches, time travel has been used in countless books, television shows and movies and seems to work just fine. In stories, of course, only one central character can perform time travel. But what if everybody could time-travel with no more effort or thought than we now expend for three-dimensional travel. Hop in a car or plane and go *where* you want. In the future, will it be just as easy to hop in a time car and zip to *when* we want, to any year of our choosing? Back to 1832 for breakfast and croquet, then forward to 2065 for lunch and an afternoon game of rocketball?

Is time travel possible? Is it desirable? Would it create total chaos or total freedom? These mysteries have tempted and tormented humankind for centuries.

# The Mystery: Time Travel

Rain clattered off the flat roofs of the row of low-grade, light-industrial, warehouse-type buildings streaked with rust and years of grime. They looked more like oversized storage sheds with roll-up corrugated metal garage-type doors than thriving businesses in Brisbane, California—north of both the San Francisco airport and the pulsing braintrust in Silicon Valley. In the middle of the row sat 138-C Brisbane Way, next door to an auto repair shop on one side and a garden-statue manufacturing shop on the other. The date was March 16, 1997, and a fierce spring storm was boiling low across the San Francisco Bay Area.

The interior of 138-C, however, looked more like a science fiction movie set than a grimy industrial shop. One corner looked like a substation for the electric company with stacks of finned metal power converters and ceramic capacitors with thick copper tubing snaking out of their tops. Tall banks of dazzling electronic equipment filled much of the remaining available space. Wave guides snaked along the ceiling, all of them eventually pointing toward a small, glass-enclosed chamber in the middle of the room.

James Milhouse, the thirty-one-year-old owner of all this equipment, hunched over the long table next to the door, tapping one foot, drumming his fingers on the tabletop, chomping hard on a wad of gum as he scanned the results of his latest test. Milhouse was a brilliant but high-strung physicist who seemed incapable of sitting still. He constantly paced, tapped and chewed on anything he could find—pencil, straw, swizzle stick, toothpick, gum, fingernail. Milhouse received his Ph.D. in theoretical physics from Princeton at age twenty-six and was hired by Stanford University to teach and conduct research that same year. He stood thin as a rail—probably from burning up so much nervous energy—and always wore a white lab coat.

He had rented this warehouse space to develop a time machine three years ago, when Stanford refused to give him adequate space or budget on-campus. Two years ago Stanford had fired him because he too often worked in the warehouse straight through the classes he had been assigned to teach.

Roland Gottland, a fifty-three-year-old venture capitalist whose parents had arrived in New York as penniless German immigrants in 1937, sat quietly in the lab's one chair watching Milhouse. Gottland had raised the money to back Milhouse's attempt to build a time machine. Chubby, with curly black hair and beard and a perpetual laugh, Gottland looked like a young Santa Clause.

"You're wasting your time, you know," Gottland said as he cracked open and ate his peanuts, dropping the shells on the floor. He had to raise his voice and repeat himself to be heard above the hum of Milhouse's equipment and the drumming rain on the roof. "You're wasting your time, James."

Milhouse answered without looking up. "Successful time travel will make me more famous than Bell and his telephone, than the Wright brothers and their airplane, than Fermi and his nuclear reactor! *And,* it will make *you* rich."

Gottland seemed as disappointed as a child who had just been told that Santa wasn't real. "I've just realized time travel will never work."

"Why not?"

"Because if it ever does work at some time in the future, a time traveler would have traveled back to our present. But no one has seen or met a time traveler. So, that means it will never work."

Milhouse shook the computer printout pages holding his latest test results as he replied. "You're wrong. I don't know why we haven't already seen a future time traveler. Maybe they pass laws against traveling back to tamper with the past. But I know the concept is correct. Einstein proved it was theoretically possible. And here I have proved that it can be made real."

"People at Stanford didn't think so when they fired you."

Milhouse snapped, "I was fired from Stanford because I refused to give the university the patent on my time machine and because the older professors were jealous of my genius and my discovery of a way to amplify the microscopic natural wormholes in quantum foam into a macro-sized wormhole!"

"That, and you kept missing classes you were supposed to teach."

Milhouse began to pace, having to carefully thread his way over snaking bundles of cables and between blocks of equipment. "My

work is too important. I couldn't stop for a bunch of whiny students."
He pointed at the mound of shells on the floor. "And sweep up that
mess. I don't want peanut shells ruining some piece of equipment."

Gottland scratched his head. "That's the fourth time I've heard
you mention quantum foam. What *is* it?"

"It's the answer!"

"But what *is* it?"

Milhouse hated to waste time explaining himself. It was why he
detested teaching. So he huffed loudly and wrinkled his face like he
was eating sour lemons before answering. "Between the subatomic
particles that make up the core nucleus of a proton or neutron there
exists a field of tiny bubbles called quantum foam."

"Has anyone ever seen this foam?" asked Gottland, stroking his
Santa Clause beard.

"It's too small to literally be seen. It would take trillions of billions of quantum foam bubbles to stretch across one proton. But we
can detect the foam, measure it and observe its effect on subatomic
particles. We *know* it exists. And some of the bubbles naturally form
handles we can detect, like on a teacup, that link different bubbles
together, forming microscopic wormholes."

"Wormholes?" repeated Gottland.

"Links between two points in space and time. If each end of a
wormhole is linked to a different moment in time, it becomes a time
machine."

Gottland's eyes narrowed. "That's subatomic quantum physics.
Will it work in the real world?"

Again Milhouse shook the printout pages. "It already has. My
last test was a success. I'm ready to attempt a major demonstration."

Gottland almost fell off his chair, a look of stunned disbelief on
his face. "Speak up. The rain is too loud, James. I misunderstood you.
I thought you said you had made this time machine work."

"I did, and it does."

Gottland bounded to his feet, his face beaming, his words tum-
bling out in a blur. "You built a real time machine? It's here? In all
this ... stuff?"

As if delivering a boring lecture he had presented a hundred
times, Milhouse said, "My time machine does four things. First, it

isolates and collects the quantum foam bubbles. Second, it combines and enlarges the quantum wormholes to useful size." He jabbed a thumb at the equipment piled in one corner. "Those panels and boxes create a controlled energy field to separate, link and amplify quantum foam micro-wormholes into a practical, working wormhole." His thumb jabbed at the power generators on a far wall. "Third, I must hold the wormhole open long enough to use it. That power grid and those sets of parallel metal plates create a reservoir of negative energy—"

"You mean like an electron?" Gottland interrupted.

"No, no. Negative energy is the energy of exotic matter—really, anti-matter. Negative energy, it turns out, is far more effective at holding a wormhole open than is positive energy."

Gottland rubbed his forehead. "Positive energy is energy from positive matter?"

"Exactly."

"And what's the fourth thing a time machine must do?"

Milhouse shrugged. "Link each end of the wormhole with a different time, of course."

"But ... but, how?" Gottland stammered.

Milhouse began to explain. "I use one of Stanford's accelerators to—"

"You just carry the wormhole down to Stanford in a cardboard box?" interrupted Gottland.

Milhouse smiled momentarily. "I carry only one end of the wormhole, in a portable energy field."

"You can do that?"

"The two ends of a wormhole are amazingly independent of each other."

"Remarkable," Gottland whispered.

"At Stanford, I accelerated one end of my wormhole to 0.99999 times the speed of light for twenty-five hours."

"Why accelerate the wormhole? We want to keep it right here so we can jump through it to see a dinosaur!"

"Time slows as you near light-speed." Milhouse answered as if he were explaining simple arithmetic to an ignorant child. "By accelerating one end of the wormhole, I shift that end to a new time reference so that the two ends link with different moments in time. The accelerated end is now one day behind of the other end. Hence, the wormhole becomes a time machine."

"That sounds like double-talk," Gottland muttered. "But will it work? Can we transport into the past?"

Milhouse forced his most gracious smile, which still looked more like a sneer. "I asked you to come today to witness my grand demonstration. Today I move the world into the era of time travel."

Gottland clapped his thick hands like a six-year-old on Christmas morning. "How? What will you transport? To when?"

Smug satisfaction spread across Milhouse's face as he pointed at an empty table inside a glass chamber in the middle of the room. "At precisely noon tomorrow, I will place a bunch of flowers on that table, where they will enter one end of my wormhole. When the flowers arrive at the other end, they will have traveled back in time twenty-four hours to today—that is, they will arrive here, on the same table, at exactly noon today."

Gottland's heart pounded and his hands fumbled with excitement as he dragged out his pocket watch. "Noon today ... Noon today. Egad! That's in two minutes!"

"I know," answered Milhouse as he began to pace and drum his fingers on the long worktable.

Seconds lay like a heavy, wet blanket over the room as time marched toward noon. Gottland stared, transfixed, at the table in the glass chamber, holding his watch in front of him so that he could observe it as well. Suddenly he sucked in his breath and stiffened as a faint, radiant glow bathed the glass chamber. His lips moved, "Five ... four ... three ... two ... one ..."

There was no explosion, no clap of thunder—as if Milhouse's wormhole had broken the sound barrier. Suddenly, a vase of seasonal flowers sat on the table. It felt to Gottland that he had blinked and missed the frame when the flowers arrived. Suddenly they were just there.

Milhouse smiled and shrugged as he unlatched the glass chamber. "The flowers have successfully traveled through the wormhole. I guess tomorrow my time machine will work."

Gottland stretched out his fingers to touch the bright petals. His hands shook as if he were touching the world's most precious gem. "These are really from the future?"

"The flowers already exist in some garden," said Milhouse. "But they won't be cut, wrapped and trucked to the corner store until tomorrow morning. I won't buy them until tomorrow and I won't place them on that table for time transport until late tomorrow morning."

Gottland couldn't rip his eyes away from the flowers. It felt like looking at aliens, at ghosts, at magic, at something that violated the natural laws that governed the world.

Milhouse pulled a bottle of champagne from a small refrigerator. "I think this calls for a toast!"

The next morning at 8:15 A.M., James Milhouse stood waiting outside the corner flower shop. It was late in opening. A slight, dark-haired woman finally unlocked the door. "I know. I'm late this morning. But ..." Milhouse ignored her and rushed into the shop. "A large bouquet of seasonal flowers! Quick!"

The woman apologized. "I'm so sorry. The truck is damaged and the flowers will not arrive until lunchtime."

"What? I have to have those flowers now!"

She shrugged. "No truck, no flowers."

Milhouse tore down the alley to his shop and raced inside. There the flowers sat on the worktable, looking very much like ordinary flowers. He began to wonder what would happen if the truck didn't arrive and he couldn't send the flowers. What would happen to the flowers that arrived yesterday if he was unable to send them today?

"Time paradox," he began to mutter as he chewed on a handy pencil. Then he sucked in a deep breath to calm himself. "Don't panic," Milhouse muttered. "There's still plenty of time."

He clicked on the master circuit breakers and punched on the power grid and other banks of equipment. Their familiar hum filled the room. Then silence. A circuit breaker had kicked off. Milhouse shoved it back on. With an electric flash, it shut off.

A short! This could take hours to find. He didn't have hours! Panic began to creep into James Milhouse's thoughts and movements.

Damp, sticky perspiration began to sheen across his forehead. He raced from bank to bank testing his equipment with a meter.

At 9:45 A.M. Roland Gottland arrived and instantly sensed the fear of a trapped animal. Sweat now dripped off Milhouse's nose.

Milhouse screamed, "Help me find the short!" and tossed a second meter to Gottland. "Start over there!"

At 10:15 A.M. they isolated the problem in a power converter box. "I'll have to replace it. There's an electronics store two blocks over," called Milhouse as he dashed out to his car.

At 10:50 A.M. Milhouse was back, frantically stripping wires out of the old converter, loosening screws and dragging the converter out of its rack. By 11:20 A.M. the new converter had been installed and tested. Milhouse shoved the circuit breaker back on. Indicator lights on the rows of equipment blinked to green. The hum of motors filled the room. The breakers held.

"I'll be back in five minutes with the flowers. Unclamp the latches on the glass housing," called Milhouse as he sped back out the door.

"Sorry," apologized the owner of the flower shop. "The truck still isn't here yet."

"What?!" screamed Milhouse. "I need those flowers!"

"The driver just called," she said. "He'll be here in five minutes, if you'd like to wait."

"Five minutes?" Milhouse slammed his palms against his thighs and began to pace the small shop like a caged animal.

At 11:33 A.M. they heard the squeal of the delivery truck's brakes. Milhouse raced out the door. "I need flowers!"

The driver unfolded himself from his seat. He was a tall, thick man. "First I got to inventory the bunches with the owner. Then she's got to sign for them. Next we got to display—"

"You don't understand!" screamed Milhouse. "I can't have gotten flowers yesterday if I don't send them today!"

Both the driver and the owner of the flower shop gazed at Milhouse as if he had lost his mind.

"Never mind. I need seasonal flowers NOW!" He threw open the back of the truck, snatched a bunch still dripping from their tub of water and threw a twenty-dollar bill at the owner of the flower shop. "Keep the change!"

His car hit 60 miles per hour in the two blocks of industrial alleyways between the flower shop and 138-C Brisbane Way. Inside, Milhouse stuffed the flowers into the vase he had bought for the occasion and slid them onto the table. He slammed the glass chamber closed and clicked the latches.

11:46 A.M.: Milhouse paused to catch his breath. He had done it. He only needed five minutes to check the calibration on each of the units and three more to power up the electric energy grid. He had six minutes to spare.

11:53 A.M.: All systems checked, synchronized and calibrated. Gottland's heart raced as it had the day before. History was about to be made. Would the flowers disappear as quietly as they had appeared yesterday? Would there be some cosmic thunderbolt as they finally broke the time barrier? Milhouse slowly turned the two big knobs that powered up the electric grid.

11:54 A.M.: One of the power units began to crackle and smoke. Sparks, first like sparklers, then like gushing Roman candles, sprayed from the unit. Gottland grabbed a fire extinguisher and blasted the smoking black box. A circuit breaker clicked off and the room was plunged into blackness. Milhouse screamed in frustration. He stumbled along one wall and clicked on the emergency lighting. The lab was bathed in a greenish glow. Flashlight in hand, Milhouse assessed the damage. "That's only a backup unit. We can bypass it and rely on just the primary. Help me disconnect it and rewire the relays!"

11:58 A.M.: Loose wires dangled like tangled spaghetti across the front of the rack where the faulty equipment had been. Milhouse sucked in a deep breath and clicked on the main circuit breaker. The main overhead lights blinked on. The equipment hummed to life. The breaker held. Milhouse cranked the power knobs on the electric grid to full.

11:59 A.M.: "Come on!" Milhouse ordered. "Sixty percent of full charge … Seventy percent … Faster, please! reach full power in time!" Gottland sat in shock, staring through the smoky haze left from the electrical fire.

The lab's atomic clock gonged 12:00 noon. "Eighty-five percent power. It'll have to do. I'm firing!" called Milhouse. His hand reached for the red knob that fired the wormhole into action. A thin, blue lightning bolt arced across the electric grid's capacitors with an eerie hiss. The breakers clicked off. The room sputtered back into darkness.

Milhouse stood frozen in disbelief; his hand still poised over the red knob. His voice was a mere whisper. "I didn't do it ..."

Gottland switched on the emergency lighting and unlatched the glass chamber, his head cocked quizzically to one side. "Hey, James. You bought the wrong bunch of flowers."

Milhouse's mind was still a confused jumble. "What?"

"This is not the same bunch of flowers as the ones that arrived yesterday!"

"How can that be?" Milhouse stammered, now noticing the differences in the mix of flowers in the two bunches.

"How can *any* of it be?" added Gottland. "You never transported anything back through the wormhole. So how could *any* flowers have arrived yesterday?"

Milhouse began to laugh with a flash of understanding. "Not today, I didn't. But *sometime* I'm going to buy that bunch of flowers and transport it back to yesterday to prove to myself that it works!" He glared at Gottland. "It will work! You were there yesterday. It already has worked!"

Gottland shook his head. "But how much longer must I coax the investors into supporting your work? I can't show them a bunch of ordinary flowers and expect them to hand over more money. And how much more is your time travel going to cost?"

Milhouse didn't bother to respond. He was already inspecting the scorched junctions in the electric grid and dreaming of the modifications he would install to bring him one step closer to sending himself a simple bunch of flowers.

As of December 1999, Milhouse still has not successfully sent his flowers back to March 16, 1997. But he continues to try.

# About This Story

The science in this story is real and has been tested at a subatomic level. No one, however, has been able to successfully amplify the natural micro-worm-holes in quantum foam into a practical time machine. The methodology to do so is described in detail in the scientific literature, as are the systems that would be needed to do it.

But this methodology has not yet been successfully scaled up to allow for practical use. In order to portray what it might be like to go that one critical step beyond science's current accomplishments—to imagine how even the most preliminary and rudimentary attempts at time travel might work—the story had to be fictionalized. Although the story is based on available state-of-the-art information (taken to the next logical step—a step science might well accomplish in the near future), the actual events of this story and the main characters are fictional. The person and personality of Milhouse have been drawn from a composite of the several researchers who were interviewed to gain a better understanding of the mind-boggling science of wormholes.

# The Science

Einstein's theory of relativity showed that time was variable. As an object speeds up, time slows down. The effect has been measured by placing an atomic clock on an airplane in London and flying it across the Atlantic Ocean at 500 miles per hour. The clock arrived in Washington reading a tiny fraction of a second behind clocks on the ground. Why? As the plane (and the clock) sped up, their time slowed down, so less time elapsed for them than for stationary clocks on the ground.

If a person lived for exactly eighty years and lived their whole life on a jet plane circling the globe at 500 miles per hour, they would live a full minute longer than someone who lived exactly eighty years on the ground at sea level. Admittedly, the effect is tiny at such slow speeds. But if the plane could fly at 0.99999 times the speed of light for eighty years, thousands of years would have elapsed on the ground by the time the plane landed. In effect, the plane would have been thrown far into the future.

Scientists knew that this sort of forward time travel was mathematically, theoretically possible. But no one paid much attention because there was no way to accelerate anything to near light-speed. Then, in the 1960s, black holes became a reality. Some theorists began to wonder if a traveler would be accelerated to near light-speed and jump into some other time if they flew into a black hole.

Still, black holes and time travel were little more than an oddity, because scientists couldn't study, let alone reach, a black hole, and they couldn't create or simulate that powerful a gravitational field on Earth to conduct laboratory studies. Worse, the notion of time travel as a serious scientific topic was badly muddied because many claimed to have magically traveled through time. It seemed that every few years someone claimed to have just visited Catherine the Great, or to have had dinner on Atlantis, or to have spent the weekend in seventeenth-century England. None of the reported incidents could be authenticated, and the vast majority were easily shown to be pure hoaxes.

So the scientific notion of time travel sat on the back burner until the early 1980s, when two of the world's greatest theoretical physicists—Stephen Hawking and Kip Thorn—and one of the world's greatest science writers—Carl Sagan—collaborated to see if they could create a plausible time-travel scheme for a book, *First Contact,* that Sagan was writing. What emerged from this study were three possible theories, or schemes, for how time travel could work. All were based on Einstein's Special Theory of Relativity.

First, a spaceship could skim along the edge of the intense gravity well of a black hole. The immense gravitational forces would accelerate the ship to near light-speed. At 0.999 times the speed of light, time slows to one seventy-fourth of what it is for a stationary observer. (Travel for one month at 0.999 times the speed of light, returning to the spot of departure, and you will have jumped more than six years into the future. One month's travel at 0.99999 times the speed of light would throw you 150 years forward in time.)

This scheme only allows for forward time travel and comes with a built-in problem that eventually ruled it out as a practical possibility. Einstein's relativity equations showed that, as speed increases toward light-speed, time slows but mass increases. A 1-pound weight accelerated to 0.999 times the speed of light would weigh 100 pounds! By the time a spaceship approached the speed of light, it would weigh so much that it couldn't carry enough fuel to keep itself going.

For the second scheme, Einstein's equations appeared to allow a traveler to compress and expand, or warp, space. This could lead both to faster-than-light travel and, possibly, to forward time travel. Einstein said it was theoretically possible, but no one has been able to even conceive of how it could be done.

The third scheme required the creation of a wormhole. Once scientists began to study the notion of wormholes in the 1980s, they realized that wormholes were the logical, practical answer to time travel. It suddenly appeared likely that natural wormholes already exist, scattered throughout our universe. Naturally occurring, random wormholes could explain most of the well-documented claims of time-slips (temporary, accidental time travel), for which there seems to be no explanation other than that someone magically flipped back in time for a brief period.

There are forty to fifty recorded time-slips that seem totally legitimate. But the notion of jumping backward or forward in time seems so fantastic that scientists had—until wormholes came along—simply refused to believe it was possible. But if wormholes exist, and if a person accidentally stepped into an invisible, naturally occurring, mini-wormhole, they could easily slip back several hundred years for the weekend. Scientists still don't know how to detect a wormhole, but it is theoretically plausible that most unexplained claims of time travel are really cases showing the effects of wormholes. The problem is that no one has actually seen a wormhole. Scientists suspect that they could be created by the intense forces of a black hole. But that is still pure theory.

In the late 1980s, a fourth theory emerged. Einstein theorized that a black hole (something that sucks everything in) might be coupled to a white hole (something that spews everything back out). The black hole–white hole combination could instantly flip someone across space and time. Time travel and warp drive all rolled into one.

Frank Tipler at the University of Maryland then discovered that a rotating singularity (a kind of a black hole–like object called a pulsar) seemed to form a wormhole-like tunnel through the fabric of space and time. Astronomers have found a number of pulsars in space. Could these be models for how to build a working wormhole time machine?

These theories by serious scientists began an instant debate. Many argued against the possibility of time travel using three general concepts. First, although time travel may be theoretically possible, it would require materials that don't exist and that have never existed, and would require more energy than our Sun will produce over the rest of its lifetime. (Proponents countered, saying, "Give us a few decades and maybe we will create the materials and reduce the energy requirements.")

Second, opponents argued that, if backward time travel were ever to become possible, we would have met time travelers who came back to visit our time. They haven't, which means backward time travel through wormholes never works. Proponents countered that such was not necessarily the case at all. If future generations have the technology for time travel, they may also have personal cloaking devices and be good at covering their tracks.

Third, opponents said that backward time travel opened the door to unthinkable time paradoxes that nature tends not to permit. So nature prevents time travel from happening—somehow. Proponents scoffed that nature could not stand in the way of Einstein's relativity equations. Then, in the 1990s, Kip Thorn and Stephen Hawking began developing a theory called quantum gravity, an attempt to bridge the great chasm between Einstein's relativity theory (which deals with the endless space of the universe) and quantum mechanics (which deals with the infinitesimal spaces inside subatomic particles).

Even though they helped to launch the time-travel debate, Thorn and Hawking now say that, when quantum gravity theory is completed, it will probably indicate that the opponents of time travel were right. Nature will not allow backward travel through a wormhole. Rather, natural forces will cause the wormhole to explode before it can be used. Still, their results are very sketchy and very preliminary.

The final wrinkle in the time-travel debate has arisen recently with the theory of parallel universes. This theory says that wormhole time travel will be possible because the backward end of the wormhole will not connect to our universe, but to a parallel universe, one exactly like ours. When a time traveler affects history in a parallel universe, the time traveler, and the time traveler's origins, wouldn't be affected, because the action would take place in that other universe. The parallel universe theory holds that there must be billions of parallel universes, some almost identical, but some radically different because of ancient past events that happened differently in each universe.

Opponents vehemently object. There is no evidence to support the existence of other, parallel universes, and there isn't enough matter to make up the ever-expanding number of universes. Still, the debate rages on—and will continue until black holes, wormholes and pulsars are visited, studied and tested.

# Fact or Fiction?

The verdict is still out on two counts related to time travel. First: Has it already happened? Are there naturally occurring mini-wormholes that have caused people to experience temporary time-slips into the past or future? Scientists are generally very skeptical of this possibility, but can't know for sure until they are able to create and study a wormhole. The best-guess answer is, yes, wormholes could account for the few, well-documented cases of inadvertent time-slips, but only if scientists were able to make a wormhole act as a time conduit to other points in time. But that is still only speculation.

Second (the big question): Can humans move in a controlled manner at will through time? The keys are pulsars and wormholes. The best current guess is that, yes, at some time we will be able to intentionally move through time—at least forward in time—by accelerating to near light-speed. Moving backward in time using wormholes is another, more difficult, matter. The best current guess is that backward time travel will not, cannot, ever happen. But scientists also once said this about breaking the sound barrier and about heavier-than-air flight.

It is likely that time machines will never become an ordinary household appliance like a car. They require far too much energy. Still, give humanity a century or two to understand black holes and pulsars better, then we'll see. Do all times exist simultaneously at every spot? Will walking from time to time be as easy as stepping from room to room—once we learn how to do it? At the dawn of a new millennium, time travel has moved out of science fiction and into mainstream science and has become a more tantalizing and frustrating mystery than ever.

## Follow-On Questions to Explore

1. If you could travel in time, where and when would you go? Why? What would you do? Would you want to change anything? What could that do to the timeline and your present?

2. If time travel were possible, and you were in charge, what rules would you create to control it? What would you worry about? Why? How would you control ordinary people's use of time travel? What is the worst thing that could happen if someone traveled back in time?

## Follow-On Activities

1. Pretend that time travel is possible and that it is controlled by a government agency. Write a time-travel request justifying your choice of time destination and the action you would perform. To what year would you go? Why? What would you do? How long would you stay? Be sure to

describe the benefits of your trip and the consequences of your proposed actions for the rest of the timeline between that past and the present.

# References

Finney, Jack. *About Time.* New York: Scribner, 1986. (excellent fictional stories of time-slips and time travel)

———. *Time and Again.* New York: Scribner, 1982. (excellent fictional stories of time-slips and time travel)

Hawking, Stephen. *A Brief History of Time.* New York: Bantam Books, 1990.

Krauss, Lawrence. *Beyond Star Trek.* New York: HarperCollins, 1997.

MacVey, John. *Time Travel.* Chelsea, Mich.: Scarborough House, 1993.

McMaster, Joseph. *Time Travel.* Boston: WGBH and NOVA, 1999. Videocassette.

Pickover, Clifford. *Time: A Travelers Guide.* New York: Oxford University Press, 1998.

Rucker, Rudy. *The 4th Dimension.* Boston: Houghton Mifflin, 1984.

Thorn, Kip. *Black Holes and Time Warps.* New York: W. W. Norton, 1994.

———. "Wormholes, Time Machines, and the Weak Energy Condition." *Astrophysical Journal* 61, no. 13 (September 1986): 122–128.

White, Michael. *Weird Science.* New York: Avon Books, 1999.

# UFOs
## Eager Hope or Foolish Fear?

## At a Glance

We humans have always been fascinated by the heavens—countless washes of stars in countless galaxies sprayed over countless millions of light-years. Compared to that, we are but tiny specks on one tiny planet circling one mediocre star near the edge of one average galaxy. We are forced to wonder: Are we alone? Is anyone else out there?

Human eyes seem to turn forever skyward. We are fascinated by things that soar through the heavens: comets, meteors, stars, birds, clouds and planes. But we are especially fascinated by the things we can't identify: UFOs (unidentified flying objects), often called flying saucers. The term *flying saucer* was coined on June 24, 1947, when businessman Kenneth Arnold flew his plane across western Washington and observed a formation of flying objects he said looked like saucers. The term *UFO* was created by the Air Force the next year to describe the mass of reported sightings.

In the second century B.C., reports of strange flying disks and wheels in the sky were recorded in Egypt and Greece. The Indian poem *Mahabharata*, written twenty-five hundred years ago, describes "a blazing missile of smokeless fire and radiant light that crossed the sky with scorching heat." Ancient rock pictographs show what looks like men in modern space suits. The Nazca Plain in Peru is laid out with huge drawings created centuries ago that can only be seen from the sky and whose lines look like a modern landing strip.

In biblical times, people called them glowing disks and giant wheels in the sky. In A.D. 1290, English monks wrote of "a large, round, silver disk that flew slowly over them." Woodcarvings from the 1500s show rocketlike objects soaring across the sky with smoke and fire trailing behind them.

All of these independent depictions and descriptions feature some basic similarities: the object is always spherical or cigar-shaped, and is always shiny, bright and glowing. Modern UFO sightings include the same elements. UFOs have been sighted in every part of the globe. More than a hundred thousand sightings have been reported!

After movies like *Close Encounters of the Third Kind* and *ET*, it's hard to remember that extraterrestrials are still the stuff of fiction, and that the term *UFO* does not mean "alien spaceship." The title *UFO* only means that that something is flying in the sky and that it cannot be immediately identified by the observer. Classifying something as a UFO doesn't say what it is. It only says that the observer can't tell what it is. If a flying object were identified as an alien spacecraft, it wouldn't be a UFO. It would have been identified.

That brings up a problem. For many, asking whether there are UFOs is synonymous with asking whether there are extraterrestrial advanced beings who visit Earth. However, the two questions are not the same. Aliens could visit without driving their ships through the lower atmosphere to be spotted and identified as UFOs. In *Star Trek* people beam down to planets from high orbits out in space. If such a ship came here, it would never be seen and, so, would never be labeled as a UFO. On the other hand, an object cruising through the atmosphere doesn't have to be an intelligent alien being to be unidentified, or unidentifiable, when it flies past an observer. It simply has to be an object which flies and cannot be concretely identified by a human observer.

We want to ask: Where did UFOs come from? Why are they here? What do they want? But first, we must wonder with both eager hope and dread: Do they really exist? Are there really UFOs buzzing about our planet? More precisely, we should ask: Can rational, scientific explanations of known phenomena account for the reported UFO observations?

If the answer is yes—that is, science can explain all the UFO sightings—then we can say that there are no UFOs, and we can begin searching for extraterrestrial life in other ways. But if the answer is no—that is, science can't explain all the UFO sightings—then UFOs truly are a mystery worthy of our best scientific attention.

# The Mystery: UFOs

The night shift goes on duty at 11:00 P.M. at the Trumble County emergency dispatch center. As she usually did, Roy Anne Rudolf brought several magazines to read during the slow early-morning hours of her shift. She checked in and eased into her chair at her wraparound console on the evening of September 28, 1994. Trumble County is a quiet, rural county north of Youngstown, Ohio, a sleepy collection of small farm towns where nothing more exciting than the weather ever seemed to happen.

Roy Anne scanned the dispatch logs for the evening shift, just going off-duty—a couple of routine, minor calls. Nothing exciting or out of the ordinary. It looked likely to be a typical, quiet night. Roy Anne liked the night shift. It gave her time to read.

Shortly after midnight, the first of the calls flashed on Roy Anne's board. A woman was screaming that strange lights were flying over her house. Roy Anne took the report while she rolled her eyes and told the woman it was probably a plane and to go back to bed.

Even before she hung up, the next call blinked onto her board. A man very casually and calmly wanted to report that strange lights were drifting overhead. They seemed to change colors and to be flying low along Sampson Drive. Roy Anne thanked him for the call and concluded it was either an elaborate prank or some sort of weather balloon.

By 12:10 A.M. she had fielded eleven calls—some hysterical, some curious, all describing intensely bright lights that seemed to be drifting or flying along, or near, Sampson Drive.

Roy Anne decided it had turned from a crank call or two into either mass hysteria … or something odd buzzing the Sampson Drive area. A prickle of fear edged down her spine. This didn't sound like a prank, and it didn't sound normal for quiet Trumble County.

She called car 914 to investigate.

Car 914 was driven by eight-year veteran Sergeant Toby Melora, a practical, no-nonsense cop with curly black hair and a warm, small-town smile. He and two other officers were in a local donut shop on a coffee break when Roy Anne called.

All three officers laughed when they heard her call.

"Is this a joke, Roy Anne?" Toby asked over his portable radio.

"No joke. I have multiple calls."

"Of lights?"

"Bright lights."

"Slowly flying down Sampson Drive?"

"That's what they all tell me."

Toby Melora shrugged at his two friends. "Guess I better investigate lights on Sampson Drive." He fixed his nightstick back into his belt and, with a final shake of his head, stepped outside to the car.

Near the top of Sampson Drive, Toby met an old man wandering dazed and disoriented and leading a dog by a leash. The dog's tail dragged between its legs and its body trembled as if it were mortally terrified. The man ranted about strange lights that had flown over his house and tried to suck him up.

Toby felt the same creeping pangs of dread that Roy Anne had felt. He proceeded cautiously, red and blue lights flashing, wearily scanning the sky.

He saw nothing out of the ordinary—until, rounding a gentle curve across the top of a slight rise in the road, everything electronic in his car blinked out. The radio, the lights, the engine—they all stopped.

There followed a long single second of deathly dark and silence. Then a light, brighter than a hundred spotlights, snapped on directly above his car. Toby fumbled with the door handle in his rush to get out, and stepped into a flood of light far brighter than daylight.

Toby blinked into an intense white light above him, struggling to survive its intensity, awed by its immense size. Slowly his cop's mind became aware of three things: First, there was a ring of small, red lights surrounding the giant white one. Second, there was no sound—no sound at all. Whatever it was, it hovered silently. Third, whatever it was, it hovered *directly* above him, watching him, studying him.

Yet Sergeant Toby Melora couldn't do anything except blink into the blinding light, shading his eyes with one hand, while his mind frantically spun trying to understand what was happening.

For ten seconds, twenty seconds, thirty seconds—it seemed a lifetime—the light hovered, slowly spinning, in total silence above him, seemingly close enough that he could jump up and touch it.

Then it moved off to the northeast across trees and fields, wandering leisurely on its path of exploration.

Instantly Toby's car started back up—all on its own. The lights clicked on. The chatter of police banter returned to the radio.

Toby shook off the stunned immobility left by his encounter. He had seen … something, something he had never encountered before, something he had never heard of before, something out of the ordinary and potentially dangerous. He was a cop and it was his duty to find out what it was.

He bounded into the car and stomped on the gas to pursue the lights as closely as the roads would allow. Gravel kicked up behind his tires as he roared down Sampson Drive, siren wailing.

As he drove, hunched forward over the wheel to keep the flying lights in view, Toby grabbed his radio mike. "Nine-fourteen to dispatch."

With a static hiss, Roy Anne's voice came back to him through the speaker. "Go ahead nine-fourteen. You find out about my lights, Toby?"

Toby sucked in a deep breath to keep his voice from trembling. "Roy, I saw something … a huge light with a red glow."

There was a short pause before Roy Anne answered. "Toby, you're scaring me. What is it?"

"It's … huge. Easily a hundred feet across. And so bright. Wait. The lights are changing colors."

"The lights change colors?"

"Red and then blue … It's—I don't know—it's something BIG! Heading up toward Brookfield."

Roy Anne began to sweat in her dispatch chair. Suddenly it felt like she was in the middle of a science fiction movie. She started to put out a general call for assistance. But there was no need. Other officers had been listening. Three had already spotted the lights. More than a dozen cars were converging on the area, sirens wailing.

Roy Anne found she was too shaken to calm and comfort the flood of callers who continued to pour in their panicked reports. All she could say was that they were aware of the lights and that officers were in pursuit. Sometimes callers were satisfied and hung up. Sometimes they asked what the lights were. Roy Anne gulped and lied that she didn't know. But in her heart, she felt dead-on certain about what those lights were.

Every dispatcher in the center hovered around Roy Anne's station, staring at the speakers that carried the police radio traffic. Fourteen officers from four precincts had now reported seeing the lights. It sounded to Roy Anne like a chase scene from a horror movie.

"I've got it, south of old 82 now, moving east."

"Roger. I'm just north of it. It's changing colors again. Going to yellow."

"Looks like it's heading toward Liberty. Can anyone intercept it before it reaches town?"

"Can we set up a blockade?"

"I got binoculars on it. I see a saucer and dome-shaped structure above the lights ... And now I see a parachute-like appendage hanging below."

"Has anybody notified the Air Force or the Army?"

Roy Anne's fingers trembled as she dialed the Youngstown airport tower. She identified herself and asked if their radar picked up anything flying low over Trumble County.

"Nothing shows on radar," was the answer.

"Are you sure?" Roy Anne pressed. "Nothing *anywhere* over Trumble County, say up near Brookfield or Liberty?"

"Lady, there's nothing flying within 60 miles of Youngstown."

An icy stab of fear jabbed at Roy Anne's stomach. She had twenty officers seeing, watching, chasing, ready to shoot at something that didn't show up on radar.

Lieutenant James Baker of the Brookfield Township police had been listening to the radio reports in his duty office. He decided he had to see this thing for himself. He dashed out of the police station and raced a squad car to the old radar tower just outside Brookfield. At 70 feet tall, it was the highest structure in the county.

Panting and beginning to sweat, he pounded up the rusting iron stairs that wound around the legs of the Erector Set–like tower. When he reached the tower platform, he was glad there was a railing to hold onto. Lieutenant Baker could clearly see the lights less than 2 miles from his position. But there wasn't one set of lights. There were three.

His knees wobbled as he grabbed the rust-covered railing and stared. The three sets of lights formed an upside-down V, with one set being positioned above and between the other two. The reports were true. The lights *did* shift colors—in unison—from red to yellow to green to blue. As the formation of lights drifted over the county landscape, the lights in every house, at every intersection, in every barn and store below them blinked out until after the lights had passed.

Lieutenant Baker radioed in his report. Roy Anne asked him, "But what *is* it, Lieutenant?"

Lieutenant Baker's reply was, "Please let it be a plane. Oh please, oh please, be a plane."

But as he said the words, the three sets of lights split apart, each choosing a different vector as they streaked into the heavens. Behind them, the mysterious lights left a dozen police cars with lights flashing and sirens blaring, and twenty police officers staring into an empty sky.

## About This Story

This story is true. The characters and events were all recorded on the police dispatch logs. Much of the dialog was also taken from actual police records. Those records were sufficiently complete and detailed that there was very little left to infer and create in order to present a complete story.

## The Science

Most scientists dismiss UFOs as pointless fiction, as a silly attempt to prove extraterrestrial life and as mass hysteria. Worse, many dismiss UFOs as pure hoaxes, as a long series of frauds not worthy of any consideration.

Those scientists who have divorced UFOs from any consideration of extraterrestrials, focused instead solely on a systematic study of UFO sightings, fall into two opposing camps. In one camp are those hard-line skeptics who insist that there are no UFOs and that every sighting that is not a hoax is the result of honest ignorance and mistake by an untrained observer. Known natural phenomena, these scientists claim, explain all legitimate sightings.

The other camp agrees that there are many fakes and hoaxes and that most of the remaining UFO sightings can be reasonably explained by known natural phenomena. However, this group contends, there remains a group of more than a hundred sightings that defy all rational explanation and therefore deserve serious, rigorous study. Most in this camp contend that—although nothing can be concluded until complete studies are conducted—this body of UFO sightings seems to imply the existence of intelligent beings of unknown origin who possess technology significantly more advanced than our own.

Which camp is more believable? Although thousands of sightings have been studied and debated, it will be useful to quickly review a few of those incidents in detail. The 1994 Trumble County sighting is an excellent place to start, as neither camp will budge in its assertions. Both claim to have the more convincing evidence.

Skeptics claim that Sergeant Melora saw either a weather balloon or an exceptionally bright meteor. That it never showed up on radar is proof, they say, that it wasn't a metallic-structured craft. After the initial report, other officers, expecting to see a UFO, mistook either Venus or a bright star low in the sky as moving lights. Several known atmospheric phenomena can cause low, bright stars to shift colors and appear to move. The steadily shifting colors are a tip-off that the officers were watching a star badly distorted by unique atmospheric conditions.

The other camp says this theory is ridiculous. The lights were seen from too many angles by too many observers to possibly be mistaken for a planet or star. Investigations have shown that there were no weather balloons released in the area that night. Nor were there any storms or other atmospheric disturbances in the area. They also point out that no recorded celestial fireball or meteor ever appeared nearly as bright as Sergeant Melora reported the light to be, nor has one ever hovered stationary at all, much less for such a long period. Finally, no known natural phenomenon could account for the disruption of electrical systems reported by several officers and hundreds of civilians.

The most famous of all UFO sightings happened on July 1, 1947, in Roswell, New Mexico. An unidentified object was tracked on three radar screens to where it crashed during a thunderstorm. The next morning two campers, a sheepherder and a group of archaeology students, all of whom had seen a bluish light streak overhead and all of whom had heard a crash, each found that crash site. They each described what they found as a delta-winged spacecraft. The spacecraft had been ripped open and three or four nonhuman bodies lay on the ground—they had large, hairless heads and wide-spaced eyes.

Rancher Mac Brazel found strange debris scattered across his ranch just northwest of the crash site, and along the trajectory of the crashing vehicle. He described paper-thin, tinfoil-like metal that couldn't be scratched or dented and that acted like rubber and bounced back into shape when compressed. He also described metal support beams that weighed almost nothing and that were marked with hieroglyphics. He turned over boxfuls of the stuff to the county sheriff.

Within two days the Army seized all debris and closed off access to the crash site. The day after the crash, the Army Air Corps announced that a spaceship had crashed. The next day they retracted that statement and claimed it was an advanced weather balloon. The next day they claimed that the crash was really secret tests of a new parachute system and that the bodies civilians had seen were test dummies. The "crash" was just debris from the parachute tests.

No one was ever allowed to view the wreckage again. Rumors have persisted ever since that the debris and alien bodies were eventually moved to Wright Patterson Air Force Base in Ohio. Recently, pro-UFO researchers have claimed to have interviewed more than 125 people who either saw the original spaceship and its debris, or had a part in moving, storing, studying and cataloging it in later years. All of these people, they claim, agree that it was a spaceship.

The government still says it was a weather balloon—or a new parachute system. The "secret" parachute system, however—as best anyone could determine—was never tested or used again. Many people remain convinced that it was a spacecraft that crashed and that the government has kept the craft and the bodies hidden all these years.

On January 7, 1948, Air Force pilot Thomas Mantell died while chasing "something he couldn't identify" in an F-51 fighter. A Kentucky state police unit radioed the air base that a UFO had been sighted. The tower staff saw a disk-like object fly over the base and scrambled three fighters to give chase. Mantell reported that he was at 10,000 feet and climbing to pursue a huge metallic object. One minute later he crashed. The official explanation was that he blacked out from lack of oxygen while chasing a bloblike light created by light dispersion through a thin, upper-atmosphere ice cloud. The object seen by tower staff was never adequately explained, nor was the fact that Mantell and his plane were both rated to fly much higher than 10,000 feet without worry about lack of oxygen.

In May 1950, McMinnville, Oregon, farmer Paul Trent took a now famous photograph of a saucerlike disk flying over his fields. The photo shows the corner of Trent's house, a power line and, just above that, the clear, sharp image of a flying saucer. Skeptics claim that the photo is just one more in the long line of faked photos and that close analysis of the photo will reveal thin wires holding up the dummy flying saucer.

In 1992 the photograph was computer analyzed and authenticated by the renowned Brooks Institute of Photography. They studied microscopic grain structures and patterns in the photo and reported that there were no strings, wires or other attachments to the flying saucer. They reported that the photo had not been altered or enhanced in any way, and that the picture was in no way a fake. Paul Trent snapped a picture of something more than 100 feet across hovering approximately half a mile from his house.

On July 17, 1957, Air Force Bomber RB-47 was en route to Forbes Air Force Base in Kansas when it picked up a fast-moving object approaching on radar. This sighting was confirmed by ground-control radar. The crew of that plane reported that a barn-sized, blue-white light played cat and mouse with them for two hours before it streaked straight up into space—darting here and there across their path. Stopping, starting. Drifting above then below them. Skeptics claim that it was reflected moonlight that the crew saw. No one ever explained how moonlight would show up on radar, or how the crew could see the same reflective aberration from a variety of angles and perspectives.

Finally, UFOs have been reported by a number of astronauts while in space. Scott Carpenter reported strange bright objects in 1962 from his *Aurora* space-craft. In 1965, Frank Borman and James Lovel took photos of two mushroom-shaped UFOs during their *Gemini 7* mission. *Apollo 8* and *11* both reported sight-ing UFOs. The most startling sighting of all came during a *Discovery* shuttle mission in 1993. The crew filmed the curve of Earth from space. But the tape showed a white dot that flew toward Earth, stopped, turned and accelerated at an amazing speed off into space. Skeptics claim that it was just a speck of space junk, or debris from the shuttle that was affected by a thruster blast. Careful analysis by aerospace engineers has shown that neither explanation is possible. That speck of light moved, turned and accelerated—all under its own power.

There has been one official government study of UFOs. The Air Force's Project Sign, in 1948, concluded that UFOs could be extraterrestrial spacecraft. The project was shut down within weeks of the release of its report. It was re-placed by Project Grudge in 1949, which turned into Project Blue Book in 1952. Project Blue Book's final report was issued in 1969. Project staff had studied more than 10,000 UFO sightings and had been able to create plausible expla-nations for all but 701. That's a lot of unexplained UFOs by a staff ordered to satisfactorily explain *every* sighting! The Air Force terminated Project Blue Book because, according to the Air Force, it could not be justified for the purposes of either national security or science. UFOs simply didn't warrant further study.

Some skeptics say that extraterrestrial travelers are unlikely to visit our world because the distances between stars are too great. It would take hundreds of years at light-speed to get here. Radio astronomers say that they have been searching deep space for years to find radio waves that would indicate intelligence—but they have found nothing. They have studied our entire galaxy. If there were intelligence out there, they say, it would broadcast itself using those same radio frequencies, and so radio astronomers should be able to hear it. Because they haven't heard anything, there isn't likely to be any intelligent life out there.

Still, Project Blue Book left us with 701 UFOs they couldn't explain. Hundreds of examples, like those listed above, remain officially unexplained. If they are not alien spaceships, what could they be? Researchers list four possibilities:

1. **Hoaxes.** Ninety-six percent of all studied UFO photos have been shown to be fakes.

2. **Natural phenomena.** Some sightings are really meteors, some are atmospheric distortions, some are simply navigation beacons reflecting off clouds, some are lens-shaped clouds (lenticular clouds), which look very much like saucers. Some (especially those at night) are really blimps. Some are ball lightning (intensely bright, spherical lightning that appears to hover). Some are weather balloons. Some are really sightings of a "mock Sun"—caused by sunlight bouncing off ice crystals in the sky. Sometimes a planet—most often Venus—will appear exceptionally bright. Weather inversions cause mirage images. Swamp gas can appear as a glowing light near the horizon. Radar beams can bounce off the boundaries between small air masses and look like a UFO on the radar screen. There is even a theory that sightings of "bright lights" tend to group around geologic faults and tend to precede minor earthquakes. (Research by the U.S. Bureau of Mines has shown that granite rocks do emit both bursts of plasma light and radio-frequency emissions when stressed to the breaking point; although the emissions are extremely small, they could be significant around the time of a major earthquake event.)

3. **Optical illusions.** Ice crystals and thin, high-altitude fog layers cause distortions that make natural phenomena appear to be supernatural.

4. **Mass hysteria.** Psychologist Carl Jung said that flying saucers come from the human need to believe in the supernatural. Historical records show

that every original sighting is followed by a cluster of other sightings. Many may simply be people wanting to see a flying saucer so badly that they convince themselves they have seen one.

# Fact or Fiction?

Are there UFOs? Certainly. There are easily hundreds of sightings that have been unidentifiable. But that isn't the real question.

Are there UFOs for which there is no possible scientific, rational explanation? Again the answer appears to be a solid yes, even though some die-hard skeptics claim to be able to explain all sightings. But their rationale too often rings false or so improbable as to be ridiculous. But that still isn't the real question.

Are there intelligent alien life-forms flying spacecraft around our planet? With the possible exception of the Roswell crash, we have no direct evidence to suggest that any UFOs are aliens, or that alien races have the capability to fly to Earth. However, after all the fakes and mistaken identities and routine natural phenomena are filtered out, there is still a large body of well-authenticated, well-corroborated, well-documented sightings that currently cannot be explained in any other way than to assume some intelligent being was flying a spaceship.

Does that prove that alien spaceships exist? No. Proving that these UFOs are spaceships will require some solid, tangible evidence—a ship, better photographic documentation or recorded electromagnetic radio contact. With more than a hundred thousand claimed sightings on record, not once has such evidence been produced.

# Follow-On Questions to Explore

1. Have you seen a UFO? Do you know anyone who has? Do you think UFOs are really intelligent alien beings? If so, why do you think they haven't made contact with us yet? Why haven't they landed? Why haven't they wanted to exchange ambassadors? Why do you think they came? What do they want?

2. If UFOs aren't aliens, what else do you think they could be? Make and keep a list. Search for other possible explanations to add to your list. Why do you think the Air Force decided that UFOs weren't worth pursuing? Do you think it was because they thought that their list of possible explanations covered every situation?

# Follow-On Activities

1. Find local pilots and astronomers who have had UFO contacts. Bring them into class and interview them about their UFO-related experiences. What do they think they saw? What do they think UFOs are? Compare the answers from different individuals. How would you feel if you saw something you couldn't explain? How did/do they feel?

2. Pick one famous UFO incident, such as the Roswell crash, and investigate it as thoroughly as you can. Be skeptical. Search for logical, natural explanations. Can you explain all or part of this UFO incident without having to assume the presence of intelligent alien beings? Why do you think the government isn't putting any effort into UFO studies?

# References

Angelo, Joseph. *The Extraterrestrial Encyclopedia.* New York: Facts on File, 1991.

Asimov, Isaac. *Unidentified Flying Objects.* Milwaukee, Wis.: Gareth Stevens Publishing, 1989.

Avery, Michael. *UFO's: Opposing Viewpoints.* San Diego, Calif.: Greenhaven Press, 1989.

Cohen, Daniel. *The World of UFO's.* New York: J. B. Lippincott, 1978.

Craig, Roy. *UFO's: An Insider's View of the Official Quest for Evidence.* Denton: University of North Texas Press, 1995.

Herbst, Judith. *The Mystery of UFO's.* New York: Atheneum Books for Young Readers, 1997.

Kettelkamp, Larry. *ET's and UFO's: Are They Real?* New York: Morrow Junior Books, 1996.

Korff, Karl. *The Roswell UFO Crash: What They Don't Want You to Know.* Amherst, N.Y.: Prometheus Books, 1997.

Landau, Elaine. *UFO's.* Brookfield, Conn.: Millbrook Press, 1995.

Marsh, Carole. *Unidentified Flying Objects and Extraterrestrial Life.* New York: Twenty-first Century Books, 1996.

Ortzen, Len. *Strange Stories of UFO's.* New York: Taplinger, 1987.

Randle, Kevin, and Donald Schmitt. *The Truth About the UFO Crash at Roswell.* New York: M. Evans, 1994.

Ritchie, David. *UFO: The Definitive Guide to Unidentified Flying Objects and Related Phenomena.* New York: Facts on File, 1994.

Sachs, Margaret. *The UFO Encyclopedia.* New York: Putnam's Sons, 1985.

Story, Ronald. *UFO's and the Limits of Science.* New York: William Morrow, 1988.

White, Michael. *Weird Science.* New York: Avon Books, 1999.

Williams, Richard, ed. *UFO: The Continuing Enigma.* New York: Reader's Digest, 1991.

# Warp Drive
## Space Speed Limit
## or Ticket to the Stars?

## At a Glance

Jet airplanes were first flown in the early 1940s. As their top speed inched toward 700 miles per hour and then toward the sound barrier, some scientists warned of dire and cataclysmic consequences of attempting to fly faster than the speed of sound. Some claimed it was impossible to fly faster than sound and that it would violate the laws of physics. Some predicted that breaking through the sound barrier would create energy waves of mass destruction that would wreak havoc across the land. Cartoons pictured people arriving places long before the sound of their voice traveling at a paltry 720 miles per hour.

In 1947, Chuck Yeger broke through the band of vibrations that threatened to tear planes apart as they neared the speed of sound and crossed over to supersonic flight. Suddenly the limit dissolved. Supersonic flight existed. Faster-than-sound travel became, if not an everyday occurrence for ordinary people, at least a part of our normal, everyday reality.

As a new century dawns, scientists and engineers are creeping ever faster and can visualize the not-too-distant day when their machines smack into the greatest speed limit of all, the speed of light. Einstein decreed that nothing can travel faster than light. His equations show that it is impossible to exceed lightspeed. It would violate the laws of physics and nature.

But would it really? Warp speed and hyper drives are the stuff of science fiction—today. But, then, rocket ships and trips to the Moon were pure science fiction a century ago. Is the speed of light a fixed speed limit? Will humans find a convenient way to smash through it? Will future flyers find that it is a paper, rather than a concrete, barrier when they finally get there?

It's hard enough to grasp just how fast light travels—about 300,000 kilometers per second (more than 186,000 miles per second). How fast is that? Earth is about 25,000 miles around at the equator. A photon of light could zip almost eight times around Earth in one second. New York to Los Angeles is almost 3,000 miles. It takes less than one-sixtieth of a second for light to make the trip. Light needs only one and one-third seconds to reach Earth from the Moon, 240,000 miles away, and only eight minutes to make the trip from the Sun, 93 million miles away. It takes several *years* for our space probes to near the Sun after blasting off from Earth.

Speed is the one, great limit to space travel. If ships are limited to traveling slower than light-speed, then humans will only be able to explore a tiny corner of the vast universe. Light takes 4.3 years to travel to us from the nearest star (Alpha Centari) outside our own solar system. It is hundreds of light-years to other stars in our own corner of the Milky Way. That means it would take hundreds of years to get there.

Any crew that headed out on a spaceship would all die before they got anywhere! Their children or their children's children would have to finish the trip—assuming that the crew had enough children who were capable of running the ship. By the time the voyage got somewhere, explored it for a year or two and returned, almost three hundred years would have passed on the ship (twelve generations of people) and, because of relativity, thousands of years would have passed on Earth. No one would even remember (or care) that the ship had been launched eons earlier. The whole concept of space exploration suddenly makes no sense—unless scientists can sneak past light-speed and travel hundreds of light-years in a few weeks, or seconds.

Thus, the interest in shattering the light-speed barrier is growing intense. Our space program hinges, at some not-too-distant point, on being able to speed through space at hundreds or thousands of times the speed of light. It's just that no one has even the vaguest clue as to how humans are supposed to do it.

At least, no one used to.

# The Mystery: Warp Drive

The physics building at the University of Cologne, Germany, sits near the end of tree-lined Mozart Strasse. Early one glorious spring afternoon in mid-May 1995, Professor Guenter Nimtz ambled down the third-floor, neon-lit hallway toward his office and the office room next door he had taken over as a lab to "tinker" in during free moments. Nimtz's two graduate-student assistants were both hunched over his workbench and electronic test equipment as he entered.

"Idle play two weeks before your exams?" asked Nimtz as he hung his tweed sport coat on a hook.

"Just a curiosity," answered Frederick Minter, a tall, thin, serious student from Munich, Germany, with jet-black hair and oversized, black, horn-rimmed glasses. Minter had a knack for making everything sound mysterious.

"A curiosity, eh?" repeated Nimtz, scowling, as he peered over their shoulders. "Sounds like you're hiding something from me."

"Not at all, Professor!" answered twenty-year-old Harvel Schuester, turning beet red. Schuester seemed incapable of deceiving anyone and cringed at the mere thought of disapproval. "We were just curious …"

Nimtz frowned. "About what?" It was a demand, not a question.

Short, blond Schuester still seemed embarrassed and flustered. "To see if we could send a laser signal through a solid barrier."

Nimtz shook his head and laughed. "A laser is just light, a stream of photons. Light won't penetrate solid brass. Why on Earth would you want to try that?"

"Just for fun," answered Frederick Minter, still concentrating on aligning the lab laser gun.

"Obviously your classes are too easy and I don't give you enough work to do."

"But Professor," Schuester whined. "It's a lab experiment."

Nimtz waved his hands. "Go outside and get some fresh air. It's a lovely day. Go study for your finals. Do something productive."

"This *is* productive," Minter answered, now calibrating the electronic signal receiver and oscilloscope, a picture tube that produces a two-dimensional image of an electronic signal.

Professor Nimtz folded his arms. "All right. Prove it. Why is slamming a laser into a solid-brass barrier a productive use of your time and my lab equipment?"

Schuester nervously answered, "The idea just sort of ... came to me in Professor Grossler's quantum mechanics class. If, at the subatomic level, everything is just probability and chance, then ... well—"

Minter interrupted and finished the thought. "Then there is a certain finite probability that *some* of the laser's photons will actually penetrate through this barrier and arrive to be detected on the other side, even though standard physics says light can't possibly penetrate through solid brass."

"So," nodded Nimtz. "This is a quantum mechanics experiment to test the effect of the Heisenberg uncertainty principle, which establishes that subatomic particles, like photons, can act in unpredictable and illogical ways."

Schuester's face beamed. "Yes! That's *exactly* what I was thinking. Isn't that a worthwhile experiment, Professor?"

Nimtz shrugged and nodded. He scanned the equipment they had dragged out and assembled, his mind envisioning the experiment they would be able to conduct as they had set up the lab. "I don't think you'll be able to prove anything this way."

"Why not?" Minter demanded.

"I'm sorry, Professor," Schuester blushed. "We can change it if you think we should."

Nimtz thoughtfully rubbed his upper lip. "First, I'd split the laser beam into two separate beams with a mirror before firing one at the barrier."

"Why?"

"So that you'll still have some of the original light beam that didn't have to fight through the barrier as a reference with which to compare any signal you happen to detect through the barrier. That way you'll know it really is the laser signal you are detecting."

Schuester asked, "Do you really think we'll get some signal through the barrier?"

"Probably not. Why do you think you will?"

Schuester blushed and, looking very deflated, dropped his gaze to the floor. Minter defiantly glared at his professor. "Because quantum probability says that some of the individual photons should pass through."

"*Could* pass through … *Might* pass through," corrected Nimtz.

"But you can't say that they definitely won't," Minter insisted.

Nimtz shook his head. "That's 14 centimeters of solid brass you're trying to send a light signal through. There may be some mathematical probability of it, but, at that distance, the probability will be infinitesimally small."

"But we *could* get some of the signal through," Minter insisted.

Nimtz smiled. He had chosen his assistants well this year. "What you really mean is that you want to see if you can create quantum tunneling," muttered Nimtz. "But I don't think my laser has enough power to force photons to tunnel through such a great distance."

"Quantum what?" repeated Schuester.

"Seemingly impossible things happen all the time at the subatomic level. The ability of subatomic particles and energy to apparently tunnel through solid barriers they shouldn't be able to penetrate is called quantum tunneling. True, only a tiny fraction of the photons make it through. But a few do, and a sensitive receiver might detect them—"

"But how do light particles get through solid brass?" interrupted Schuester.

Nimtz shrugged. "They shouldn't. They should all be reflected or absorbed by the surface of the brass. But somehow, in the wacky quantum world of subatomic particles, there are always a few that don't act the way they are supposed to and seemingly materialize on the other side of the barrier."

Minter smiled triumphantly and crossed his arms. "So, you admit we *will* send photons through the barrier?"

"*Might,*" laughed Nimtz as he shook his head. "There is a remote chance that you might." Then he nodded toward the lab workbench. "Let's try it and find out."

Nimtz crossed to the lab closet and fished through his ring of keys to find the one that unlocked the door. "First we'll need a more sensitive electronic signal receiver than the one you're using. And we should use one that can monitor a wide frequency spectrum in case some of your photons lose energy during transit and shift their frequency below the visual range."

He wheeled out a cart with his most sensitive and expensive equipment on it. "We'll also use this better scope to create a graphic image of the signals, because we can shift it into multiple graphic modes." Nimtz rubbed his chin for a moment before pointing at a pair of additional mirrors on a shelf across the room. "Bring both those mirrors over, Harvel. If we send one of the two laser beams through 14 centimeters of brass, we should send the other through the same distance of open air so that both laser beams will have traveled the same distance before reaching the electronic receiver and the display oscilloscope."

The lab burst into a flurry of activity as the three men excitedly snaked connecting cables between pieces of equipment, aligned the barrier and broadcast horns and tested individual components.

"I think that does it," concluded Nimtz, wiping his hands on a clean rag. He nodded toward Harvel Schuester. "This was your idea, Harvel. Switch on the laser. Frederick, you monitor and adjust the scope."

Schuester flipped on the laser. With a loud hum, a brilliant, emerald-green beam flashed across the room.

The beam struck an angled mirror that split the beam in two. One half was bounced between Nimtz's mirrors before reaching the receiving antenna of the signal receiver. There it was converted into an electronic signal and sent to the oscilloscope Minter watched, where it appeared as a tall spike in the scope's pulsing green line.

The other half of the laser beam was directed at the end of a 14-centimeter-long, rectangular block of brass. The end of the block glowed green, as the laser beam seemed to splash off its smooth surface and dissipate into the air. Nimtz's most sensitive receiver was hooked to the far end of the block to catch any stray photons that happened to penetrate through almost 6 inches of solid metal. This receiver also converted any detected photons into an electronic signal that was amplified and sent to the oscilloscope to appear as a second spike.

"Getting anything?" Nimtz called out to Minter.

"I think so," he answered. "But something's wrong."

Nimtz stepped around the central lab bench to peer over his student's shoulder.

"I have two separate spikes," Minter reported. "One from each signal, I guess."

"Then the uncertainty principle is right!" cheered Schuester. "Some photons *do* penetrate solid substances!"

Minter continued to stare at his scope. "But that means that by the time the signals get here they are different. I thought they would be the same and appear as just one large spike. Why do I have two signals on the scope instead of just one? I think something is wrong. Why are the signals coming from the two laser beams different?"

Nimtz peered over his student's shoulder. "Show me what you mean."

"Something is wrong," repeated Minter, pointing at the two spikes on his scope's image. "The two signals should have reached the scope at the same time. Their spikes should appear at exactly the same place on the graph. But one seems to be shifted forward as if it reached the scope before the other."

"The laser beam must have been slowed passing through the brass barrier," said Schuester. "That *has* to be why one set of pulses reached the scope after the other."

"Are you sure, or just guessing?" asked Nimtz.

"What else could it be?" Minter demanded. "Everyone knows nothing can travel faster than light. Einstein said so. So if one of the signals was delayed and took longer to reach the receiver, it *had* to be the one traveling through the barrier."

Nimtz countered, "But that signal was also light. It should have traveled at light-speed."

Both graduate students paused. Suddenly they weren't sure what was happening. Was one beam of light slowing down below light-speed? Were they somehow slowing light? Schuester began to blush and fidget. "But what else could it be, Professor?"

"Any one of a dozen things," he answered. "A bad connector. A signal echo in one of the pieces of equipment. A faulty processor—"

"So you think it was an equipment problem?" Minter interrupted.

"I think it *could* be. And I think you should stop guessing and, like responsible scientists, find out!" Nimtz pointed at Schuester. "Turn the laser back on." He turned to Minter. "Hand me that piece of cardboard. First, we'll make sure that one of the spikes on the scope corresponds with each of the two laser beams."

Nimtz blocked the signal that traveled straight through air with his piece of cardboard. The second signal spike faded from Minter's oscilloscope.

Schuester muttered, "So the signal that arrived later at the oscilloscope is the one that traveled through air—at light-speed?"

"That can't be," Minter muttered.

Nimtz shifted the cardboard to block the laser beam aimed at the brass barrier. The lead spike faded from Minter's scope.

"That's impossible!" he cried. "The photons tunneling through the barrier *can't* reach the scope *faster* than light-speed!"

Nimtz wrinkled his forehead as he thought out loud. "The signal pathways are the same length ... No connector problems or delays ..." He gazed sternly at Frederick Minter. "Don't say 'can't,' Frederick. I think it has."

"But ... but, that would mean the photons traveled faster than light-speed while they passed through the barrier," Schuester stammered.

Nimtz nodded, still lost in thought. "It would appear so."

"No!" insisted Minter. "Einstein said. Nothing travels faster than the speed of light."

"But Einstein never incorporated quantum mechanics effects into his equations." Nimtz eagerly rubbed his hands together. "This little curiosity of yours could prove to be amazingly important. But first, we have lots of testing to do to make sure that what we *think* we're seeing is what we really *are* seeing." He smiled at his assistants. "You both have plenty of free time over the next couple of weeks, don't you?"

Two weeks later Guenter Nimtz announced that he and his assistants had sped laser photons through a solid-brass barrier at twice the speed of light. Most of the scientific community scoffed and ridiculed Nimtz, saying that only a fool would think that light-speed could be exceeded.

But a few scientists well-versed in the oddities of quantum mechanics admitted that it seemed possible to momentarily exceed light-speed. Most prominent among them was Professor Raymond Chiao of the University of California at Berkeley, a specialist in quantum tunneling. He wrote back to Nimtz that they, too, had gotten an occasional random photon to exceed light-speed. But, Chiao continued, it was just a trick of quantum physics and was not a significant accomplishment, as Nimtz would never be able to transmit any useful information with these superaccelerated photons.

Guenter Nimtz was outraged. It was one thing to have his work challenged. It was another to have it casually dismissed as insignificant and meaningless. He gathered his group together in late June and set out to prove that he could send real information faster than light and erase all doubt as to the importance of their accomplishment.

As he often did, Nimtz played classical music softly in the background during this group meeting. Today he played Mozart's Concerto no. 40, one of his favorites.

"What kind of information will we send?" asked Minter.

Nimtz's forefingers waved through the air like batons in time with the music as he thought.

"What about a mathematical formula?" Schuester offered.

"What about a photograph?" added Minter. "We could digitize it and send that data stream on the laser beam."

"I think we should start by sending music," said Nimtz. "That's complex information, and it will be easy to tell if it arrives undistorted at the receiver."

"*What* music?" asked Minter.

Nimtz shrugged and pointed at his office stereo. "*This* music. Mozart's Concerto no. 40."

They had to borrow additional equipment to modulate the laser beam to carry the electrical signal of the music. Then they found they needed a better, more precise, laser generator. It took two weeks to set up the experiment.

When they played back the recording they made of the signal that had tunneled through 14 centimeters of solid brass, it sounded just like Mozart's Concerto no. 40 being played through a cheap pair of speakers. It wasn't as good as the original. But it was definitely Mozart's Concerto no. 40. The scientists had transmitted complex information at faster than light-speed.

They then calculated the maximum speed at which they could get their photon signal to tunnel through its barrier—4.7 times the speed of light. Guenter Nimtz was able to transmit a signal with complex music at almost *five times* the speed of light!

Nimtz brought in other professors at the University of Cologne and challenged them to find fault with his methodology or results. They couldn't.

Nimtz published his results and met icy skepticism. He was treading on one of the most sacred elements of Einstein's great legacy to science. Most physicists said they would need far more proof than a simple lab experiment with music to believe that travel beyond light-speed was possible. Raymond Chiao scoffed that music didn't count as sending real information faster than light.

But those who have studied the data grudgingly admit that, in the summer of 1995, Guenter Nimtz and his two graduate assistants successfully smashed through the ultimate speed limit. The light barrier had been broken! It is now up to the rest of science to decide how to take best advantage of this breakthrough.

## About This Story

The events and principal characters of this story are real. The story is historically accurate and is based on published reports in scientific literature and on video interviews with Guenter Nimtz.

## The Science

American physicist Albert Michaelson was the first human to accurately measure the speed of light. He made his first measurements in the late 1800s and refined his estimate up through his retirement in the mid-1920s. Along the way, his efforts earned him the Nobel Prize in physics—making him the first American to win that coveted award.

But Michaelson and others struggling to measure the speed of light noticed an odd thing. No matter how they measured it, the speed of light always remained the same. They could be moving toward a light source, or away from it. It should have made a difference in the measured speed. But it didn't. They always measured the same speed. The struggle was to explain this apparent contradiction.

Einstein, in his theory of relativity, provided an explanation. He theorized that the speed of light was a universal constant. He also said that it was the greatest possible speed in the universe. He even showed that time could vary—speed up or slow down—as a function of velocity and gravitational forces in order to keep the speed of light a universal constant. The speed of light, about 300,000 kilometers per second, became an absolute and unbreakable speed limit. Virtually all scientists accepted Einstein's theory.

Everyone but science fiction writers let the idea of faster-than-light travel drop. There was no point in any further investigation. But science fiction writers had to envision far enough ahead of science to realize that space travel required speeds greatly in excess of light-speed. Soon they had invented warp drive, hyper drive, space folding and all manner of other fictional schemes to allow humans to contact alien—and very distant—species and worlds.

Until the 1980s, exceeding light-speed was just a pipe dream. The laws of science and physics said that light-speed was the maximum speed in the universe—period. But in the early part of that decade, three prominent physicists—Kip Thorne, Carl Sagan and Stephen Hawking—began a serious exploration of ways to beat the universal speed limit. They proposed three possible methods: black holes, wormholes and compressed space—all ways to sneak around, rather than smash through, the universal speed limit.

They first turned to Einstein's notion that any matter that entered a black hole would almost instantly be ejected from a white hole somewhere else in the universe. Who needed to fly faster than light-speed if a black hole–white hole tunnel in space and time could zip you instantly across the universe?

But calculations based on quantum mechanics theory showed that it wouldn't work. First, it seemed that a singularity (a spot where matter became infinitely dense and gravity grew infinitely large) existed inside every black hole. Surely anything entering a black hole—even an atom—would be ripped apart by these monstrous gravitational forces. Second, it appeared that anything that made it beyond a black hole would emerge through a white hole only as a stream of subatomic particles. And these particles probably would not emerge into our universe, but into some parallel universe, or into a new universe being created by the black hole. So black holes were scratched from the list.

Thorne, Sagan and Hawking next explored wormholes (shortcut tunnels through time and space that allow a traveler to step from end to end almost instantly, no matter how far apart those ends are). Step into one end of a wormhole and emerge out the other a few seconds later, even if that end were 50 light-years away. That, surely, would count as traveling faster than light!
But no one had ever found or studied a wormhole (or even confirmed that they actually exist in the universe). So this idea remained theory and guesswork.

Some attention has recently been directed at pulsars, which are rapidly spinning neutron stars. Calculations indicated that pulsars could act as wormholes through space, or, more correctly, as one end of a wormhole. However, serious questions remain: Where is the other end? Can a traveler ever return? More practically, because the nearest pulsar is hundreds of light-years away, no one knows how to get to a pulsar to see if it could work as a wormhole conduit to speed travelers along faster than light.

Worse, Thorne and Hawking made calculations in the mid-1990s that appeared to show that wormholes—if they did exist—were inherently unstable and would self-destruct before they could be used. Wormholes weren't scratched from the list, but they were pushed to the back burner as being an unattainable means of travel given current technology and theory.

Finally, Thorne, Hawking and Sagan studied space compression, or space folding. Einstein's equations seemed to show that it was physically possible to compress and expand space. Launch a ship into Earth orbit and then use its "space compression machine" to compress the 4.3 light-years to Alpha Centari to a couple hundred thousand miles and arrive there in time for dinner. If it took a minute to complete the compression and expansion, it would take a minute to travel 4.3 light-years.

Although Einstein's equations seemed to indicate that this process of space folding was possible and physically permissible, no one had even the vaguest idea of how to go about doing it. Initial attempts to study space folding showed that it would require such immense amounts of energy that the lifetime energy output of our Sun would be barely sufficient for one trip.

Einstein's universal speed limit still seemed rigid, unyielding and inescapable. Mild interest was rekindled in the early 1990s when new work at Lawrence Livermore Lab in California suggested that, possibly, the unfathomably large amount of energy stored in a black hole could be tapped to power one of these modes of space shortcuts. It was a nice theory, but was still little more than a vague idea. It would remain worthless until someone could find a nearby black hole and a nearby wormhole that could be studied up close. It seemed that the effort to make deep-space travel practical was at another dead end.

Then Guenter Nimtz shattered the speed of light. True, he didn't transport a person or lab monkey faster than light. But he didn't simply accelerate a random photon or two beyond light-speed, either. He sent complex music at almost five times the speed of light. Yes, it was only music, and yes, it was only through 14 centimeters of brass. But he did it. He surpassed light-speed in sending real information.

On their first flight, the Wright brothers flew for only twelve seconds, and that in a plane that needed to be pushed downhill by two men in order to build up enough speed to get it into the air in the first place. Still, the Wright brothers broke through a limit that had plagued human air travel, just as Guenter Nimtz had done. Through his work in quantum physics, it has been proven that individual particles of light (photons) can exceed the speed of light through space. This is not something that will lead directly to *Star Trek's* trans-warp drive, but it has shown that the speed of light isn't the ultimate speed limit for transmitting complex information.

Guenter Nimtz's work has been studied and confirmed by several other universities around world. Light-speed has been exceeded. The question now is whether that is only a quirk of the bizarre quantum world, or whether it has practical applications for space travel. This effort will be part of the current central thrust of quantum physics: Can quantum strangeness be magnified into the macro-universe in which we live our daily lives? Physicists call it the search for quantum gravity—the unifying theory to link Einstein's relativity with quantum mechanics. Soon we may call it the ticket for a one-hour ride to the stars.

## Fact or Fiction?

Can humans travel faster than light through space? No. Not yet. Can anything travel faster than light. Yes. Photons (light itself) has been measured traveling many times faster than the speed of light. But no larger particles have been accelerated beyond light-speed.

Will humans ever travel faster than light? The best guess is yes, even though many physicists still insist that, as Einstein dictated, light-speed will never be exceeded. There are too many promising irons in the fire for at least one not to hit pay dirt. Scientists will soon complete the development of a unified field theory (quantum gravity), which may show how to translate quantum-level phenomena up to our macro-level universe.

Quantum gravity may point the way to the physics necessary to compress and expand space. Wormholes may prove to be manageable and user-friendly space tunnels. Dr. Nimtz's work may lead to faster-than-light travel of larger and more complex items than photons. Stephen Hawking's mini–black holes may be found in our solar system (one theory claims that several should be lurking somewhere in our system's tiny corner of space). Once scientists can study a real black hole, the resulting great leaps forward in our understanding may provide the keys to breaking the speed of light.

The odds are that one of these areas of study will succeed, so that, a hundred years from now, students will shake their heads and wonder how we could have ever been so ignorant as to believe that faster-than-light travel was impossible. It is most likely that working prototypes for faster-than-light travel machines (spaceships?) will be tested during your lifetime.

# Follow-On Questions to Explore

1. Do you think humans will be able to travel faster than the speed of light with as little care as we now give to exceeding the speed of sound? If you travel faster than light, how would you be able to see where you are going? Shouldn't you worry about running into planets and stars zipping along that fast? If you travel faster than light, would you be able to see anything at all? Because you would be traveling faster than the light could reach you, would everything be just black? Would you hit things before you could see them?

2. The subatomic world seems incredibly weird and unpredictable by the standards and physics of our everyday lives and world. Subatomic particles—quarks, gluons, muons, positrons, negatrons, anti-matter and quantum foam—seem totally alien and bizarre. Yet are they? Don't atoms, with massive nuclei and spinning electrons, look just like miniature versions of our solar system? Don't complex organic molecules resemble galaxies? If you were a giant observer who looked at our solar system the way we look at an individual atom, and if you therefore thought that the world was smooth and uniform (like an electron), wouldn't the complex and changing surface of the world seem pretty weird and unpredictable? Do you see similarities between the microscopic world of electrons, protons, atoms and molecules and that of vast space with its stars, planets and galaxies?

3. Research the Heisenberg uncertainty principle. It is mentioned a couple of times in the story above. What does this principle say? What does it mean? Who was Heisenberg? What impact did this principle have on the field of subatomic physics? What is the importance of this principle for quantum mechanics?

# Follow-On Activities

1. Can you detect the speed of light in your classroom? If you fired a laser at a mirror that was 5 miles away, it would hit the mirror and return to you in about one twenty-thousandth of a second. There are probably no instruments available to you that are capable of detecting a time interval as short as that. The fastest time-measuring equipment you have access to is

most likely a good 35mm camera. Usually these cameras are capable of opening and closing their shutters in either one one-thousandth or one two-thousandth of a second. Of course, in that time (one two-thousandth of a second), light has traveled 93 miles.

So, how did early-twentieth-century scientists accurately measure the speed of light? Research the subject in the library and on the Internet. Pay particular attention to the work of Albert Michaelson (see *Marvels of Science* by Kendall Haven).

Can you devise an experiment you could try at school that would at least estimate the speed of light? What would it look like? What would it do? What equipment would you need?

2.  The effort to break the speed of light is the latest in a long series of efforts to break established limits. Research as many "limits" to human activity as you can that have been broken but that were once believed unbreakable. Research a variety of fields (science, sports, engineering, etc.). List as many "limits" as you can find, and explain how and when they were broken, and why many once believed they could not be broken.

# References

Burns, Ruth Ann. *Stephen Hawking's Universe.* New York: Thirteen: WNET, 1997. Videocassette.

Haven, Kendall. *Marvels of Science.* Englewood, Colo.: Libraries Unlimited, 1996.

Haven, Kendall, and Donna Clark. *100 Most Popular Scientists for Young Adults.* Englewood, Colo.: Libraries Unlimited, 1999.

Hawking, Stephen. *A Brief History of Time.* New York: Bantam Books, 1990.

Krauss, Lawrence. *Beyond Star Trek.* New York: HarperCollins, 1997.

MacVey, John. *Time Travel.* Chelsea, Mich.: Scarborough House, 1993.

McMaster, Joseph. *Time Travel.* Boston: WGBH and NOVA, 1999. Videocassette.

Pickover, Clifford. *Time: A Travelers Guide.* New York: Oxford University Press, 1998.

Rees, Martin. *Before the Beginning: Our Universe and Others.* Reading, Mass.: Addison-Wesley, 1997.

———. "Exploring Our Universe and Others." *Scientific American,* December 1999, 78–83.

Rucker, Rudy. *The 4th Dimension.* Boston: Houghton Mifflin, 1984.

Thorne, Kip. *Black Holes and Time Warps.* New York: W. W. Norton, 1994.

———. "Wormholes, Time Machines, and the Weak Energy Condition." *Astrophysical Journal* 61, no. 13 (September 1986): 122–128.

White, Michael. *Weird Science.* New York: Avon Books, 1999.

Wilson, Robert. *Astronomy Through the Ages.* Princeton, N.J.: Princeton University Press, 1998.

# Index